POROUS CITY

Contemporary Hispanic and Lusophone Cultures

Series Editor
L. Elena Delgado, University of Illinois at Urbana-Champaign
Richard Rosa, Duke University

Series Editorial Board
Jo Labanyi, New York University
Chris Perriam, University of Manchester
Lisa Shaw, University of Liverpool
Paul Julian Smith, CUNY Graduate Center

This series aims to provide a forum for new research on modern and contemporary hispanic and lusophone cultures and writing. The volumes published in Contemporary Hispanic and Lusophone Cultures reflect a wide variety of critical practices and theoretical approaches, in harmony with the intellectual, cultural and social developments that have taken place over the past few decades. All manifestations of contemporary hispanic and lusophone culture and expression are considered, including literature, cinema, popular culture, theory. The volumes in the series will participate in the wider debate on key aspects of contemporary culture.

1 Jonathan Mayhew, *The Twilight of the Avant-Garde*:
Contemporary Spanish Poetry 1980–2000

2 Mary S. Gossy, *Empire on the Verge of a Nervous Breakdown*

3 Paul Julian Smith, *Spanish Screen Fiction: Between Cinema and Television*

4 David Vilaseca, *Queer Events: Post-Deconstructive Subjectivities in
Spanish Writing and Film, 1960s to 1990s*

5 Kirsty Hooper, *Writing Galicia into the World: New Cartographies, New Poetics*

6 Ann Davies, *Spanish Spaces: Landscape, Space and Place in
Contemporary Spanish Culture*

7 Edgar Illas, *Thinking Barcelona: Ideologies of a Global City*

8 Joan Ramon Resina, *Iberian Modalities: A Relational Approach to the
Study of Culture in the Iberian Peninsula*

Porous City

A Cultural History of Rio de Janeiro (from the 1810s Onward)

BRUNO CARVALHO

LIVERPOOL UNIVERSITY PRESS

First published 2013 by
Liverpool University Press
4 Cambridge Street
Liverpool
L69 7ZU

Copyright © Bruno Carvalho 2013

British Library Cataloguing-in-Publication data
A British Library CIP record is available

ISBN 978-1-84631-975-4 cased
ISBN 978-1-78138-164-9 paperback

Typeset in Borges by
Carnegie Book Production, Lancaster

Contents

List of Maps

List of Figures

A Note on Translation

Translations are my own unless otherwise noted. Words in languages other than English first appear in italics, followed by a translation. I have preferred the Portuguese form of 'mulatto' because it is more colloquial and conveys gender (mulato/a). In some cases, I follow the Brazilian convention of referring to an author by the first name.

Preface

I

When the Italian architect Lina Bo Bardi arrived in Rio de Janeiro in October 1946 she used a single word to describe her initial impression: *incanto* ('enchantment').[1] Few have remained indifferent to views of the city from the ocean or from above. Born in Rio, I often wondered what it might feel like to experience its nature, rhythms, or streets for the very first time. It was always easy, even as a child, to understand how the city's uncommon beauty and liveliness can seduce visitors. But throughout my early life and adolescence, in the 1980s and 90s, Rio seemed stuck in an endless downward spiral of violence, urban poverty, corruption, and dysfunctional government. Any sense of *incanto* had to be quickly shielded by nostalgia, a frustration for anyone born 'after the fall'.

Rio's contradictions caused an impression on me very early on. I was first unsettled by enigmas that now seem almost mundane: in the city of my childhood, strangers with vastly different incomes and backgrounds hugged effusively in the stands of a football stadium. These same strangers might have also paraded side by side during carnival, engaged in casual conversation at the beach, or treated street children as if they were invisible. In a place where finding common ground can be so effortless, how could so many be comfortable with striking socio-economic inequities?

The naivety did not last long. It would eventually become clear that mobility and segregation sometimes coexist. Socio-racial mixture and cultural inclusion can abet other forms of exclusion, just as stratification does not preclude fluid boundaries. I would learn that the disenchantment of modern life has been a constant theme in the social sciences and in cultural theory. I also learned that Rio's history had no original sin, or fall, and that the paradisaical city of Bossa Nova songs never quite existed (at least not for all of its residents). Eventually, life abroad altered my relationship to a city that, at the same time, has never stopped changing.

Nonetheless, Rio's capacity to enchant kept surprising me. Over the past several years, I have seen countless colleagues, students, and friends react, much like Lina Bo Bardi, to their first experiences in the city. Sometimes I found myself wanting what they have. This book, written largely while living away, allowed me to reconcile disparate desires. It has to a degree brought to fruition the promises of experiencing Rio as if 'for the first time'. It has also generated a more layered understanding of the city's past, its role in the making of Brazilian culture, and its significance to key debates about modernity and urban cultural practices.

II

Porous City focuses on one of the most compelling spaces in the history of modern cities: Rio de Janeiro's Cidade Nova, or New City. The Cidade Nova was created by royal decree in 1811 and razed for the construction of a monumental avenue during the Second World War. This area has since been largely neglected, but it was critical to Rio's development and to the emergence of musical genres that came to define Brazil's national identity. Once known as both 'Little Africa' and a 'Jewish neighbourhood', the Cidade Nova attests to the multi-ethnic, multiracial, and multilayered character of Brazil's former capital. It was an important reference for foreign travellers, prominent writers, and pioneering social scientists. Adjoining the city's first favela, it played a crucial role in foundational narratives of Brazil as 'the country of carnival' and as a 'racial democracy'.

Through a granular view of particular urban spaces, our perspectives expand.[2] As a case study of the Cidade Nova, this book reflects about how the absence of ethnic ghettoes relates to circulation practices and cultural exchange. As a history of Rio over a span of several decades, it shows the city's transformations from a port town into a bustling metropolis. And although no single site could ever be representative of a nation so diverse and complex, focus on the Cidade Nova seeks to shed light on how initially marginalized expressions – like samba music – became emblematic of Brazil. In the process, a more universal story emerges, about how urban changes can shape language, just as language itself can shape the development and experience of cities.

None of that was at all conceivable when I visited the Cidade Nova's Vila do Éden, or Eden Villa, in the beginning of 2007. At the time I had become interested in the construction of President Vargas Avenue during the 1940s. The multi-lane avenue cut through a great swath of Rio, including the Praça Onze, the Cidade Nova's former central square. It was a place that only resonated with me because of references in popular music. The area now stood as a testament to the failures of modern urbanism. Where a neighbourhood once existed, cars and buses reign while pedestrians do what they can. Any sense of the Cidade Nova as an actual place appears to have vanished.

Amidst my research, I read in one of the free newspapers distributed in Rio's downtown area that the director Sérgio Bloch was making a documentary about the avenue.[3] We met, and Sérgio invited me to be interviewed for the film. I spoke about how the press covered the urban reform, and was followed by an architect, Paulinho Fonseca. Paulinho is a singular type of intellectual, not rare among Cariocas, as Rio de Janeiro natives are known: one whose understanding of the city owes as much to books as it does to the street corners and characters that make up its daily life. After our interviews, we had a spirited conversation in one of the many bars that sprawl onto Rio's sidewalks.

Weeks later, I received a call from Paulinho on a Sunday morning, asking me whether I could meet him at a party in the Eden Villa, 'what remains of the old Praça Onze'. I went. The villa is a cul-de-sac of over fifty single-storey terraced houses lodged in between an elevated highway, a police station, a rarely visited concrete modernist cultural centre, and President Vargas Avenue. Only informally known as Eden, it is indeed an oasis of sorts amidst a desolate, disfigured urban landscape. The party was held in front of Pinduca's and Celi's house, and brought together family, friends, and neighbours. Much about the environment was familiar: the *mocotó* (a bean stew made from cow's feet), the *cachaça* (a sugar cane liquor), the lively music, and philosophizing conversations. But Paulinho invited me because the septuagenarian couple – one an Ashkenazi Jew, the other Afro-Brazilian – had grown up there, in the heart of the Cidade Nova. They – he expansive and excitable, she affable and measured – made quite an impression on me. I left determined to study this peculiar confluence of Afro-Jewish cultural spaces.

As I became increasingly fascinated by the types of encounters that had taken place in this New City, my research began to reach back into the early nineteenth century, and to involve an array of subjects, from the Emperor of Brazil to a red-light district, from Gypsies to Orson Welles. It was a process rife with re-enchantment. I discovered that references to this area's landmarks were found throughout major works of literature, music, and the visual arts, as well as in obscure archives and long-forgotten texts. Little could I know, when meeting Pinduca and Celi on a Sunday afternoon, that their union would set me off in an adventure that culminates with this book. But that was not the only surprise reserved for this researcher: in my memories of that party, Pinduca had been the Afro-descendant, and Celi the daughter of Russian Jews. Only upon visiting them again two years later, this time in the more formal capacity of interviewer, did I realize that it was the other way around. Pinduca, Jewish-born, proudly recalled Yiddish words from his childhood; Celi, Afro-Brazilian, traced her lineage to migrants from the country's rural interior.

Something about the mix-up was disconcerting, yet it served to illustrate a lesson: there are as many ways of remembering urban experiences as there are ways of representing them. It can always be possible, after all, to render familiar places anew. This book, then, is in part also about the various forms through which writers, artists, and urban dwellers can perceive, remember, manipulate, and imagine a given city. Conversely, it is also about how we can read things past, and about some of the ways in which they keep speaking to us, if we return to them.

III

Reference to an Afro-Jewish neighbourhood might seem more provocative than precise. The neighbourhood that the reader will encounter in the following pages, in fact, was even more heterogeneous. But drawing attention to this combination serves as a way of highlighting how the Cidade Nova appears in contemporary scholarship: studies dedicated to this area tend to deem it either African or Jewish. A recent book calls it a 'foreign landscape' (Fridman 2007). On the contrary, I argue, the Cidade Nova was instrumental to the making of Brazilian culture. The more theoretical introduction touches on that and other issues raised in this preface. It revisits the idea of the 'city as palimpsest', explains how the book incorporates strategies from a myriad of disciplines, and articulates the concept of a 'porous city'.

The first chapter, 'At the Centre of an Imperial Capital: Swamps, Yellow Fever, and Gypsy Parties', opens with the 1808 arrival of the Portuguese royal court in Rio de Janeiro. As a geographic centre, between the administrative quarters of the Old City and the residence of Brazil's emperor, the Cidade Nova received major infrastructure investments and caught the attention of many foreign travellers. A surge in yellow fever epidemics, however, pushed wealthier residents elsewhere. The swamp-filled neighbourhood became consolidated as a home to the lower classes, including newly arrived migrants, freed slaves, and Gypsies. Analysis focuses on Manuel Antônio de Almeida's seminal *Memórias de um sargento de milícias* (Memoirs of a Militia Sergeant), a mid-nineteenth-century precursor of the realist novel. The story's narrator portrays the Cidade Nova as a distant space of parties, Gypsies, and perilous indigenous witchcraft. The descriptions of what happens *way over there* paradoxically contain a level of detail that betrays the author's own familiarity with those practices. Building on an influential reading of a dialectic between order and disorder both in the narrative and in nineteenth-century Brazilian society, the chapter proposes this interplay as expressive of a type of 'spatial porosity'. In the process, several questions pertaining to Rio de Janeiro's socio-racial relations surface: what does it mean when a city's most oppressed inhabitants are also its most visible? And how do those exploited under a slave-based system leave a deep and irrevocable imprint on dominant cultural practices?

'A Master on the Periphery of a Periphery: Popular Music, Streetcars, and the Republic' picks up around the 1870s, when Rio de Janeiro's streets gain tram (streetcar) lines, the contours of what we could call Brazilian musical forms begin to take shape, and abolition as well as the end of the empire are on the horizon. As the Cidade Nova increasingly turns into a site of crowded tenements and precarious housing, associations between the neighbourhood and 'blackness' become commonplace – along with racially tinged notions like insalubrity and the threat of 'dangerous classes'. Mostly outside the scope of novelists, the neighbourhood goes on to have an important function in the fiction of Brazil's most prominent nineteenth-century writer, Machado de Assis, a mulato who circulated ably among the lettered elites. The chapter argues that through specific spatial references (streets, public places), his writings meticulously plot the complex socio-cultural landscape during the transition from the empire to the republic, established in 1889. Some of his celebrated short stories, traditionally read as restricted to a domestic and private sphere, shed light on the author's relationship with the city, allowing for a discussion of social tensions, racial relations, and the dynamics of economic mobility.

'Beyond the Belle Époque: On the Border of a "Divided City"' concerns the first two decades of the twentieth century, when a drastic Paris-inspired urban reform in the Old City helped to create the idea (and to an extent the reality) of 'two Rios de Janeiro': one modern and beautiful, the other uncivilized and inhabited by the undesired. The chapter focuses not only on the 'other' city, but on mediating figures that frequented its different spaces, like the composer Chiquinha Gonzaga, and two mulatos and prominent writers whose works assume critical importance: João do Rio, a mixture of flâneur and investigative journalist, and the 'damned' novelist Lima Barreto, an active critic of the republic and its urban reforms. Less-well-known texts, like the travel accounts of João Pinheiro Chagas (a future prime minister of Portugal), also generate broader insights about urban development, and into the Cidade Nova's role as a type of contact zone between expanding suburbs, the commercial and political centre, the port, and nascent favelas, or shanties built on hillsides.

In the 1920s, 'Little Africa' shared the Praça Onze with a burgeoning

'Jewish neighbourhood'. The public square grew to be the focus of its popular street carnival, and the adjoining Mangue canal became the site of a red-light district. At the same time, these locales entered the aesthetic imaginary of a generation of modernist writers and painters. After discussing the Ashkenazi presence in the area, 'Afro-Jewish Quarter and Modernist Landmark' explores its potential intersections with the Afro-Brazilian milieu. The chapter incorporates readings of crucial texts by major authors like Murilo Mendes, Mário de Andrade, Manuel Bandeira, and Vinicius de Moraes, as well as works by visual artists Lasar Segall and Oswaldo Goeldi. With the Cidade Nova as its focus, the book confronts questions related to how a Brazilian artistic modernity coped with the fast-paced modernization and urbanizing processes undergone by the city, as well as to how these artists engaged cultural expressions (dance, language, music) and/or ethnic groups widely seen as antiquated, uncivilized, and a hindrance to the country's progress.

The fifth chapter, 'Writing the "Cradle of Samba": Race, Radio, and the Price of Progress' analyses the role of the Cidade Nova's street carnival in incipient racial discourses, through close readings of now much forgotten but influential texts during the 1930s: Graça Aranha's *A Viagem Maravilhosa* (The Wonderful Journey) and Arthur Ramos's *O Folk-lore Negro do Brasil* (Black Folklore of Brazil). Several broader transformations are considered, like the 1930 coup that brought Getúlio Vargas to power and the development of radio, instrumental to samba's emergence as a national genre. Amidst this context, the chapter explores how socio-cultural paradigms and urbanism went in seemingly opposite directions: the country became widely accepted or even celebrated as mixed, but city planning further sought to segregate urban spaces. Our discussion then turns to the first comprehensive plans for Brazil's capital after the so-called belle époque, commissioned to a pioneering and at the time prestigious French urbanist, Alfred Agache. His vision in the late 1920s of an avenue across the Cidade Nova came into fruition after the Vargas regime's 1937 dictatorial turn, incorporating fascist elements and privileging the motor car. The tightly controlled and censored press welcomed President Vargas Avenue as a sign of progress, modernity, and cosmopolitanism.

'"It's (Mostly) All True": The Death of a Neighbourhood and the Life of Myths' discusses the President Vargas Avenue's construction in the context of changes happening elsewhere in the world, and retrieves the voices of local musicians who opposed it. Orson Welles's experience in the city, in 1942, provides insight into some of the foreseeable consequences of the urban reforms, and captures part of the public sentiment around them. The chapter focuses on the director's fascination with samba, his relationship with popular musicians, and prescient realization of the soon to be razed Praça Onze's great importance to Rio's cultural landscape. Combining existing scholarship and original archival research, it argues that the square would be an integral component of his aborted film, *It's All True*. The analyses bring to light unpublished studies on Rio commissioned by the director, his portrayal of Afro-Brazilians, informed references to places well outside of the usual foreigner's itinerary or contemporary cinematic gaze, and innovative use of musical forms to structure the film. One of the main scenes in Welles's film would have been a performance of the song 'Praça Onze', by Herivelto Martins and Grande Otelo. Amidst a nationalist and authoritarian state, they composed one of carnival's most memorable songs to lament the demise of the public square. That and other sambas will help us reflect upon issues of memory and cultural production.

'The Future Revisited: Where Has the Past Gone and Where Will it Go?' looks back at developments after the 1940s, when the Cidade Nova ceased to have a defining function in Rio's urban fabric. As new infrastructural interventions and cultural representations privileged other parts of the city, the neighbourhood entered a period of decadence and reconstruction. Rio itself underwent a loss of status as Brazil's capital moved to Brasília in 1960. Despite its diminished relevance, the Cidade Nova remained reflective of changes happening elsewhere. It has now become central to developments spurred by the 2016 Olympic games. This last chapter synthesizes some of the book's main arguments while introducing a more contemporary perspective. And amidst competing narratives of Rio that highlight spatial segregation, urban violence, and more recently renewed hope, the conclusion reaffirms the extent to which the Cidade Nova's past and future continue to be critical to the city.

Notes

1 Bardi's narrative of her arrival by ship can be found in 'Curriculum literário' (1999: 12).
2 We might think here of Walter Benjamin's insight about film: 'With the close-up, space expands' (2007: 236).
3 It has since been released under the title 'Presidente Vargas: Biografia de uma Avenida' (President Vargas: Biography of an Avenue), Abbas Filmes, 2009.

Introduction: In Search of Things Past: Mapping Rio

I

F ew images are as apt as a palimpsest to convey the complex layers that make up our contemporary cities. Combining the Greek *pálin* ('again') and *psáo* ('I scrape'), palimpsests designate a manuscript in which the text of the first writing is scraped off so that the parchment or clay tablet may be written on again. They have served as a fertile metaphor to the fields of architecture, archaeology, planetary astronomy, forensic science, psychoanalysis, geology, and literary criticism, and likewise populate the imaginary of urban historians and theorists.[1] Urban spaces are like a palimpsest in a palpable, physical sense: as a city undergoes reforms or development, its tangible, visible signs – buildings, streets, parks, trees – are 'scraped off', demolished, or razed to allow for the new. But the past, in cities as in a reused manuscript, can make itself present even when it appears to have been discarded. In that way, palimpsests provide a suggestive metaphor to enrich our reflections of any twenty-first-century metropolis, especially those that have been torn apart and rebuilt over wars, natural disasters, and large-scale reforms.

Rio de Janeiro, founded in 1565, never experienced major destruction caused by bombings, earthquakes, hurricanes, or fires. Brazil's capital from 1763 until 1960, the city might seem young by the standards of the Old World, but it is difficult to imagine a place that has been more 'scraped off' during the last 200 or so years. Some of Rio's central streets had three or four generations of buildings occupy the same site in the twentieth century alone, and the image of a palimpsest becomes particularly fitting. As the most visible city of a nation eager to establish itself as modern and cosmopolitan, the former capital often acted as a showcase – or laboratory – for numerous architectural, city planning, and urbanism typologies. That alone might not set it apart, but as we will soon see, throughout this process Rio's cityscape gave shape to remarkable urban forms, social relationships, and cultural expressions.

In the context of Rio de Janeiro's urban history, the Cidade Nova was at once full of particularities and representative of the city as a whole. The period during which it served this dual role spans from the 1810s, when the neighbourhood was created by royal decree, until the monumental President Vargas Avenue spelled the destruction of its core in the 1940s. If we are to stick with social groups associated to the place, or who laid a claim to one of its landmarks, the Cidade Nova was inhabited by Gypsies, African-born freed-persons, runaway slaves of various ethnicities, Afro-descendants, and Ashkenazi Jews. It harboured many others, including impoverished migrants from rural parts of Brazil and Western Europe, mostly Portugal, Italy, and Spain. Out of encounters enabled by an urban environment, perhaps only possible in the Americas during a period of intensive transatlantic diasporas – in this New City of a so-called New World – emerged some of the musical genres (maxixe, choro, samba) that would define Brazilian national identity in the twentieth century and beyond.

Through much of its history, Cidade Nova referred to nearly everything beyond the bounds of planned but unbuilt city walls, meant to surround the colonial-era 'Old City'.[2] Like nowhere else in Rio de Janeiro, the neighbourhood was intimately connected to the city's first inhabited *morros* (hills, later called favelas), the port area, the bohemian quarter of Lapa, the downtown (Centro), and early working-class suburbs. As its borders contract over time, and as it is pushed further west, the cartographic material contained here should give readers an adequate sense of the places discussed (see Maps 1–4). An effort has been made to include relevant streets and landmarks in these maps. During most of its existence, the neighbourhood's area corresponded roughly to Manhattan's Lower East Side, extending over a length of a little more than one mile, and a width of about two-thirds of a mile.

What Cariocas now label Cidade Nova denotes a much smaller portion of the city, and one that no longer includes the area of its former main square, the Praça Onze. Today's Praça Onze metro station is about 600 yards to the west of where the square was actually located. It is not only the geographical area, however, that interests us. This does not intend to be a book about a single neighbourhood, a term conceived broadly here. The spaces on which we will dwell, after all, stand out not only for the mixtures within their populations, but for the extent to which they were critical to the city's development, for the functions they acquired, and for their place in citywide and national imaginaries.

Somewhere along the line the 'new' of the Cidade Nova lost its newness, and the neighbourhood became referred to as the 'old New City'. In recent years, a cluster of shiny glass box towers has been added to the landscape. These constructions in general do not seek to integrate the surrounding fabric, parts of which remain abandoned to obsolete warehouses, decrepit buildings, or parking lots. The busy President Vargas Avenue, and perpendicular to it an elevated highway dating from the 1970s, both transformed places where people met and lived into non-places that they pass through. The names of some of the Cidade Nova's former landmarks persist as a connection to forgotten, vanished pasts: the Praça Onze metro station, as we have seen, alludes to the long-gone vibrant public square, once the focal point of the Jewish neighbourhood and of Little Africa. Over the years, the locale's original designation of Praça Onze de Junho (June Eleven Square), marking the date of the Riachuelo Battle, got shortened and turned into something else in everyday use. Rather than the 1865 military victory over Paraguay, the current station's official name commemorates the square's memory.

The Praça Onze's role in early carnival festivities and its later mythic status as the 'cradle of samba' are evoked in the location of the Sambódromo, a mix of stadium and parade-ground where today's grandiose carnival processions take place, televised for the entire country.[3] A state school, the Escola Municipal Tia Ciata, inaugurated in 1984, honors a black woman from the state of Bahia who lived in the square, known as Aunt Ciata. Her house became a gathering place and reference point for musicians, writers, politicians, and an assortment of people interested in Afro-Brazilian religious ceremonies during the 1910s and 20s. Nearby stands a bust of the Zumbi dos Palmares, the leader of a seventeenth-century *quilombo*, a maroon community in the country's north-east. The national Day of Black Consciousness has been established on the anniversary of his death, and the monument marks the area's significance in the struggles and heritage of Afro-Brazilians. Or so goes the logic of those that had it installed there in 1986, lodged between lanes of traffic.[4]

Located in the vicinity of the Mangue canal, the City Hall, a seventeen-floor reinforced concrete and glass building, has been nicknamed by the populace as the 'Piranhão' – the augmentative of an expression used to describe prostitutes.[5] Besides more obvious insinuations, the term references the nearby red-light district of the Mangue, which remained in the area for several decades after its heyday of the 1920s and 30s. Mangue, meaning marsh or swamp in Portuguese, itself unearths the ecosystem that preceded the area's development. No monuments or place names refer to the extensive Jewish presence in the neighbourhood's past.

To be sure, mentions of the Cidade Nova today do not bring to mind synagogues, samba dance halls, or prostitution, at least not to those without a personal history tied to it. The immediate associations are to a new metro station bearing its name, or to the address of the Prefeitura (the

City Hall). Except for sparse patches of terraced houses and a couple of churches that avoided demolition, little remains recognizable of the former neighbourhood. To write about its previous lives and evolution, to search for its past and articulate its significance in Rio de Janeiro's cultural history and Brazil's formation, could indeed be understood as a process akin to attempts of reading the erased layers of a palimpsest.

Palimpsests suggest a number of analogies to urban spaces. If medieval Christian monks, for example, re-inscribed over pagan texts for reasons that were economic as well as ideological, city planners and administrators of urban modernity have often operated with an analogous combination of aesthetic–political motivations.[6] Both shared a sense of entitlement as they proceeded to reconstruct or remake physical spaces. But one could also postulate that urban spaces are not only like a palimpsest, they are a palimpsest: in their capacity for absorbing elements from the past amidst transformations, in their mechanisms of recording, or in the involuntary remembrances that permeate everyday language and practices.

Sigmund Freud famously explored a comparable concept in a different context. In an essay from 1925, he approximated the *Wunderblock*, or the Mystic Writing Pad, to 'the structure of the perceptive apparatus of the mind'. The contrivance essentially consisted of a reusable writing tablet, where the contents could be cleared by raising a transparent covering-sheet. Freud describes how 'a pointed stylus scratches the surface, the depressions upon which constitute the "writing"'. Like in a palimpsest, after the 'erasure' one can discover that 'the permanent trace of what was written is retained upon the wax slab itself and is legible in suitable lights'. Freud equates the wax slab with the unconscious (1961: 227–32). Scientific techniques have been developed to render legible those traces behind the scraped-off layers of an ancient manuscript. As we know, psychoanalysis has devised its own methods.

We can attempt to transpose that analogy onto reflections about urban spaces and memory in imaginative ways. What Freud deems 'writing' can be posited as the intersection of spatial functions and personal stories. In other words, the static snapshot of street layouts, infrastructure, and place locations as represented in a map, as well as the multiple everyday practices, paths, or trajectories of individuals within a city – that which Michel de Certeau theorizes as indeed akin to linguistic discourse.[7] The dimensions, design, and proper name of a public square, for instance, but also the stories it accumulates over time: holding annual religious processions, the occasional political manifestation, or the bench where lovers meet.

Surface 'erasures' evoke the demolitions of urban reforms or the destructions of wartime. They also implicate irrevocable structural changes

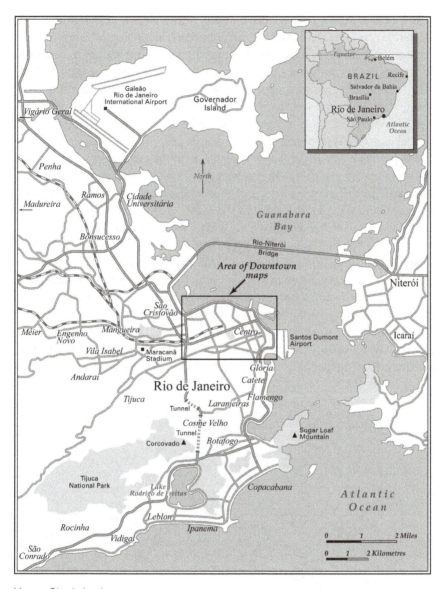

Map 1   Rio de Janeiro, *c.*2010

in *how* individuals can experience or 'write' themselves into cityscapes: new infrastructure, socio-economic transformations, technological innovations, demographic shifts, vertical and horizontal growth, introduced or redrawn streets, walkways, buildings, etc. The 'permanent traces' become legible when cultural, architectonic, and toponymic vestiges activate shared meanings, for example, or when historians, literary critics, and theorists perform a certain type of 'excavation'.[8] It is an enticing metaphor that helps put into relief the rich texture of cityscapes.

But just as cities suggest a wonderful array of metaphors, they can as easily elude or resist them. Throughout this book we will encounter limits and perils in different traditions of representing urban spaces. In the city as organism, what is the lifeblood? People, cars, capital, dreams? Who diagnoses 'ailments' and administers a 'cure'? In the city as text, who reads, what gets to be read, how do we agree upon a 'language'? And in the city as Mystic Writing Pad or palimpsest, what does it mean for things past to resurface? How do we listen to a 'trace'? Which practices persist because they adapt, and which vanish because they cannot change? From dance to music, literature to history, urban reforms to everyday life, 'writings' and 'erasures' in cities multiply, affect each other, produce 'traces' that are as ubiquitous as they can be opaque. Even the most plastic metaphor succumbs to the multifaceted dimensions of cities as lived and imagined spaces.

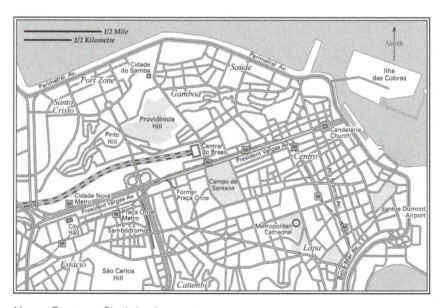

Map 2   Downtown Rio de Janeiro, *c*.2010

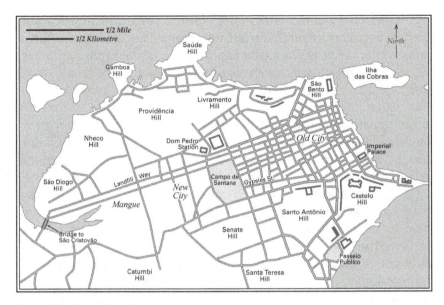

Map 3   Rio de Janeiro, c.1850

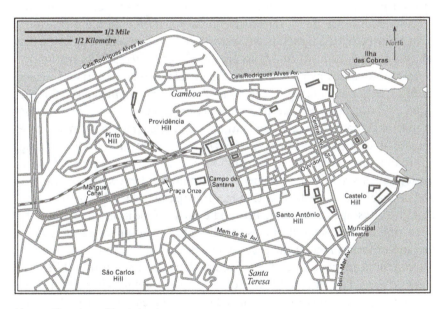

Map 4   Downtown Rio de Janeiro, c.1910

To understand and represent Rio de Janeiro's cultural history in a way that does not flatten its multiple layers, we combine concerns and approaches from a variety of disciplines. And to account for the dynamism of urban life, we bring together materials usually kept apart. Plays, novels, short stories, poems, music, paintings, essays, and film are essential to this study. But sources more often used in the social sciences than in the humanities are also present throughout, including transportation records, censuses, city plans, ordinances, maps, political speeches, oral testimonies, memoirs, family archives, letters, travel accounts, newspapers, magazines, and scientific treatises.

The Cidade Nova poses a set of methodological challenges that can be turned into opportunities. For much of its life, the neighbourhood paradoxically entered lettered imaginaries owing to practices that escaped the immediate concerns of most lettered elites. Until being embraced by modernists, Afro-Brazilian religions, immigration, popular music, carnival, and prostitution were often considered unfit for writing about. So how does one write a cultural history of urban spaces based on sources that in most cases represent them as marginal or incidental, if at all? The question in itself provides an initial answer: the linguistic markers of how authors – or fictional characters – internalize a place can be even more revealing than descriptive passages. It is not just adjectives that concern us, then, but adverbs as well: is the Cidade Nova portrayed as *here, there*, or *way over there*?

Textual analyses play a more prominent role in this book than in most cultural histories. Taking a cue from Freud's spatial metaphor for the mind, we can describe our procedure as an attempt to reconstruct the cognitive mappings of a given author. Cognitive or mental maps have become associated with Kevin Lynch's *The Image of the City* (1960), denoting an individual's internal representation of the city, as opposed to a 'cartographer's map'.[9] City planners usually employ the concept as positive and desirable: it suggests orienting features (paths, edges, landmarks, etc.) that give cityscapes a visual quality and a sense of meaning, as opposed to alienation or confusion. If our use of the concept encompasses more than just urban forms, mental images can also denote biases and unrecognized projections. A neighbourhood perceived as dangerous might in fact be safe, and vice versa. Legibility to Lynch means 'the ease with which [a city's] parts can be recognized and can be organized into a coherent pattern' (1960: 2–3). Yet a city can be misread, and a pattern can be coherent while revealing hidden prejudices and misperceptions.

Close readings throughout this book seek to shed new light on major works of literature while also advancing historical analyses and theoretical reflections. We will consider both how the written sources of a period represent urban spaces and the actual spaces that literature occupies. This is a historical as much as a theoretical matter: the historian José Murilo de Carvalho, referring to Brazil's nineteenth-century imperial elites, writes of 'an island of the lettered in an ocean of the illiterate' (1980: 51). Readers and writers were in fact more likely to live and work in certain zones of the city than in others.[10]

We will pursue a twofold interest in lettered cartographies and in cultural geography. The first concept resonates with *La ciudad letrada* (*The Lettered City*, 1996), where Ángel Rama studies how the written word was employed to impose order and enact power in Latin American societies, particularly during the colonial period. Here, lettered cartographies imply patterns gleaned from cognitive maps of 'knowledge-producers' (newspapers, government, radio, etc.). Although necessarily reflective of the views of urban elites, they may be dominant without being monolithic, often involving complex variables like private experiences, local politics, aesthetics, race, gender, class, etc. In the process of tracing Rio de Janeiro's lettered cartographies through several historical transitions and technological developments, the concept itself undergoes profound change, becoming progressively less cohesive as new means of cultural production emerge – along with writers from more varied backgrounds.

Lettered cartographies are often in dialectic tension with cultural geography.[11] The latter remains closer to the empirical or physical realities of how infrastructure, material resources, and cultural spaces (theatres, houses of worship, bookshops, carnival parades, etc.) are distributed in a city. Mapping this dimension of the cityscape helps us to access the perspectives of the multitudes that frequented, inhabited, or belonged in a place, but seldom left traces. The understanding of a city's cultural geography cannot be restricted to 'the lettered eye'. To that end, a study of Rio de Janeiro with focus on the Cidade Nova widens the horizon of possible readings for a number of 'canonical' texts, generates insight into what it meant to live in the city under different conditions or periods, and allows us to re-evaluate established narratives about Brazil's former capital.

But, before we proceed, a final note concerning methodology: this book returns to several sources familiar to Brazilians as well as scholars of Brazil, and brings to light materials that have been unknown or overlooked until now. At the same time, this project would not have been possible without the rich bibliography of urban, social, economic, cultural, political, and intellectual histories of Rio de Janeiro, along with studies by anthropologists, sociologists, musicologists, biographers, literary critics, and architects. Even where my interpretations diverge, I often build on prior work and remain indebted to the research and many leads left by previous authors.

II

If each of the following chapters can be read as a historical layer – or a set
of layers, what Gilles Deleuze might call a diagram[12] – in the palimpsestic
landscape of Rio de Janeiro, then the relationships between these pasts
could be described as porous: full of passageways, cumulative, marked by
unfixed boundaries. In an essay on Naples, first published in 1925, Walter
Benjamin writes that 'porosity is the inexhaustible law of the life of this city,
reappearing everywhere' (1989: 168). Something similar could be said of Rio
de Janeiro. It is a metropolis without a past of defined ethnic boundaries,
a city permeated by a history of often fluid frontiers between order and
disorder, popular and erudite, black and white, nature and urban, public
and private, sacred and profane, centre and periphery.

Along with the convergence of several 'undesirable' social and ethnic
groups, these categories overlapped in the spaces of the Cidade Nova. The
neighbourhood was uncharacteristically porous in the context of modern
cities, and to some degree characteristic of Rio de Janeiro as a whole. Despite
the historical framework, porous here should be understood as more of
a spatial than a temporal quality. The term derives from the Greek *poros*,
meaning 'passage or way'. It is part of the etymology for the skin's pores,
and for a city's port, which might itself say something about the types of
interactions found in such places. Portugal, and by extension the Portuguese
language, incorporates into its name the Latin *portus*, for port.

The concept provides a new way to interpret one of the persistent enigmas
of Rio de Janeiro and Brazil: how does a culture and self-image defined by
mixture coexist with stark socio-economic disparity? This study hopes to
offer insights into how in an environment of inequality and asymmetrical
exchanges, in a country where slavery was not abolished until 1888,
multi-ethnic encounters and a permeable cultural life were able to flourish.
These questions remain urgent as Brazil continues to confront problems of
urban violence, uneven infrastructure, and poverty. Rio's virtues should
not cover up for its problems, but neither should the discussion of its faults
ignore a vital and exciting cultural memory. The idea of porosity, in this
context, seeks to add to longstanding debates among those who study or
think about Brazil. It also unveils an arena where the Brazilian experience
can make a real contribution to global debates about racial diversity, urban
juxtapositions, and social divisions.

Variants of porous have begun to appear more frequently in discourses
of the humanities and social sciences in recent years.[13] At least one critic,
Beatriz Jaguaribe, uses the adjective form in relation to Rio (2007: 114).
More often adopted in scientific literature, the term provides a less loaded

alternative to syncretism and miscegenation, helping to avert the celebratory connotations these descriptors have acquired in the Brazilian context since the 1930s. Both are linked to the affirmation of a supposed racial democracy that dangerously overlooks the country's long history of racism and social injustice. Porous can be used more broadly than syncretic or even *mestizo*: it describes, for example, an institution with a loose sense of membership, where individuals come and go. Porosity, at the same time, lends itself to some more precise uses than hybridity. In the most direct sense, hybrid could be applied to all cultural practices.[14] Every musical form or religion, for instance, can be understood as composed of heterogeneous elements, regardless of how pure they might seem in the eyes of practitioners. That does not mean, evidently, that all musical forms and religions should be considered porous.

Porosity is often positive and desirable, but it is not necessarily so: its clearest expressions in Rio de Janeiro's history are to be found not only in a vibrant and multiracial music scene, where people of different social classes mingle and collaborate, but also in a dreadful red-light district, populated by Afro-descendants and Jewish women alike, and frequented by the rich as well as the poor. Due to this ambivalence, it is appropriate to recall the 'cordial man' of Sérgio Buarque de Holanda's seminal *Raízes do Brasil* from 1936 (*Roots of Brazil*, 2012). Cordiality, in his writings, speaks to an incapacity to comprehend the distinction between private and public domains, where those performing public functions are chosen according to personal trust, family ties, or friendship rather than their capacity (Holanda 2006: 140–51). It can be interpreted as a conservative category – the veneer of cordiality occludes a system that does not favour merit or change. If we pursue the logic, Rio de Janeiro's porous cultural forms serve to sustain the vast distance that separates the material conditions of its social classes.

José Miguel Wisnik, in his recent *Veneno remédio: o futebol e o Brasil* (Poison Cure: Football and Brazil, 2008), proposes yet another way to articulate this ambivalence. His essay of national interpretation resorts to the *pharmakon*, containing at once the possibilities of curing and poisoning.[15] These dual potentials are embodied in Rio de Janeiro's porosity, and I argue that the Cidade Nova's history and its representations provide a key to help us unlock some of the city's dilemmas. Rio de Janeiro has been known since the early twentieth century as the *cidade maravilhosa*, the marvellous city, and those familiar with its natural beauty will find any explanation of the adjective to be superfluous. To those accustomed with the images and realities of urban violence, and with the intense contrast between favelas and upper-class buildings, it might also not be necessary to explain Rio's more recent epithet as the *cidade partida*. The expression could be translated as 'split city', 'broken city', or 'divided city', though the last will be preferred here.

The phrase gained currency after appearing in the title of a book by Zuenir Ventura, published in 1994, a moment of acute crisis in Rio. Zuenir wrote *Cidade partida* in the aftermath of a massacre in the Vigário Geral favela, when twenty people were murdered by off-duty policemen. This followed another tragic event, in July 1993, when six street children and two homeless men were killed on the steps of the Candelária Church. Amidst a climate of deep disenchantment, the journalist's narrative intertwines two sides of the so-called divided city. Over a ten-month period, Zuenir Ventura spent time with residents, social leaders, and drug traffickers from Vigário Geral. Simultaneously, he chronicled the incipient efforts of civil society leaders to respond to Rio's growing violence. The movement led to the creation of the Viva Rio NGO. If Zuenir refers to Vigário Geral as 'a world where the Republic never arrived' (12), Viva Rio brought together some of its most influential members from the media, business, activism, and academia.

At a time when many in public opinion voiced the desire to combat violence with more violence, Viva Rio's founders reached a consensus that any solution to Rio's crisis would have to involve the approximation of its 'two cities'. Although most of *Cidade partida* focuses on contemporary developments, the author carefully disarms a nostalgic imaginary of the upper classes, where the 1950s is perceived as Rio's golden age of Bossa Nova and innocence. The book opens with a catalogue of violence, corruption, and 'divisions' from that era. Throughout *Porous City*, we will see earlier precursors to the notion of a polarized place, tracing discourses of Rio de Janeiro as 'two cities' to the beginning of the twentieth century.

As Zuenir Ventura's work recognizes, nonetheless, even where disparities between areas of the city are indeed glaring, reified categories often prove to be more porous than apparent. The idea of Rio as a city of mixtures and encounters coexisted with the imprecations of a *cidade partida*. To deem Rio de Janeiro a 'porous city', in other words, does not intend to suggest an opposition to the 'divided city'. On the contrary, mixture and division here are frequently like the different sides of a coin, the two faces of Janus, reminiscent of the ambiguity central to Georg Simmel's 'Bridge and Door'. In that essay, Simmel argues that by designating things as separate, we have already connected them in our consciousness. Conversely, in order to connect things, they must first be separated: the door represents how dividing and connecting are two sides of the same act.[16]

A divided city, then, can be argued to presuppose a porous city, and vice versa. Representations of Rio de Janeiro as a city split between *morro e asfalto* (hills and asphalt, literally), on one hand, carry the risk of obscuring the extent to which their histories and challenges remain interrelated.[17] To speak of porosity, on the other hand, accounts for the connections implicit in the city's socio-spatial segregation, manifested most visibly in (seemingly) unrelated realms: widespread urban violence and popular culture. At the same time, it points to the unfulfilled possibilities of mixture, only partly realized in some of Rio de Janeiro's more open cultural expressions: football, samba, funk carioca, carnival, beach-going. If only we could add to this list further examples from education, business, law, medicine, government, etc.

As Rio de Janeiro's history unfolds over the next couple of hundred pages, readers will notice the argument for a gradual decrease in the city's porosity. It may be so, as spaces of mixture became a target for state-sponsored modernization projects, hygienist practices, intellectual discourses, and city planning. Through much of the nineteenth and twentieth centuries, governing elites were intent on confining, domesticating, eliminating, or driving out those aspects of fluidity and interchange that paradoxically marked the formation of Brazil's dominant cultures and which were frequently concentrated on the Cidade Nova and similar spaces: the musical scene, prostitution, as well as undesirable ethnic and social communities.

Discomfiture with the city's mixtures – not absent of racial overtones – particularly after the establishment of a republican regime in 1889, must be tied to a Brazilian search for order and progress. Above all while it remained a national capital, the ideals outlined by the positivist motto in the country's flag defined much of the urban planning and government measures directed towards Rio de Janeiro. There has been a longstanding desire to 'govern by straight lines', as Maria Alice Rezende de Carvalho shows in a text about engineers during Rio de Janeiro's belle époque (1994: 65–91). Discourses echoing that past have resurfaced throughout the city's more recent history. It must not be forgotten, then, that despite all associations between order and reason, the pursuit of order can be at once liberating, empowering, but also systematic, rigid, and even delirious or cruel. As the past century taught us, sometimes tragically, urban reforms and renewal programmes can be blinded by ideology, divorced from the complexities of city life, and impose stifling conditions on the everyday social needs of its inhabitants.

A last meaning of porosity deserves to be unpacked: in spite of the perversely unequal systems of distribution of resources or infrastructure behind the ethos of openness and inclusivity that Rio de Janeiro's residents sometimes cultivate about themselves, there remains a dimension of porous having to do quite simply with an ability to absorb elements from the most diverse traditions, across the multiple Afro and Jewish transatlantic diasporas, for example. While avoiding the many traps provided by Rio de Janeiro – those that lead towards impairing seduction, as well as towards inexorable indignation – it also seems prudent to avoid what Marshall

single neighbourhood rather than a continent – while our interests will be much broader.

11 Their relationship can be explored through the notion of a 'cartographie vécue' (a lived cartography), responsive both to the subject's spatial representations of cognitive mapping, and to what Henri Lefebvre means by 'l'espace vécu' (lived space), at once practiced and socially produced spaces (1991). We may also think of Jonathan Raban's 'soft city of illusion, myth, aspiration, nightmare [...] as real, maybe more real, than the hard city' (1998: 4).

12 Tom Conley writes, citing Deleuze's *Foucault*, that 'a historian can work in the context of what Deleuze calls a cartography of becoming: "A diagram is a map, or rather [a set of] maps superimposed upon another. And, from one diagram to the other, new maps are drawn [tirées]. Thus no diagram fails to bear, next to the points it connects, other points, relatively free or unbound, points of creativity, of mutation, or resistance; and we move from them in order to comprehend the totality"' (2007: 13).

13 In very different contexts, Taylor writes of 'porous selves' (2007), Chambers refers to a 'porous modernity' (2008), and there has been at least one conference with 'Porous City' in its title, organized by *urban interface* and held in Oslo in 2010.

14 For a more nuanced discussion of the concept, see Canclini 1995.

15 In English, see Wisnik 2006. *Pharmakos* assumes an important role in Derridean deconstruction. See 'Plato's Pharmacy' (Derrida 1981).

16 In most Romance languages, the word for door (*porta* in Portuguese) also shares its etymology with porous. Janus, not coincidentally, is sometimes considered the god of doors.

17 I refer to the contemporary paradigm of hills, designating favelas, versus asphalt, used as a metonymy for the 'rest' of the city – itself revealing of how a post-Fordist urban order equates the spaces of motor cars to the formal, non-favela city.

CHAPTER ONE

At the Centre of an Imperial Capital: Swamps, Yellow Fever, and Gypsy Parties

He who knows one of the cities, will know them all, so exactly alike are they, except where the nature of the grounds prevents.

Thomas More, *Utopia*

I

By 1808, when the Portuguese court arrived in Rio de Janeiro after fleeing Napoleon's troops, it was a port city of 40,000 to 50,000 inhabitants and the major trading centre of a predominantly rural country.[1] The colony's capital since only 1763, Rio de Janeiro was unprepared to become capital of the United Kingdom of Portugal, Brazil, and the Algarves, a title obtained in 1815.[2] Besides the Royal family, the newly acquired status brought key changes: opening of the ports for trade with foreign markets, the establishment of Brazil's first bank and printing press, as well as the creation of institutions like a Royal Library, Botanic Garden, and Academy of Fine Arts. The only American city ever to serve as the seat of Metropolitan power, Rio would undergo rapid growth during the period following the court's arrival. In twelve years alone, the population just about doubled to around eighty thousand.[3]

The colonial capital made perfect sense as a port city. Located in a naturally protected and calm bay, it connected inland through routes that led to the gold-mining interior regions of Minas Gerais. The British merchant John Luccock, who lived in Rio from 1808 until 1818, remarks that 'when the court first arrived [...] the city was circumscribed within very narrow boundaries' (Luccock 1820: 38). It was surrounded by the ocean to the north-east and east, swamps to the west and north-west, and several hills elsewhere. Although they made the capital notoriously easy to fortify, these natural boundaries also constrained its ability to expand – and Rio remains to this day a city in many ways shaped by geographical peculiarities.

Dom João VI, the Portuguese regent, had little alternative but to mandate city growth towards the swamps of São Diogo. By a royal decree in 1811, tax incentives were granted to those who built on the swampy terrains, which were gradually land-filled. One-storey houses were not allowed, and exemptions were greater for *sobrados* – larger houses with more than five doors or windows in their facades.[4] Some of these buildings would become the infamous and overcrowded tenements of later decades. In any case, thus was born the area known as the Cidade Nova, the New City.

Besides helping to solve a severe housing crisis, the provision to stimulate construction in that area had another convenient reason for the royal family. A few months after their arrival, a local nobleman offered his quarters in the semi-rural neighbourhood of São Cristovão, and Dom João decided to move the royal residences there. The property, known as the Quinta da Boa Vista, was a bit removed from the centrally located Royal Palace, past the yet to be drained swamps. A land-filled New City, besides giving the city a place to grow towards, considerably shortened the path from the city's administrative centre to the royal residences of São Cristovão. As Luccock attests, in 1813, a new road 'was in progress across the marshes West of the city, to the village of St Cristophe, whither the royal family frequently retired' (244).

In 1819, it took around an hour and a half to reach the royal villa from the city's centre, through the tortuous Mata-Porcos Road.[5] By 1821, another visitor to Rio notes that 'The road of the Cidade Nova, being the daily route of the royal family, is kept in pretty good order' (Henderson 1821: 74). That new road connected the city's centre to the imperial residences by cutting through the entire length of the New City, an extension of roughly one and a quarter miles.[6] It became known as the Caminho do Aterrado (Landfill Way) or the Caminho das Lanternas (Lantern Way), owing to the installation of fish-oil lanterns. On that subject, an impressed Revd Robert Walsh remarked in the late 1820s that 'lamps [...] are now sufficiently numerous, and the town is as well provided as most cities on the continent of Europe' (Walsh 1831: 254).

Foreign observers had a very acute perception of the extent to which Rio was divided as an Old City and a New City. The Campo de Santana (Santana Field), named after the small St Anne Chapel built during the eighteenth century on the edge of town, formed the boundary between them. This was the site where Dom João's son, Dom Pedro I, was acclaimed as the country's first emperor, following his declaration of Brazilian independence in 1822. Officially renamed Acclamation Field, it became a privileged place within Rio's political history and cultural formation, as we will soon begin to see. The New City began to develop in the area adjacent to the Field. While its boundaries would gradually come to be defined, through much of the first half of the nineteenth century, Cidade Nova referred to nearly everything beyond the limits of the Old City, much of it still consisting of unoccupied marshes well into the 1860s. An almanac would define it more rigidly as 'the district comprehended from the Acclamation Field to the São Cristovão street' (Laemmert 1854: 195).

It is because of the Cidade Nova's 'accidental' central location that we have any mention of its early days, especially in the accounts of foreign visitors to Brazil. Throughout the nineteenth century, European travellers in Rio were often invited to see the king and later emperors D. Pedro I and D. Pedro II. Several wrote about their impressions of the way to the Quinta da Boa Vista. Absent the account of Brazilians, we must rely on their descriptions to get a sense of how the area developed. A few years after Luccock's stay in the capital, for example, Revd Walsh noted that 'Already, in the memory of persons residing there, the most extensive and almost incredible accessions have been made to the city; – the whole of the space about the Campo de Santa Anna was a stagnant marsh; it is now drained, and covered with streets' (253).

The Cidade Nova's beginnings were rather auspicious. In 1817, Luiz Gonçalvez dos Santos (better known as Padre Perereca), defending his interests as a Canon, urges that a 'sumptuous' church be built in the centre of the new neighbourhood, 'to crown and beautify' its recent growth. The small Santana Chapel, he argues, became insufficient to serve a part of the city where 'so many noble and magnificent houses shine' (Santos 1825: 162). More contained, the French painter Jean-Baptiste Debret, who arrived in 1816 and remained throughout the 1820s, remarks that the Cidade Nova's constructions were of much 'better architectonic taste' than those of the Old City (Debret 1954: 290).[7] A prominent contemporary historian praised the area's increasing population and 'beauty' (Silva Lisboa 1834–5: 174). To the Cidade Nova's residents, particularly those living further from the Campo de Santana, these glowing descriptions might have seemed to conceal at least part of the reality: the English naturalist Charles Bunbury writes of the swamps being filled with all sorts of refuse, including dead animals (1981: 21).

Several of Rio de Janeiro's very first urban plans, intent on rendering the colonial town worthy of its newly acquired functions, sought to capitalize on the Cidade Nova's geographical location. When the court architect and captain of the Royal Corps of Engineers, José Joaquim de Santa Anna, proposed a plan concerned with the city's drainage, he took the Campo de Santana as its central point (Santa Anna 1815: 8). At the time of its writing in 1811, the blank slate provided by the Cidade Nova held the promise of allowing Rio de Janeiro's urbanization to start anew. Since the neighbourhood's streets remained unpaved, for example, they could more easily incorporate new techniques to facilitate draining (13).

During the 1820s, there were plans to develop and 'beautify' the Cidade Nova, drafted by the French architect Grandjean de Montigny.[8] And in 1843, the engineer Henrique de Beaurepaire Rohan, employing the latest draining and paving techniques, was responsible for what could be deemed the first comprehensive urban plans in the country's history.[9] All of these proposals envisioned the city expanding westward in the direction of the swamps, and gave the Campo de Santana a status as the capital's centre, which Montigny thought should function as a 'forum'. Both plans also shared a preoccupation with imposing a grid-like system for the Cidade Nova's streets. This recalls Lisbon's Pombaline Baixa, a downtown neighbourhood reconstructed after the 1755 Earthquake. Unusual in the context of Portuguese urbanization, such grid-like designs presented a stark contrast to the irregular layout of streets in the Old City.[10]

These plans would not be implemented, and although they produce echoes in later urban interventions, their broad vision for the city remained largely unfulfilled. It is not inconceivable that the Campo could have assumed a role comparable to Mexico City's Plaza Mayor as a stage of national manifestations and as a symbolic centre, in which case the Cidade Nova would have turned out to be a very different type of neighbourhood. During the 1810s alone, after all, important institutions became located there, like the Army Headquarters and the Royal Museum (later the National Museum). While the latter, on the Cidade Nova side of the Campo de Santana, confirms the designs of city planners for the area, the former had been attracted to the field's de facto position at the edge of the city: the open spaces were ideal for military exercises (Azevedo 1877: 420).

As it so often happens, the city's future did not conform to the predictions of specialists. Even early in the century, it was already becoming apparent that the aristocracy preferred areas further outside of the city.[11] The seafront *chácaras* (country houses) in Botafogo began to stretch the city in the direction of the future South Zone, to this day home to much of Rio's affluent populations and to its world-famous beaches. By the mid-century, it seemed less likely that the Cidade Nova would become a neighbourhood for the wealthy, or a site planned according to the latest European ideals of what a city should be like. Rio de Janeiro, against the wishes of some, could never be a European city. Like capitals from the so-called Old World, it had to contend with 'undesirables', among them Gypsies. Unlike its counterparts, however, Rio also had to confront tropical diseases, and was irrevocably defined by having the 'largest urban slave population in the Americas' (Karasch 1987:

xxi). These three elements, to varying degrees, would be instrumental in shaping the Cidade Nova's later role in the making of a national, Brazilian culture.

II

Besides references in travel narratives, and most of them in passing, the Cidade Nova does not appear often in Rio de Janeiro's mid-nineteenth-century literature or historiography. Few of the city's residents (at least among those able to write) cared to describe or even mention the area – Joaquim Manuel de Macedo's famous *Um passeio pela cidade do Rio de Janeiro* (A Promenade through the City of Rio de Janeiro), from 1862, ignored it altogether. But one of the earliest exceptions happens to be the now canonical *Memórias de um sargento de milícias* (Memoirs of a Militia Sergeant), a work that can offer great insight into how this newly inhabited zone would function within the city's lettered cartographies and cultural geography – as a space perceived and represented as marginal while paradoxically being in the geographic centre.

Manuel Antônio de Almeida's narrative opens with a declarative phrase that both locates the action in a recent specific history and evokes the language of fables: 'It was back in the time of the king' ('Era no tempo do rei').[12] The text right away establishes a *then* while the paratext implies a *now*. The novel's serial publication from 1852 to 1853 in a newspaper, the *Correio Mercantil*, in and of itself reinforces its contemporariness. Appearance in a medium predicated on current events, in other words, indicates the story's currency to a mid-nineteenth-century audience.[13] At the same time, it is left clear the plot will unravel during the days of Dom João's reign, earlier in the century, since the king had returned to Portugal in 1821. In the second sentence, a new paragraph, the narrator begins to also demarcate the setting along the lines of a *here* versus a *there*:

> One of the four corners that the Ouvidor and Quitanda streets form was referred to as 'Bailiff's Corner', in those days. And an apt name it was, for it was there [*aí*] the favorite meeting place of all the individuals exercising that office, which was then held in no inconsiderable esteem. (Almeida 1941: 23)

The adverbial choice *aí* instead of *lá* or *ali* signifies the place's proximity to the reader. Though all three can be translated as 'there', *aí* denotes *there, where you are*. It is no longer the meeting place of bailiffs, and thus does not merit the adverb *aqui* (here), but the text introduces the sense that we have a narrative voice originating from a central space.

The recurrent past tense emphasizes how things *used to be*, perhaps also a reminder of how fast they were changing. The verb in the present ('form') refers to the very specific coordinates that plot the scene within two major streets of the Old City, a well-known point of reference to readers familiar with Rio de Janeiro.[14] In that centre of the past, the narrator evokes right away a degree of order. The reader encounters, for example, a stable correspondence between how places were named and their function within the colonial city – something that finds echoes in the 'order of the signs' of what Ángel Rama calls the 'ordered city' (1984: 11). By the time Almeida writes, however, he must already explain how the Bailiff's Corner had gained its name. Through a metonymic displacement, then, the text creates an association of that *here*, that central place close to the readers, with the law – albeit recognizing that its latest representatives (in the first direct acknowledgement of a *now*) are no longer what they used to be: 'The bailiffs of today are but meager shadows of bailiffs in the time of the king [...]'.

As the second paragraph progresses the narrator refers to the dynamic between bailiffs and their 'opposing extreme', the appeals court judges, and in the process articulates a revealing axiom of Manuel Antonio de Almeida's literature: 'Well, the extremes, after all, touch each other [...]'. In other words, he does not set up a rigid dichotomy, but rather a dialectic relationship between opposing forces. That dialectic nature serves as the basis for a seminal reading of the book by the Brazilian sociologist and literary critic Antonio Candido. In 'Dialética da malandragem' (The Dialectic of Roguery), he argues that besides 'a first universalizing stratum' Almeida's work has a 'second stratum [...] constituted by the dialectic of order and disorder, that manifests concretely the human relations at the level of the book' (1993: 36), organized in accordance to the author's 'accurate intuitions' of the social reality of Rio de Janeiro in the period (37).

The dynamics of these human relations of Almeida's fiction, in turn, elucidate how urban spaces of Rio were experienced and internalized during the course of the century. On the surface, or on a diegetic level, the novel's Cidade Nova conforms to the expected representations of a peripheral area from the perspective of a lettered city, of a knowledge-producing centre – fitting within patterns of how the press and fiction of the period portrayed the neighbourhood. Closer analysis reveals how the narrative's mapping, at the same time, defies or resists these expectations, leaving room for more contact and exchanges between 'opposing extremes' than immediately apparent.

A couple of paragraphs into the first chapter, the narrator places the reader back in a familiar place: 'But let us return to the corner'. Its every day was predictable, almost scripted: 'Whosoever passed by on a weekday in that blessed age would see seated there on low, worn leather seats, called 'campaign chairs', a more or less numerous group of those noble people peacefully conversing [...]'. From that universe comes the protagonist's father, Leonardo, a figure presented in an unflattering light ('soft' and 'sluggish'), which allows us to identify a degree of irony in the supposed nostalgic view of that 'blessed age', of that 'noble people' (24). Leonardo was a Portuguese immigrant to Brazil who 'never left the corner', but once his unfaithful wife fled to Portugal with a sea captain, he abandons his son and the promise of a stable life.

Leonardo's son, the story's eventual protagonist, would be raised by a godfather and engage in all sorts of adventures that to many critics recall the picaresque narratives of the Iberian Peninsula.[15] But it is the father who provides our first excursion to the city's outskirts, in a revealing passage:

> Way out there at the mangrove swamp of the Cidade Nova, next to a pond, there stood an ugly-looking straw-roofed house whose dirty exterior and muddy street front clearly indicated that its interior cleanliness would be no better [...]. The house was almost always shut up tight, which cast a certain air of mystery upon it. The sinister dwelling was inhabited by a figure cut from the most detestable of molds: an aged half-breed [caboclo velho] with a heinous, dirty face who dressed in rags. (41)

In contrast to the precision of the reference to the old city, Almeida's narrator represents the Cidade Nova as something vague and distant. It is also 'way out there' ('lá para as bandas') which seems to position his voice as coming from the centre, from the lettered city of the newspaper and its readers. *Lá* (there), unlike *aí* or *ali*, denotes a distance from both enunciator and receptor. If one assumes a point of view from the Centro (as the old city became known) – in other words, from the perspective of the producers of textual knowledge – those swamps are not only marginal but also perilous, to be avoided at any cost.

The language adopted renders clear the types of associations at play, and they are predictably negative: *ugly, dirty, mysterious, sinister.* Although by Almeida's time the area had become considerably more urbanized than when the story takes place, in the novel those quarters are home to the house of the 'caboclo', a figure that adds other elements to the semantic field of the Cidade Nova. The term usually describes one of mixed Indigenous and European ancestry, and was once used more broadly to designate Brazil's native populations. It also applies to supernatural entities, and there is a variant of Yoruba-influenced Afro-Brazilian religious systems called Candomblé de Caboclo (Prandi 2001). The caboclo, nonetheless, hails from the rural portions of the country, and this particular one practises *feitiçaria* or sorcery, a 'superstition' condemned in the text as immoral, uncivilized, and belonging to the past. The narrator ridicules the caboclo's supposed powers, and the episode reinforces what Jean Franco would label the 'racial roots of magic', 'dependent on the clichéd cartography that separates "rational" Europe from the non-rational rest' (2002: 9).

The Cidade Nova swamps, then, emerge as a frontier with rural, 'non-rational' Brazil, where order seemingly begins to break down – in a reiteration of the 'Greek conception that opposed the civilized *polis* to the barbarianism of the non-urbanized' (Rama 1984: 14). Certeau's distinction between place (*lieu*) and space (*espace*) also becomes useful: place 'implies an indication of stability', 'space is composed of intersections of mobile elements' (1984: 117). The Bailiff's Corner, with its law officials 'sitting down', stood as the central place from which order emanates, doubled as a metonymy of the lettered city out of which the narrator ostensibly tells the story. We only venture outwards once Leonardo's life falls into disarray. Leonardo searches for the caboclo and his supernatural powers 'way out there' in the Mangue due to problems with a young woman he falls for – but not any woman, a 'cigana', or Gypsy.

After Leonardo meets her, we are presented with detailed descriptions of their parties, frequently suppressed by the Major Vidigal, an authority figure (based on a well-known historical character of the same name) straight from the Centro, seeking to assert the law. The narrator makes a point to remind us: 'The guard-house was in the Sé Square', in the Old City (23). The pattern of state authorities engaging Rio's peripheral zones and marginalized residents in a repressive fashion will not seem unfamiliar to those aware of the city's later history and present circumstances. At any rate, one may thus spatialize and map Candido's reading of the dialectic between order and disorder in Almeida's narrative. In other words, the pole of disorder corresponds precisely to the Cidade Nova, with its caboclos, Gypsies, and tempting festivities, while authority and the law emanate from the central city, seat of royal and military power.

Brazil began receiving Gypsies, who were expelled from Portugal (in tandem with other European countries) during the sixteenth century (Pieroni 2000). The present-day Praça Tiradentes, past the Rua da Vala, now Uruguaiana – which to some constituted the border between the Cidade Nova and the Cidade Velha (Villaça 1998: 323) – was then called Campo dos Ciganos (Gypsies Field). The street leading to the Campo de Santana was called Rua dos Ciganos (Gypsies Street). As the city expanded after the arrival of the Portuguese court, Gypsy encampments moved further out to the Cidade Nova. In the 1830s, Gypsies frequented the Campo de Santana, trying to sell items like fake jewellery to farmers or travellers from the interior, who stopped at the Campo's fountains where their mules and horses could find water (Holloway 1993: 129–30). By 1885, their association with the neighbourhood had crystallized to the point that Alexandre José de Mello Moraes would name his compendium of Gypsy popular poetry as *Cancioneiro dos ciganos: poesia popular dos ciganos da Cidade Nova* (Songbook of Gypsies: Popular Poetry of the Gypsies of the Cidade Nova).

A contemporary of Almeida, Antônio Gonçalves Teixeira e Sousa also includes Gypsies in his *As tardes de um pintor, ou as intrigas de um jesuíta* (The Afternoons of a Painter or the Intrigues of a Jesuit), from 1847. Although this novel's depictions might be less surprising, they are revealing of longstanding prejudices towards Gypsies, and of growing prejudices towards the Cidade Nova. A chapter entitled 'O campo dos ciganos' (Gypsies Field) takes the action back to the eighteenth century without specifying exactly when it takes place, setting up a *then* versus *now* similar to that of Almeida's novel. Teixeira e Sousa was equally attuned to the rapid changes that Rio de Janeiro underwent, 'a city that like an emporium of Meridional America, threatens to be an American colossus in a short time, growing without stopping, visibly, a century ago it was not even a shadow of what it is today'. Alluding to the future ahead, the narrator shifts to the present, testifying to how the conversion of marshes into a completely land-filled Cidade Nova was still underway in the 1840s: 'covering the entire terrain, a swamp of muddy and marshy waters, and thick mangroves, the escaping remnants of which we see until today at the edges of the Cidade Nova's Landfill Road'.

As tardes de um pintor then proceeds to paint the Gypsies and their community in Rio de Janeiro, tracing them from the undefined but recent past to the reader's present:

> In that time [...] Both the Gypsy Field and the [Gypsy] street did not have that name because it was given arbitrarily, no, since it was in this nascent neighborhood of the city, covered by all sorts of filth, that a multitude of Gypsies established themselves, given to all sorts of vices and bad habits; and in the proportion that education and civilization advance throughout the city, these Gypsies receded and hid themselves, as if they were antipodes of civilization and good behavior. Until this day we see them inhabiting the edge of the Aterrado, the slope of the inlet [of São Diogo], etc.

The construction and exploitation of an opposition between civilized and barbarian has of course become a familiar tale for the postcolonial reader. In the post-independence new order, nonetheless, similar patterns reproduce themselves, targeting marginalized groups. Gypsies, Jews, and Afro-descendants – all at one point associated to the Cidade Nova – would remain at the bottom of the hierarchy. Even as the number of Gypsies dwindled, and even as the Cidade Nova became geographically central in Rio de Janeiro's layout, social forces antithetic to *education, progress,* and *civilization* became indefinitely mapped on or projected to that area of the city.

Although Teixeira e Sousa's narrator adopts the past tense, suggesting there might have been some change between the period alluded to and the time of narration, his description goes much further than Almeida's in mapping the Cidade Nova as a space of lawlessness:

> Well, since this neighborhood of the city was the least frequented and the most deserted, especially at night, it was also there where hiding places were found for deserting soldiers, sailors who abandoned the royal navy, slaves escaping their masters, those evading prison, exiles (by banishment) whose exile had ended, and, at last, all sorts of bandits, who joined with the Gypsies to steal, murder, etc.

As tardes de um pintor, despite this passage, might seem to add some complexity to the negative representation of Gypsies. It includes a character suggestively named Justo, a Gypsy who yearns for justice. He is, nonetheless, introduced as an exception within that multitude prone to vice and bad customs. The narrative, in the end, perpetuates the usual stereotypes, several of which reappear in Almeida's book.[16]

As many others in *Memórias de um sargento de milícias,* the cigana exhibits little psychological complexity and remains nameless, akin to the allegorical characters that permeate medieval dramas and the Iberian folklore. On Gypsies as a social group, we read the following: they are 'the plague', 'an idle people of few scruples'. It is among these uncommendable types that Leonardo's son, the unruly boy of the same name, spends his first night away from home at a party in the Campo dos Ciganos, with two new young Gypsy friends. This Leonardo goes on to become the novel's protagonist, and, rather ironically, at the end, the militia sergeant of the title.

It is that trajectory, from outlaw to law enforcer, which in part characterizes the peculiar dialectic between order and chaos, law and disorder, which Antonio Candido identifies both in Almeida's text and in Brazilian society:

> The special stamp of the book consists in a certain absence of moral judgment and in the cheerful acceptance of 'man as he is,' a mixture of cynicism and good nature that demonstrates to the reader a relative

equivalence between the universe of order and that of disorder, between what would conventionally be called good and evil. (Candido 1995: 91)

Candido concludes that 'Order and disorder are, therefore, extremely relative, and connected in innumerable ways' (92). He could potentially be referring to the spatial arrangement of the city itself, more porous than the New City/Old City dichotomy implies. In a physical sense, the two halves of Rio de Janeiro were indeed connected by thoroughfares that cut across them. Significantly, as the novel progresses, it blurs spatial distinctions, especially in the passages where festivals and religious processions take over the streets.

Several other curious dialectic relationships can be explored, then, and they might be equally peculiar to nineteenth-century Rio de Janeiro, to a type of spatial porosity with great consequence to the city's daily life and cultural production. Some of what Walter Benjamin had to say about Naples might have found an appropriate correlative in a description of Rio: 'Irresistible, the festival penetrates each and every working day. Porosity is the inexhaustible law of the life of this city' (1989: 168). It is an attribute that seems to help shape the most enduring literature or music to come out of Rio, including *Memórias de um sargento de milícias* – a 'hybrid' text, notoriously difficult to categorize.[17] Likewise, if the narrator appears to hail from a *here*, as we have discussed, providing a perspective that stems from the Centro, Almeida himself – and ultimately his work – can be better understood as operating somewhere in between.

A certain distance between author and narrator is perhaps already signalled by how the novel appears in newspapers signed, rather abstractly, by an anonymous 'Um brasileiro' (A Brazilian). Upon closer inspection, the reader finds a measure of dissimulation in the narrator's mapping of the 'distant' Cidade Nova. As the novel advances, the city's marginal areas are not so vague for the author after all: he is more than familiar with aspects of life *way out there*. While condemning Gypsies, the text reveals a remarkable knowledge of their music, dances, and rituals. And while dismissing the caboclo's works as a farce, the novel curiously reports in detail how he invokes divinities to help bring back the woman Leonardo desired. Almeida's precise descriptions have in fact been considered an important primary source to musicologists and cultural historians interested in the development of Rio de Janeiro's musical traditions.

Mário de Andrade, an accomplished musicologist, describes the novel as 'full of musical references of great documentary interest' in an introduction (1941: 10). José Ramos Tinhorão, an important contemporary scholar of Brazilian music, deems him a 'pioneer in the collection of musical folklore'

(2000–2: 43). In Brazil's early Romanticism, according to him, writers would 'always focus on the music of the people as something exotic' – with the exception of Almeida, part of the reason he is considered a 'precursor of the realist "novel of customs" [romance de costumes]' (44). Although he supposedly relied on oral sources and acquaintances when composing characters like Major Vidigal, it seems clear that Almeida had an intimacy with the language, daily lives, and practices of an urban social layer that frequently eluded historians and went ignored by novelists: the ranks composed of white artisans and free mulatos, 'soldiers, sailors, domestic servants, handymen, vagrants (occasionally given to marginal or even criminal activities) and prostitutes' (104) – particularly the lower middle classes who resided in the Cidade Nova while he wrote.[18]

Almeida himself, in 1840, lived with his family at the very edge of the Old City. According to Marques Rebelo's biography of the author, he would have played during his childhood in the nearby Campo de Santana (1943: 16). As the son of Portuguese parents of modest means, he in a sense belonged more to the milieu of his characters than to that of his readers, part of how 'Manuel Antônio's book is perhaps the only one in our nineteenth-century literature that does not express the outlook of the dominant classes' (Candido 1993: 51). By virtue of writing itself, in a highly stratified society where few were able to read, Almeida is already a figure of the Centro, of the lettered city. Yet he is one who navigates across its social spaces, able to absorb several popular expressions that rarely 'belonged' in writing, in the sphere of intellectuals.

To Marques Rebelo, *Memórias de um sargento de milícias* was an early 'cry of reaction' against the Brazilian Romanticism, with its 'opera indianism' of Indians and blacks who 'seem as if they have come from Paris and London'. It is an 'unconscious cry' and Almeida the first 'to write approximately as people speak in Brazil' (Rebelo 1943: 42). In the combination of seemingly conventional spatial markers, colloquial language, and informed descriptions, it is as if we had an extra-diegetic narrator but an intra-diegetic author, to borrow Gérard Genette's distinction (1983). In other words, there is a definite tension between what the narrator tells us and what he shows. One gets the sense that Almeida cannot help but insert his experience of Rio's peripheral zones into the novel.

If, as Ángel Rama argues, the 'written word would live in Latin America as the only binding one, in opposition to the spoken word which belonged to the realm of things precarious and uncertain', then Almeida's work begins to break down the opposition. The relation between the language of books and the language of the streets would also function in a dialectic mode. His novel emerges as among the first to bridge 'the distance between the rigid letter and the fluid spoken word, which made a city of protocols out of the lettered city, reserved to a strict minority' (Rama 1984: 41).[19] It mediates, then, between the daily life of Rio's lower classes and the practices of a 'city of protocols', between centre and peripheries, past and present, and thus takes the readers outside and beyond the lettered city, to that 'realm of things precarious and uncertain' of not only the spoken word, but of the Cidade Nova, with its Gypsies, outlaws, and festivities.

III

In an essay in which she cites the examples of Roberto Arlt and Jorge Luis Borges in Buenos Aires, the literary critic Beatriz Sarlo asks about the experience of living, at the age of thirty or forty, in a city so completely different from where one was born or migrated to (2001: 190). The same question can be postulated of most who resided in Rio de Janeiro during the period covered by this study. Almeida, for example, sets his novel at a turning point in the city's history and writes it at another. Within those few decades, the king Dom João VI returned to Portugal in 1821. His son, Dom Pedro I, declared Brazil's independence from Portugal in 1822. He was acclaimed as Brazil's first emperor. The country then saw Dom Pedro I abdicate the throne in order to return to Portugal in 1831. At the age of five, his own son, Dom Pedro II, succeeded as Brazil's second emperor, waiting until 1840 to be declared of age to govern, which he did until being overthrown during the establishment of the republic in 1889.[20] Some of the historical changes that Rio de Janeiro underwent in the transitional period from independence to the second empire are latent in Almeida's narrative, although the action itself precedes them.

During Almeida's brief life (1831–61), he witnessed Rio de Janeiro's population more than double to around 205,000 in 1849.[21] Among other things, the city inaugurated its first public transportation system (by animal traction) in 1838, regular refuse collection in 1847, street lightening by gas (instead of fish oil) in 1854, and its first railroad station in 1858. That period also saw construction of the Mangue Canal begin in 1857, one of the major infrastructural projects of Imperial Brazil. Starting right to the west of the Rocio Pequeno (later renamed Praça Onze de Junho), the canal extended for around 1,200 yards parallel to Aterrado Street, allowing for the elimination of the Sentinela Lake and the São Diogo swamps (Azevedo 1877: 383). After its inauguration in 1860, the Mangue Canal would become one of the city's landmarks for years to come, and ushered new development towards the Cidade Nova.[22]

At the same time, while Almeida published his novel, Rio de Janeiro was undergoing some significant demographic shifts. In *Slave Life in Rio de Janeiro, 1808-1850*, Mary Karasch shows that due to fear of slave trade abolition and the rising demand of forced labour for all the construction under way, the numbers of incoming slaves increased dramatically throughout the years following the court's arrival (1987: 60-5). In 1850, the Eusébio de Queiroz law strengthened earlier legislation against the transatlantic slave trade and was followed by greater enforcement.[23] After that, it appears that a significant number of the capital's slaves were sold to the booming coffee plantations in the country's south-east, being replaced in the workforce by scores of European immigrants, mostly from Portugal (Chalhoub 1990: 190).

Between the court's arrival and the Eusébio de Queiroz law, the percentage of Rio's population comprised of slaves increased from 34.6 per cent in 1799 to 45.6 per cent in 1821, dropping to 38.3 per cent in 1849. Thereafter it would decline sharply to 21.3 per cent in 1870, while the number of Europeans increased steadily.[24] Many of those newly arrived would take residence in the Cidade Nova, but even before immigration intensified, the Santana parish (which included much of the neighbourhood) was already the city's second most populated, with 18.8 per cent of the total population in 1849.[25] At the time, the parish included 16.3 per cent of the city's slaves, less than its share of the total population. Over a quarter of Rio's freed-persons, however, and an even more disproportionate amount of the city's Brazilian-born freed-persons – 33.7 per cent – lived within its boundaries.[26]

While Almeida successfully captured the environment of Rio's lower middle classes, some critics remark that slaves and blacks are 'virtually absent' from his novel.[27] The paradigm of the artist who circulates from centre to periphery will reappear throughout the history of Rio's culture, yet the mobility allowed to an immigrant's son like Almeida, or even to a mulatto like Teixeira e Sousa,[28] could not be afforded by a great number of the city's black inhabitants. As Karasch demonstrates, there was a wide range of autonomy and differing social status within Rio de Janeiro's mid-nineteenth-century black population. Beyond the physical walls that ensured the confinement of a number of slaves whose daily lives were reduced to windowless buildings and long hours of forced labour, the city contained other intangible but no less present barriers: for slaves, 'Rio de Janeiro was a city of boundaries, one of limitations on their freedom'. Besides what was demarcated physically, 'the fortifications, walls, and iron-barred mansions', there were 'the social constructs past which they dared not trespass for fear of brutal mistreatment' (1987: 55). The slave-based system relegated blacks and their descendants to the bottom of the pyramid, generally excluding them from positions of power.[29] The conflicting nature of how access was permitted in certain places to some but not others

– with unspoken rules drawn not necessarily simply along colour lines – accompanied the complexities of competing hierarchies: African-born men of old age, for example, stood at the bottom from a slave-owner's perspective, yet were often revered by their counterparts, frequently holding important positions in religious structures.

Although Rio de Janeiro's slaves and freedmen were in many ways 'outside society' (Karasch 1987: 115), they left a deep and irrevocable imprint on the city's culture. According to John Luccock's records, for instance, around half the Brazil-born artists in the city were black or *pardo*, of mixed race (1820: 56). Some of the contradictions within a society where blacks are at once systematically exploited and ever-present appear in the reactions of travellers. Their impressions range from the indignation of Dabadie at the cruelties of slavery (1859), to R. D. White's observation of 'groups of [enslaved] water carriers [...] chattering and laughing with right good will', a 'constant stream of merry blacks' (1897: 9), to the Count of Robiano's surprise at seeing so many blacks and Indians in the 'capital of a great empire' (1878: 2).[30] In 1849, we can estimate that around a third of those living in the city had been born in the African continent.

Rio de Janeiro's status during the mid-nineteenth century, as a city largely inhabited by Africans and their immediate descendants, does lead us to question the possible effects of their dominant presence in its streets, markets, and public spaces – which so consistently impacted the impressions of foreign travellers. The French painter Édouard Manet, who travelled to Rio de Janeiro after completing his studies in 1848, wrote to his parents of how in the streets one only saw black men and women (Manet 1928). His observation appears to be confirmed by many others, including Jean-Baptiste Debret's and Johann Moritz Rugendas' depictions of the city, where both the French and German painters portray urban scenes almost exclusively populated by blacks. One of the earliest photographs of the Passeio Público, among the city's most aristocratic public places, shows a lone black boy strolling about (Ermakoff 2006: 92). It is also widely remarked that the Portuguese rarely left their homes, especially women, both as part of custom and to avoid the tropical heat. What does it mean, then, when a city's most oppressed groups are also its most visible?

Approaching that question demands that we consider its less obvious counterpart. Besides being the most visible, Rio's black inhabitants were also the city's most audible. Several visitors to the Imperial capital made remarks about the singing of porters or stevedores, frequently accompanied by instruments. Bunbury, bothered by the incessant sounds of working black men, thought Rio was the noisiest place he had ever been to (1981: 19–20). To Ernst Ebel, who hailed from Riga, this music was 'abominable' (1828: 30).

Debret narrates scenes where slaves gather around fountains and squares to sing, inspired by a longing for their motherland (1954: 252). According to him, on these occasions one could tell apart the nations of different slaves, as spectators joined the singer in the refrain, in accompanying vocals, clapping, or through instruments, both improvised – metal pieces, broken plates, sea shells, stones, cans, wood – and traditional, like the marimba and the berimbau (253).

Twenty-some years later, C. S. Stewart wrote that 'the chief human sounds' reaching the ears of a visitor to Rio are those made by blacks, whose 'cries through the streets vary with the pursuits they follow', be they coffee carriers, furniture bearers, or fruit vendors (1858: 72). These strike him as so varied 'that each kind of vegetable and fruit seems to have its own song'. The Christian missionary's largely unsympathetic account of Brazil expresses extreme discomfort with the 'incongruous mingling of races and mixture of blood', and with the 'fearfully mongrel aspect of much of the population, claiming to be white'. Upon observing a squadron of dragoons at the Campo de Santana, along with a band of sixteen performers, he notes that they included 'every shade of complexion, from the blackest ebony of Africa [...]' to 'the clear red and white of the Saxon, with blue eyes and flaxen hair' (73). It is a sight that he deems to be unfailingly 'revolting', at least to someone from the north of the United States. On the occasion of the celebrations surrounding Dom Pedro II's birthday, Stewart, who had considered the music of the street workers 'dull', 'loud', and 'monotonous', cannot help but deliver the following compliment, perhaps unable to shed a newly fledged Pan-American sensibility: 'An abundant supply of fine bands was in attendance. Negroes and mulattoes predominated in those, testifying to the gift of musical taste in the race here, as with us in the United States' (150).

A similarly vibrant soundscape would intrigue another Christian missionary, James Fletcher, who concluded that 'the harmony of sounds are sweet to him [the negro], though uncouth to others' (1868: 30). Writing about the music of Africans and Afro-descendants in the streets of Rio in less than flattering terms, he nonetheless relents, as if overpowered by sounds not quite legible yet somehow enchanting: 'the impression made upon the stranger by the mingled sound of their hundred voices falling upon his ear at once is not soon forgotten' (30). It might seem as if the experiences of such occasions only arrive to us filtered through the exoticizing and often condescending views of foreign travellers. But, naturally, Fletcher's was not the only memory upon which those musical traditions and practices impressed themselves. Within earshot of one of the main sites where slaves most often gathered, the *chafariz* (fountain) of the Campo de Santana, one found the Music Conservatory, housed in the National Museum from 1848 until 1872 (Manuel Azevedo 1877: 229–32). Regardless of what those musicians' attitudes to the nearby 'mingled sounds' might have been, we would certainly hear echoes of those singing voices in the new musical genres being formed in Rio de Janeiro at the time.

What of those men and women, carrying pianos under the scorching tropical sun, or selling fruit or sweets in the streets? How did they see those exotic pale-skinned foreigners, speaking their own incomprehensible languages? It is of course very difficult to reconstruct these perspectives, to understand the relationship of slaves and freed blacks to European practices or to Rio's urban spaces. Yet we know that it was not only formally trained musicians, local passers-by, or Christian missionaries who listened to the chorus of slaves singing and playing instruments by a fountain in a public square. It seems to have been a process marked by circularity. In 1816, the royal family employed an orchestra of at least fifty-seven slaves (Karasch 1987: 204). And, far from being confined to African music, there is ample evidence that slaves – not just those playing in orchestras or bands – incorporated other songs and traditions into their repertoire: polkas, Portuguese *modinhas*, and Latin Catholic antiphons all became part of the mix (240–1).

Likewise, Africans and their descendants assumed an important place in what we could consider Rio de Janeiro's incipient popular culture. Even in *Memórias de um sargento de milícias*, where blacks or slaves are indeed 'virtually absent' from the plot, they occupy the city's public squares, particularly amidst religious processions or festivals, when music tended to be essential. At one point, we read of a *rancho* 'that walked ahead of the procession, attracting the attention of the devout as much or more than did the saints, the biers, and the sacred emblems' (63).[31] He notes, for example, the famous wear of *baianas*, mostly black women who were natives of the province of Bahia. A few decades later, the universe of these baianas would converge at the heart of the Cidade Nova, and become a powerful socio-cultural force within the city.

Almeida also describes ranchos playing 'barber's music' during the Festa do Divino Espírito Santo (Feast of the Holy Ghost) in the Campo de Santana.[32] As Martha Abreu shows in her *O império do Divino* (The Empire of the Divine), a cultural history of religious festivities in nineteenth-century Rio de Janeiro that focuses on the Festa do Divino, it was the 'biggest and most popular' of all parties during the first half of the 1800s (1999: 37). The Holy Ghost had a special significance for the city's slaves and black residents, incurring their devotion with a fervour that seems to have been connected to the search of freedom from bondage (46–52). On his portrayal of the festivities, Almeida notes 'a large rancho accompanied by no small number of black women and girls, Dona Maria's slaves and their children, who carried woven mats and baskets of food' (74). Those baianas and especially these black girls ('negrinhas') might be without agency or marginalized, particularly from the lettered city's perspective, but they are there – and at least in one of Rio's public spaces, the Campo de Santana, some of them seemed to have found a type of sanctuary, albeit an imperfect and temporary one.

Almeida describes how during the Festa do Divino 'a great part of the field was already covered with those rancho groups seated on mats, eating, talking, singing modinhas to the accompaniment of the *guitarra* and *viola*' (75), suggesting the Campo de Santana as a privileged space of sociability for the lower middle classes. To numerous black and mulata women, some of whom appear to have been free and even owned slaves (Leithold 1966: 30), the fields also provided means to earn a living.[33] Its fountain, located closer to the Cidade Nova side of the Campo, besides supplying the district with water and being a rest stop for country folk on their way into town, also acted as the city's principal public facility for washing clothes. By the 1820s, it was already equipped with vast tanks (Debret 1954: 274). In the mid-1850s, Thomas Ewbank finds it 'ever alive with lavadeiras [laundresses]' (1856: 113), counting over 200 women engaged in activities related to washing clothes, some of them Minas and Mozambique girls. The presence of these washerwomen gave a name to one of the Cidade Nova's main thoroughfares, the Rua do Sabão (Soap Street), parallel to Aterrado Street.

Especially earlier in the century, the large fields were far enough from the Imperial Palace to provide an unregulated space where slaves could on occasion 'dance to their own music' (Karasch 1987: 58). The Campo sometimes hosted Afro-Brazilian practices like *umbigadas* and *batuques*, although at different points in the century such manifestations were prohibited or suppressed.[34] Not by coincidence, while older and wealthier churches of predominantly if not exclusively white membership were located in the Old City, most black and mulato brotherhoods and churches had been established on the outskirts, including the Santana Church. At the corner of the Cidade Nova side of the Campo, its Confraternity was formed by *crioulos*, a term that in Brazil often referred to freed-persons.

Perhaps an expression Joseph Roach uses to describe New Orleans's Congo Square in *Cities of the Dead*, 'liminality at urban center' (1996: 63), would be appropriate here. In Rio, however, African practices – frequently regarded as 'savage' by whites much as in the case of New Orleans – occurred in the same sites where slave-owners paraded their military force and where a whipping post was located. The space of liminality, then, paradoxically doubled up as a place where the 'normative' is imposed, where a slave-based society reasserts its control and the semblance of order. These juxtapositions translate to the multiple names given to the Campo throughout the nineteenth century. Almeida significantly prefers Campo de Santana in his novel, although by the 1850s it had already acquired the more stately official name of Praça da Aclamação (again, commemorating Dom Pedro I's acclamation as emperor). It was also now a 'praça', more urban than the former 'campo'. Thirty years earlier Luccock had labelled it 'Parade Ground' in a map, and some forty years later it would yet again be renamed as Praça da República, its current official designation. The place, nonetheless, throughout these changes has remained known in the city's everyday life as the Campo de Santana.

The Santana Church itself, however, was demolished in 1855 to give place to the railway station, the Estação do Campo, later Estação Dom Pedro II, and eventually Central do Brasil – as it is now known – inaugurated in 1858. That year marked the point when the Festas do Divino held in the vicinity ceased being viable (Abreu 1999: 269). It is entirely possible that these two developments were related. Construction of the new *igreja matriz* (principal church) of the Santana parish also began in 1858, in a site that had been reserved for a new prison, about a block away from the Rocio Pequeno – already known as the Praça Onze by the time the new Santana Church finally opened up, twenty years later (Santos 1907: 413). Earlier, in 1868, after ten years without requesting permits, the Brotherhood of the Divine Holy Ghost once again sought authorization to celebrate the Festa do Divino (Abreu 1999: 269). This time, however, the locale elected was no longer the Campo de Santana, but rather the open space in front of the new church, in the heart of the Cidade Nova.

Along with the Church and Festa moved some of the practices and associations that had made the fields such a central space for the city's Africans, Afro-descendants, and increasingly for the Azoreans working with them side by side: a group that also cultivated the Feasts of the Holy Ghost with particular intensity and gusto.[35] Based on complaints and observations registered in documents written by municipal inspectors, we learn that 'batuques, singing and dances' were relatively commonplace in the Cidade Nova during the 1860s, and that women and whites also participated in such events.[36] Though by no means confined to it, the spaces where these porous relations were best able to thrive appear to have become concentrated around that area of the city.

IV

During the eighteenth and early nineteenth centuries, the Campo had acted as the border where the city ended and the rural, putatively order-less Brazil began. As the city expanded, it became the landmark that seemingly divided Rio de Janeiro in two. Once the São Diogo swamps were being land-filled and urbanized at a more rapid pace, particularly with the construction of the Mangue Canal, the Cidade Nova acquired a more central status both geographically and in terms of how public buildings and infrastructure were distributed. During a period of two decades or so in the mid-nineteenth century, Rio's political axis would be dislocated towards the Campo de Santana. As a result, the Cidade Nova would be the beneficiary of infrastructural investments usually reserved for central and privileged urban areas.

Symptomatic of how the direction of the area's development remained ambivalent, the same landscape elicited strikingly different reactions from two contemporary observers. In the late 1830s, an anonymous Portuguese correspondent and the United States consul, John Martin Baker, both saw the Campo de Santana dividing Rio de Janeiro in two.[37] Yet, to the first, 'All that immense field is surrounded with small houses by and large of petty appearance' (Coelho 1965: 157), whereas Baker conveyed quite another picture: 'there are situated in this Square many splendid buildings, both public and private' (Baker 1838: 98). Indeed, besides the headquarters of the army and the National Museum, the Municipal Palace had been on the western face of the Campo since 1825, across the fields from the Senate Chamber, which moved there the following year. In subsequent decades, the Casa da Moeda do Brasil (Mint) and the headquarters of the firefighters would also move to the area (in 1863–4).

Half a block west of the Campo, the Count of Itamarati had one of Rio's grandest examples of neoclassical architecture built in the early 1850s, the Itamaraty Palace. Further out, within the same period, the Barão de Mauá's gas works was partly housed in an impressive neoclassical building. In the same style, the city's first municipal school opened in the Praça Onze in 1872, between the square and the beginning of the Mangue Canal, an area that had been reserved for a public market (Azevedo 1877: 386). Investment in the area also shows in multiple 'beautifying' measures. In 1842, while still known as the Rocio Pequeno, its limits were defined by ropes, an intervention accompanied by some betterments like a neoclassical fountain, a project of Grandjean de Montigny inaugurated in 1846 (Santos 1965: 115). And the Mangue Canal, although it had been inaugurated in 1860 – symbolically, on 7 September, the anniversary of Brazil's independence – received rows of imposing imperial palms in 1869. These would become one of the city's most photographed settings, and a common image in postcards of the early twentieth century (Fig. 1).

The empire's preoccupation with image paid off in the impression left on James Fletcher, who writes that 'the procession from St Christovao to

Figure 1   Postcards of the Mangue Canal

the Palace of the Senate [through the Cidade Nova] is not surpassed in scenic effect by any similar pageant in Europe' (1868: 210). The same visitor would praise Rio's lighting system, not noticing a difference in how it was distributed: 'The streets of few cities are better lighted than those of Rio de Janeiro. The gasworks on the Aterrado sends its illuminating streams to remote suburbs as well as through the many and intricate thoroughfares of the Cidade Velha and the Cidade Nova' (124). Of the five thoroughfares receiving the service when it began in 1854, the Rua do Sabão and the São Pedro (formerly Aterrado) were among them (Santos 1907: 315). Public illumination, of course, still occupied a central place in the imaginary of the period, tied to the eighteenth-century Enlightenment adoption of actual lights as an emblem of reason (Starobinski 1973).

More than the category of the 'divided city' that would permeate representations of the city over a century later, a notable degree of interconnectedness characterized the relationships between its two putative sides. Besides Rio's main railway station on the Cidade Nova side of the Campo, which began to run regular service to the suburbs in 1861 (Santos 1934: 482), the neighbourhood had been privileged by public transportation that linked it to the Old City. Of the five regular *gondola* lines planned in 1838, three sought to serve the Cidade Nova. Gondolas were animal traction vehicles that carried nine passengers. In 1846, two of those lines were already functioning, one of them through the Cidade Nova (241–5). By 1869, several streetcar lines criss-crossed the area (264–5). The Cidade Nova, then, emerged as one of Rio's most accessible neighbourhoods, well connected to the administrative, commercial, and political centres, as well as to the port and to the burgeoning suburbs further to the west and north.

Likewise, the city's sewage system was conceived for equitable implementation in both of the city's halves in 1857.[38] And while there did not seem to be a difference in which streets were paved or not paved (Santos 1934: 247), those of the New City were in fact more pleasantly spacious compared with the infamously crowded and dirty streets of Old Rio: 'The streets [of the latter] are narrow and unequal; [those of the former] are wide and straight. In general all the streets are paved and most have pavements'.[39] Indeed, the French traveller Dabadie found that the Cidade Nova 'was better edified than the other, with wide and well-aligned streets, and houses of pleasant aspect'. But not very busy and, to his surprise, inhabited by rather impoverished people, among which predominated the Gypsies (1859: 5).

Based on all these developments, it seems difficult to imagine that the city's most destitute, including those Gypsies seen by Dabadie in 1850, would not be pushed out further towards the suburbs. How, then, did the Cidade Nova not become an aristocratic or upper-class neighbourhood? A mostly unanticipated factor appears to have encouraged the movement of the upper middle classes and the elites towards the southern districts, closer to the ocean or mountain air, and away from the swamps of the Cidade Nova: starting in 1849, the city was hit by a series of devastating yellow fever epidemics.

Already in 1840 we read that the Cidade Nova 'was not a well chosen site in which to continue the edification of the city' due to its swampy condition and little air circulation, which would cause it to become insalubrious during summer.[40] A few years later, Dr Sigaud, one of the founders of Rio de Janeiro's Medicine Society, cites 'among the causes of insalubrity in the capital [...] the permanence of the Cidade Nova swamps, a pestilential source, true Pontine Marshes of the New World's Rome' (1844: 221). Despite these warnings, historian Sidney Chalhoub demonstrates that prior to the summer of 1849–50 yellow fever was extremely rare (1996: 60).[41] Soon after that, Rio became known as a 'foreigner's grave'. As the city tried to shed off the epithet and stamp out yellow fever and other diseases, that effort would influence much of its urban planning and development. Chief among the plans concerned with the city's sanitation were the two reports from the Commission of Betterments of the City of Rio de Janeiro (1875–6). They devoted a good deal of attention to the Cidade Nova, including the recommendation to prolong the Mangue Canal, which had not produced the desired effects.[42] That intervention, along with others like razing of the Castelo, Santo Antônio, and Senado Hills, as well as the widening and straightening of several avenues, would be revisited in later years under the republic.

When authorities invested in the Cidade Nova's infrastructure in the early to mid-nineteenth century, they did not necessarily have in mind its future functions and residents: workers of modest means, public functionaries, mulatos, artisans, newly arrived immigrants from Europe (especially rural Portugal, Spain, Italy, and later Ashkenazi Jews), as well as from other regions of Brazil, including contingents of freed blacks and runaway slaves from north-eastern provinces like Bahia. The area's proximity to jobs, not just in the commercial centre but also in the port, led to rapid population growth and a decline of living standards. Many of its large houses were split into crowded multi-family units of cheap rents, and the second half of the nineteenth century saw a proliferation of *cortiços*, or tenement housing, in the area (Chalhoub 1996: 54–6). Despite the Mangue Canal and the construction of important public buildings, the Cidade Nova's centrality would prove to be easily overpowered by the promise of 'better airs' in the city's oceanfront and more mountainous neighbourhoods. The threat of yellow fever, then, further sped up the process by which it became consolidated as a neighbourhood of the lower classes.

On the one hand, the neighbourhood reached the 1870s as a type of cross-section of Rio de Janeiro: its demographic composition was fairly representative of the city's as a whole, it stood at the geographic centre, and was easily accessible from various different places.[43] On the other hand, it was poised to become a neighbourhood of the 'recently arrived' (Fridman

2007: 24), and brought together certain exceptional characteristics that allowed the area's population and public spaces to play an oversized role in the cultural life of Brazil's capital. The Cidade Nova, despite its lower rents and concentration of tenement housing, provided better conditions than those more crowded quarters of the Old City.[44] It continued to benefit from investments that did not find a parallel in the suburbs. Not to be understated, the area remained well connected to the Centro by a network of *bondes*, or streetcars. The implementation of an efficient public transportation system has been one of the historic challenges of Rio de Janeiro, partly explained by its mountainous and irregular geography, partly due to lack of political will. Inefficient and expensive public transport constituted one of the main factors for the proliferation of favelas in the twentieth century, as people often could not afford (or did not wish) to live far from their workplaces. The Cidade Nova of the second half of the nineteenth century, then, in great part by the 'accident' of its central location, constituted a rarity within lower-class neighbourhoods: allowing for not only a more practical commute but for better infrastructure and public services. Resulting, we can speculate, on more dignified living conditions.

A series of coincidences or unrelated conditions particular to Rio de Janeiro, coupled with global technological innovations – like the development of commercially viable transatlantic steam ships in the 1870s, allowing for immigration from Europe on an unprecedented scale – would enable cultural encounters in many ways only possible in an urban environment. Perhaps even more so in the New World and in *this* New City, a place largely unencumbered by a past, by a set of hegemonic customs. In that sense too, the Cidade Nova constituted a privileged space, a heterotopia of sorts.[45] Its many displaced individuals – like the Portuguese natives in *Memórias de um sargento de milícias*, or the slaves singing around a fountain – often arrived with deeply rooted cultural baggage and to different degrees had to negotiate their identities and cultural practices in an urban milieu marked by plurality, by a mixture and overlap of languages, interests, aspirations, possibilities, and personal histories.

These exchanges – as they often do – appear to have happened without grand artistic objectives or consciousness of what was at hand. Their results, often formidable, can be traced back to some of those parties, processions, and encounters described by Almeida. Some of these meetings, perhaps by their improbability or counter-intuitiveness, escape the prying look of historians until revealed through a novel's intuitions or in a spark of memory, as in one recollection by an aged Pixinguinha (1897–1973), a grandson of slaves who was baptized in the Santana Church. Decades after the fact, the celebrated composer and flautist would speak of attending Gipsy parties in the vicinity of the Cidade Nova as a child.[46] He tells of how Sinhô (1888–1930), another seminal samba pioneer, frequently 'took' their melodic themes. The endless debates about who or what influenced what or who are not the beneficiaries of this memory's sudden resurgence. Rather, it adds yet another layer to the story of Rio's culture, to how in the socio-cultural and literary fabric of that early and much forgotten Cidade Nova lies the palimpsestic landscape out of which emerges so much of what came to be considered Brazilian.

Notes

1 For a study of the Portuguese royal court in Rio de Janeiro, see Schultz 2001. According to a census from 1799, the city had a total population of 43,376 (Karasch 1987: 61).

2 Although the title was not conferred until 15 December 1815, Rio de Janeiro became the effective seat of royal power after the court's arrival (Schultz 2001: 190).

3 More precisely, it reached 79,321 inhabitants based on data collected in 1821 (Karasch 1987: 61).

4 The decree is reproduced in *Bibliotheca brasiliense* 1907: 206.

5 So estimates a Prussian cavalry captain in his accounts of travelling in Rio in 1819 (Leithold 1966: 53). The Mata-Porcos neighbourhood corresponds to today's Estácio.

6 It led directly from the Campo de Santana to the Ponte dos Marinheiros (Sailor's Bridge, also called the São Diogo bridge).

7 Debret left Brazil in 1831, having been a favoured court painter both under the auspices of king Dom João VI and later during the empire. He taught in Rio de Janeiro's Imperial Academy and became a member of the Academie des Beaux Arts after his return to France. His time in Brazil resulted in a three-volume series of engravings entitled *Voyage pittoresque et historique au Brésil*.

8 Montigny arrived in Rio de Janeiro in 1816 and, along with artists like Debret, would be considered part of the so-called French Artistic Mission in Brazil. Lilia Schwarcz (2008) sheds new light on the presence of French artists in the court and on the episode's repercussion in Brazilian history, debunking the notion of a cohesive 'mission'.

9 The *Relatório apresentado à Ilma. Câmara Municipal do Rio de Janeiro por H. de Beaurepaire-Rohan* is reprinted as an appendix in Andreatta 2006.

10 Holanda draws a contrast between the *desleixo* (laxness) in the Portuguese planning of colonial cities, and the more systematic and ordered style of the Spaniards (2006: 95–149). Note that the Manhattan's Commissioners' Plan of 1811 also proposed New York City's expansion as a grid, on a larger scale. For a study of grid patterns that traces them back to both Roman and Chinese forms of imperialism (centrifugal in the west, centripetal in the east), see Edgerton 1987.

11 Debret writes that the richest and most elegant houses of the city's outskirts were found on the way to São Cristovão on the Mata-Porcos road, in the Engenho Novo, the Glória Hill, the Catete, and in 'the beautiful Botafogo inlet' (1954: 163).

12 I have relied on Ronald W. Sousa's translation (Almeida 1999), modifying it wherever appropriate.

13 In her afterword to the novels' English translation, Süssekind ties the novel to the emergence of the *crônica*, a literary genre frequently occupied by current events (Almeida 1999: 171–83).

14 Luccock lends historical veracity to the comment: 'My first home in Rio brought me to the near observation of a large and important class of the inhabitants. It was at the corner of Rua d'Ouvidor, where it joins the Rua da Qui Tandi [*sic*]; precisely on this spot, every unhallowed morning, the Attorneys, together with the under officers of the law, met to transact business' (1820: 102).

15 Among these, Mário de Andrade, in his introduction to the 1941 edition (Almeida 1941: 5–19).

16 Although neither of the novels mentions the participation of Gypsies in the slave market, other authors include it in their negative depictions of them (Walsh 1831: 323–7; Debret 1954: 220).

17 In his introduction to the translation in English, Thomas H. Holloway describes how 'literary taxonomists have puzzled over which category fits a work that in many ways is a literary anomaly' (Almeida 1999: xi).

18 Some early to mid-nineteenth-century residents of the neighbourhood achieved notoriety, like a famous mulatto sculptor known as Mestre Valentim (1745–1813), who lived and had his atelier in the Rua do Sabão, according to a newspaper advertisement. Another celebrated mulatto sculptor, Chaves Pinheiro (1822–84), lived in the Rua de Santana (Gerson 1965: 250; Lopes 2006: 41).

19 Chasteen's more elegant but less literal translation follows: '[the distance] that separated the written from the spoken word, the rigidity of letters from the fluidity of speech – that reserved the manipulation of all legal protocols to the tiny group of letrados' (Rama 1996: 29). The original reads: 'la distancia entre la letra rígida y la fluida palabra hablada, que hizo de la *ciudad letrada* una *ciudad escrituaria*, reservada a una estricta minoría'.

20 For excellent biographies of the emperor, see Lilia Schwarcz 2004 and José Murilo de Carvalho 2007.

21 Rio's population increased from 97,599 in 1834 to 205,906 in 1849, according to censuses (Karasch 1987: 61).

22 The Barão de Mauá, a figure of great influence in Imperial Brazil, conducted the construction. He inaugurated it along with a gas factory, also in the Cidade Nova, which deposited residues in the canal. On the Baron (later Viscount), see Caldeira 1995.

23 After an 1826 treaty with England banning the slave trade took effect in 1831, contraband became common. On laws against the Atlantic slave trade in the context of Brazilian politics and foreign policy, see Needell 2006.

24 According to studies by Luiz Felipe de Alencastro, over 200,000 Portuguese immigrants arrived in Rio between 1844 and 1878 (Chalhoub 1990: 199). In 1849, 17.6 per cent of the city was already composed of foreign-born free persons, a number that excludes both freed-persons and the two-thirds of slaves born in Africa. All included, 46.7 per cent of the city's inhabitants had been born outside of Brazil. Demographic calculations in this paragraph are based on census data found in Karasch 1987: 61–6.

25 In 1821, it had been the least populated of the city's urban parishes. By 1849,

38,717 people lived in the Santana parish, behind Sacramento, located on the other side of the Campo de Santana.

26 Freed-persons comprised around 5.2 per cent of Rio's residents. We encounter in the Cidade Nova at least one protagonist of what Chalhoub deems the *cidade negra* (black city), formed in 'the process of blacks struggling towards the institution of *a politics* – in other words, the search for freedom – where there had previously been *a routine*' (1990: 186). In 1835, Manoel, a man known as a 'curandeiro' (medicine man), described as a 'preto mina' and resident of Formosa Street, was considered 'suspicious' due to meetings held in his house with other Minas, most likely because authorities feared a rebellion (199).

27 Holloway, after establishing their 'virtual absence', notes that they create a situation for the free lower classes that plays a major role in the novel: 'no one in the book works', as he writes (Almeida 1999: xvii).

28 Teixeira e Sousa was the son of a 'ruined small merchant' (Tinhorão 2000-2: 55). Süssekind expands on how other critics (Candido, Roberto Schwartz) maintain that 'what distinguishes this novel are its characters and the privileges these free, unremarkable, property-less men enjoyed in a slave holding society such as nineteenth-century Brazil' (Almeida 1999: 181).

29 Karasch puts in perspective the many reports of foreigners surprised at seeing blacks in high positions, as those tended to be exceptions (1987: 123-5).

30 Berger 1980 remains the most complete bibliography on foreign travellers prior to the twentieth century.

31 This is one of the first mentions of *ranchos*, musical groups that like the *cucumbis* and *congos* combined influences from African expressions of Banto origin with elements from popular Iberian cultures. Later in the century, ranchos developed into carnival groups, leading to organized, competitive parades as early as 1911. See Gonçalves 2003.

32 For the role of groups composed of barbers in the development of Rio's music, see Cavalcanti (2004: 109) and Tinhorão (1998: 155-76). A barbershop headed by two freedmen is among Debret's most famous depictions of Rio (1954: 17).

33 Other black and mixed-race women, both slaves and freed, controlled a good deal of Rio's street economy, selling food or produce (Karasch 1987: 58). Of the 249 female *quitandeiras* (street vendors and market women) included in the 1834 census, 201 were free blacks, and 33 were listed as free *pardas* (73). Whereas 58.6 per cent of the city's inhabitants were male in 1849, 56.3 of the freed persons were women.

34 Batuque refers to various practices, more commonly denoting music and dance of African origins, marked by percussive elements, often loosely organized around a circle, and sometimes containing religious significance. Umbigadas belong to a similar realm, where the etymological root (*umbigo*, for belly button) evokes a move through which one replaces another inside a circle. At different moments in the century, these gatherings were more tolerated, controlled, or persecuted by authorities (Abreu 1999: 36, 199, 225-9). Holloway also discusses the relationship of the police to these public events (1993: 161). Around 1822, Augustus Earle painted a lively 'Negro Fandango Scene at Campo de St Anna [...]', held at the National Library of Australia.

35 In the 1850s, former slave ships began to transport immigrants from the Atlantic islands (Chalhoub 1990: 200). Karasch discusses slaves increasingly working

beside Azoreans and Portuguese peasants (1987: 65), while Abreu notes their major role in the continued presence of the Festas do Divino (Abreu 1999: 45).

36 Citing several examples from the Santana parish, Abreu convincingly argues that these events sometimes counted with the complicity and support of neighbours, being thus tolerated by authorities (Abreu 1999: 280-7).

37 The report in the *Universo Pitoresco*, a Portuguese magazine (1839-40), reads: 'The Campo de Santana [...] is a vast parallelogram that divides in two the capital of Brazil' (reprinted in Coelho 1965: 157). Baker writes: 'The City is divided into the Old and New Town, separated by the Campo of St. Anna' (1838: 98).

38 Construction began in 1862, contemplating the neighbourhoods of the Catete, Glória, Botafogo, the commercial centre, and the Cidade Nova (Santos 1907: 385).

39 In *Universo Pitoresco* (1839-40), reprinted in Coelho 1965: 124.

40 In *Universo Pitoresco* (1839-40), reprinted in Coelho 1965: 153.

41 Chalhoub mentions estimates that a third of Rio's inhabitants contracted the fever during that first epidemic. It was followed by a major epidemic of cholera in 1855-6, adding another scourge to a list that also included tuberculosis and smallpox. Although there were competing medical interpretations about their transmission, miasma theories generally held swamps to be undesirable places. For a history of how the epidemics were controlled, see Benchimol 1999. In 1870, of the 5,902 deaths recorded due to yellow fever, 1,118 were in the Santana parish (Souza 2009: 13).

42 The reports from the Comissão de Melhoramentos da Cidade do Rio de Janeiro can be consulted at the Arquivo Geral da Cidade do Rio de Janeiro. Among its members was the engineer Francisco Pereira Passos, who would spearhead the capital's urban reforms less than thirty years later. The Mangue Canal became obstructed a few years after its inauguration, and was criticized in the press for 'infecting the air' (Azevedo 1877: 385).

43 By 1872, the Santana parish – the city's most populated – had been dismembered into the parishes of Espírito Santo and Santo Antônio, both of which included parts of the Cidade Nova. The Santana parish still roughly corresponded to the neighbourhood, however, and its census data can be considered representative. According to the 1872 census, of its 38,903 inhabitants (14 per cent of the city's total), approximately 31.6 per cent were foreign-born, 44.2 per cent were women, 61 per cent were white, 17.4 per cent were pardos, 21 per cent were black, 0.39 per cent were caboclo, and 69.8 per cent were illiterate. The numbers for the entire city (population almost 278,000) are, respectively, 30 per cent foreign-born, 42 per cent women, 55.2 per cent white, 20 per cent pardos, 24.1 per cent black, 0.33 per cent caboclo, 63.9 per cent illiterate. Of Santana's blacks and pardos, 50.4 per cent and 83.8 per cent were free versus 42.9 per cent and 80 per cent for the entire city.

44 In 1868, a fifth of the parish's residents lived in cortiços, accounting for 29 per cent of the total population living in that type of housing (Carvalho 1980: 37-8). Maps of tenement housing in Rio during the 1870s and 80s, produced by Unicamp scholars and Stanford University's Spatial History Lab, available online in 2012, show that rent was lower in the Cidade Nova than in the centre, although prices increased in the vicinity of the railroad station.

45 A 'heterotopia', in the Foucaldian sense, can be understood as a heterogeneous or 'different space' but also as something 'imagined'. See Foucault's 'Different Spaces' (2000).

46 According to the flautist, these Gypsy parties took place in the Catumbi, most probably less than a mile from the Praça Onze. We will revisit Pixinguinha (Alfredo da Rocha Viana Filho) and Sinhô (José Barbosa da Silva) in Chapter 4. Their importance to the history of Brazilian music is widely recognized, but their indirect role in the country's literary history, through their relations to writers like Mário de Andrade and Manuel Bandeira, among others, should also not be understated. The interview in question, more of a recorded conversation, took place on 10 June 1966, with the participation of several samba specialists. The recording can be consulted among the Depoimentos held at the Museu da Imagem e do Som in Rio de Janeiro (hereafter MIS).

CHAPTER TWO

A Master on the Periphery of a Periphery: Popular Music, Streetcars, and the Republic

Not everyone can claim to know an entire city.

Machado de Assis, *Esau and Jacob*

I

Rio de Janeiro would reach the last decades of the nineteenth century marked by porosity. Order/disorder, colony/metropolis, centre/periphery, black/white: not much seemed to fall along the lines of a neat dichotomy. Nowhere does this seem clearer than in the formation of Brazil's earliest urban musical genres, through processes that broke down yet another binary, popular and erudite. Quite a bit has been written about how multiracial marching bands and church-related orchestras created fecund exchanges between so-called popular and erudite music and musicians, to the point that it becomes difficult (or arbitrary) to draw a distinction.[1] Rio was already a city of extremes of wealth and poverty, but these extremes were placed under close and constant contact. If social relations were nothing to idealize – frequently brutal and exploitative – they did seem to have consequences to the development of musical expressions like maxixe, choro, and eventually samba.[2]

In his essay 'Machado Maxixe', José Miguel Wisnik argues that the short story 'Um Homem Célebre' (A Famous Man) by Machado de Assis (1839–1908) – perhaps Brazil's most eminent writer – is 'a curious and penetrating analysis of Brazilian musical life at the end of the nineteenth century' (2004: 21). It tells of Pestana, a successful composer of beloved 'polcas' with maxixe-evoking titles, who remains unable to fulfil his dream of creating classical music in the mold of his masters Mozart and Beethoven. To Wisnik, Machado de Assis intuitively perceives and articulates how Rio's popular music appropriated European genres, converting them to Brazilian patterns of a largely African syncopated rhythmic base (41). The essay goes on to propose the Brazilian rhythmic solution as homologous to the oscillation between order and disorder seen by Antonio Candido in *Memórias de um sargento de milícias*. We can extend the observation to how some of Rio's finest writers spatialize their fictions, or fictionalize the city's spaces. Wisnik further compares the Brazilian musical condition to the condition of the mulato, citing composers like José Maurício Nunes Garcia (1767–1830) and Ernesto Nazareth (1863–1934). Not by chance, a number of the aforementioned finest writers who will be discussed in this and the upcoming chapters also happen to be mulatos: Machado de Assis, the 'master' of this chapter's title, Lima Barreto, João do Rio, and Mário de Andrade.[3]

Permeability to Wisnik – an accomplished composer himself, besides literary critic – is the mark of Brazilian music. The trait relates to the spatial porosity we have discussed as characteristic of Rio's urban landscape during much of the nineteenth century. Besides the number of blacks on the streets and the overwhelming natural beauty of the Guanabara Bay, another feature of Rio de Janeiro that consistently earned a mention from foreign travellers was the quantity of pianos in its households.[4] With the court's arrival Rio had already developed a vibrant musical culture, yet its most original and enduring musical forms would arise out of the intersection between practices common to the Cidade Nova, and the demand for popular musicians in Central Rio.[5] Pestana, the protagonist of Machado's 'Um Homem Célebre', lives in the Cidade Nova's Aterrado Street, and when the story opens had just played in an 'intimate soirée' in Areal Street, an address close to the Senate Palace.

In Luís Guimarães Júnior's *A Família Agulha* (The Agulha Family, 1870), a novel that critics approximate to Almeida's, we find the neighbourhood presented as a source of musicians who would entertain festivities throughout the city. In a scene describing the preparations for a baptism party within the petit-bourgeois family of the title, the musician who was to enliven the occasion arrives along with his *violão* (guitar). The instrument had by then displaced the viola, and by virtue of its mobility relative to the piano, would increasingly define Brazil's popular music. The player is immediately introduced merely as 'Clementino, from Cidade Nova', as if those were his credentials. The physical description of the character as toothless and of mixed race further locates him in the city's peripheries:

> The guitarist was a tall *pardo* [mixed race] man, cross-eyed and with complete lack of teeth in the upper gums. One of these types found during festival days in the countryside, amidst the booze [aguardente] of a bunch of happy creatures who do not know the existence of

grammar, and who prefer the *cateretê* and the *fado* to the pleasures of Jouvin and the scissors of Dason!

Tinhorão observed the *fado*'s association with the more rural *cateretê* as an indication that it was no longer fashionable (1998: 167). We must also add the broader connection between a dance and song-form practised by the Portuguese, the fado, and the suggestion of a rural origin: most Iberian immigrants to the Americas experienced an abrupt transition from a rural to an urban environment. And, more pertinently, to Tinhorão the partygoers' requests both for recent polka favourites and for anachronistic fados 'could only be granted because the guitarist hailed from the periphery [...] where old customs and habits [...] still coexisted with the new fashions' (168). We have yet another dichotomy that the Cidade Nova defied: there the rural overlapped with the urban, and its musicians seemed like repositories of new and old music forms.

This porous quality appears to have manifestations beyond the musical realm. One of these exceptional cases became the subject of Eduardo Silva's *Prince of the People* (1993): the lieutenant Cândido da Fonseca Galvão (?1845–90), born in the state of Bahia, son of a freed African father, and known in parts of Rio as Dom Obá. *Obá* in Yoruba means king. Silva documents Obá's presence – often first to arrive – at the public audiences conceded by the Emperor Dom Pedro II in his São Cristovão palace (1997: 72). An active voice in the press (he bought space for newspapers to print his articles), Obá was looked down on by white elites. He was revered as a true prince, however, among a considerable portion of the population: especially slaves, freed-persons, and free peoples of colour. Dom Obá received tribute from his subjects, and even from the emperor (104). He had volumes of poetry sold in bookshops of the Old City, and his writings, full of Yoruban and some Latin, were recited at gatherings in taverns (135). Exotic to some contemporaries, a typical figure to others, such a character strikes as less probable after the 1888 abolition and the soon to follow First Republic, counter-intuitive as that may seem. Declared in 1889, the new regime was brought about in part by political interests that sought to end slavery only to replace freed blacks with white European labourers.[6]

Dom Obá died in Barão de São Felix Street, which connected the Cidade Nova and the port. It was known for its crowded lodgings, some of which served as a sanctuary for runaway slaves before abolition (Chalhoub 1996: 26). Obá reigned over the area to be known as Rio's Little Africa, which also comprised the Saúde and Gamboa neighbourhoods. Constrained by a series of hills, these portside neighbourhoods were well connected to the Cidade Nova through several streets and a tunnel that opened in 1879 (Santos

1907: 289). The centre of this milieu was the Rocio Pequeno, the public square that, as we have mentioned, was renamed as Praça Onze de Junho to commemorate the date of Brazil's victory in the Battle of Riachuelo (1865), during the War of the Triple Alliance.[7] We can surmise the importance to Dom Obá of the Divine Holy Ghost, which now had its yearly celebrations at the Santana Church, in the vicinity of the square. His 'official portrait', sometimes published or reproduced alongside articles and letters, contained a drawing of the dove of the Holy Ghost. In a testament to the mixtures taking place in Brazil at the time, that symbol was identified with Oxum, a Yoruban *orixá* (deity or 'saint'). Oxum was joined in Obá's portrait by two other orixás, Ogum and Oxossi (Silva 1993: 149–51).

The portrait also depicted a royal crown, topped with a Christian cross, and Dom Obá wearing military garb. Obá's ability to serve as a link between the official world of the empire and Little Africa could in part be attributed to respect, on the part of Dom Pedro II and others, of his service in the War of the Triple Alliance (90). During the conflict and immediate aftermath, it appears that many ex-volunteers of colour obtained public jobs (113). Not unlike music circles, military life was marked by an intensification of interactions across race, region, and class. The system's limitations, however, earned the following quip from Dom Obá: 'Can it be that [white] Brazilians will always be doctors, priests and engineers [while blacks and browns] are only good for hanging their heads low as cornet players and private soldiers?' (140). Twelve years after the war ended, Dom Obá – who was frequently supportive of the empire – expressed indignation at how 'the government [...] had all of us going to fight the war, [and] today we see our brothers die of hunger, without having enough for our subsistence'.[8]

As war veterans, freed slaves, European immigrants, and others came to the country's capital looking for opportunities and a better life, the population of Rio almost doubled, from 274,972 (1872) to 522,651 (1890). By 1890, Rio's population was roughly three times greater than that of Salvador, Brazil's former capital, and almost five times that of Recife, Brazil's third largest city (Santos 1993: 23). Close to half the city's inhabitants had been born elsewhere. About a quarter were from the interior of Rio de Janeiro or from other provinces (Bahia, Minas Gerais, Pernambuco, and São Paulo, in that order). Around 23.7 per cent were foreign immigrants mainly from Portugal, Spain, and Italy. Although the percentage of foreigners had been higher in 1872 at around 30 per cent, their raw number more than doubled to 155,202 in 1890, despite en masse naturalizations during the first few months of the republic (Menezes 1996: 62–3). Even greater internal migration explains the decrease in their participation of the population's total.

The massive influx contributed to the increase of those 'without a stated profession', from 30 per cent of the population in 1870 to 44 per cent in 1890 (Silva 1993: 55). In other words, the ranks of those without a job or working at the margins of an official economy seemed to grow significantly as the slave-based system fell apart. A disproportionate number of freed-persons and their descendants found themselves unable to integrate the marketplace. At the same time, if one goes by information provided in the censuses, the percentage of blacks in Rio drops from 24.13 per cent (1872) to 12.34 per cent (1890), while that of *pardos* (mixed-race) increased from 20.66 per cent to 24.94 per cent. These changes reflect European arrivals and miscegenation, but they are also a product of inaccuracies and ideological biases in the census criteria.[9] After abolition, in any case, blacks were still at the end of the line. Many of those who, like Dom Obá, came to Rio in search of a better life had to make do in woeful housing conditions.

If in *A Família Agulha* (1870) one could still refer to the Cidade Nova as a semi-rural periphery, during the following decades the neighbourhood would be surrounded by burgeoning suburbs and new development, including industry, at a rapid pace. The Cidade Nova, due to its relatively good public transportation and key location near the port and the Centro, continued to receive a great number of new residents. These newcomers would be cramped into recently built lodgings as well as in some older, once comfortable multi-storey houses. Although the Cidade Nova had a high concentration of the city's tenements (cortiços) and lodgings (estalagens), by 1890 its overall housing density appears to have been lower than elsewhere, and its lodgings seemingly had somewhat better sanitary conditions.[10] At the dawn of republican Brazil, the area's residents were disproportionately illiterate and foreign-born.[11] The gender and racial composition remained comparable to the city's as a whole, but it was considerably less white than the Old City.[12]

Based on the limited and sometimes contradictory information available to us, it is an almost unsurmountable challenge to reconstruct the make-up and social structure of the city. Attempts to isolate particular areas based on cultural rather than administrative criteria can prove to be even more elusive. Several scholars of Rio de Janeiro, nonetheless, document the difficult conditions found in working-class districts like the Cidade Nova at the turn of the century (see, for example, Graham 1988; Lobo 1989; Damazio 1996; Menezes 1996; and Vaz 2002). Despite all the hardships, and however lettered elites might have thought of them, we also know that these urban dwellers were not reduced to misery: vibrant and diverse religious practices, economic aspirations, and musical cultures enriched the social lives of many. They would go ignored or marginalized by most, but certainly not all contemporary and subsequent Carioca writers.

II

Even as the Cidade Nova stood at the centre of the city and served as a residence of so many, it would seldom appear as a central place in the literature of the period. And, increasingly, portrayals of the neighbourhood connoted not just popular, musical culture, but also carried certain prejudices. Aluísio Azevedo (1857–1913), author of an important novel that we will return to (*O Cortiço*, 1890), along with his brother, the playwright Artur Azevedo (1855–1908), penned *Fritzmac*, a major success once it took to the stages of Rio de Janeiro in 1889. In a subgenre of the *teatro de revista* (revue theatre), drawing from vaudeville and cancan, the show incorporated musical numbers, spicy humour, and satire of events and people that marked the previous year.[13] The play thus deals with abolition, growing immigration, and other more topical or less memorable controversies of the period, aside from certain 'universals' like love and the seven deadly sins. All in a light fashion, in a series of loosely bound skits.

In the second scene, the Mademoiselle Fritzmac – Fritzmac in the language of the time denoted a fake or artificial person – and the Baron of Macuco receive characters named after some of the main Grandes Sociedades Carnavalescas (Great Carnival Societies).[14] First came the Clube dos Fenianos, attempting to convince the Mademoiselle to join their ranks. Soon after, the Clube dos Democráticos arrives. Both were by then traditional Societies, located in more central areas of the city and catering to a wealthier, more 'prestigious' crowd. They engage in a shouting match to see who could offer more money to entice the Mademoiselle to participate in their parade. Then we hear from the maid that the Clube dos Progressistas da Cidade Nova has also arrived.[15] The reaction of the other two combines incredulity with a sense of superiority:

BOTH (standing up):	Huh?
O CLUBE DOS DEMOCRÁTICOS:	So madam, you trust that type?
O CLUBE DOS FENIANOS:	Even the Cidade Nova! ...

Significantly, the Clube dos Progressistas da Cidade Nova introduces himself not in a mere *copla* or couplet like the previous two, but in a *copla-lundu*, incorporating the African-based musical form to its verses.[16] The character embodies the general qualities associated with the neighbourhood, and presents himself as of more modest means. In a punch line surely to be savoured by the audience, he concludes by improbably offering an even larger sum of money than the others:

I am no blowhard;
I am modest, rightly so;
The simpleton cannot give
More than he has got.
If the missus wants to ride my car
Dressed up in omolu (mosaic gold)
I will right away cough up
Thirty grand. (Dance.)

Despite the monetary promise ('trinta mil réis'), the contrast could not be clearer. The Cidade Nova representative was by his own admission the most 'pachola' (roughly, a simpleton). The colloquial and crude language was most likely meant to generate laughter as an object of ridicule. Indeed, membership in the Cidade Nova Club might have diverged from other more elitist organizations, but, at any rate, Sociedades hardly characterized the neighbourhood's carnival. It was rather dominated by entrudos and rancho processions favoured by the lower classes. In the case of the rowdy entrudos, the rise of more French- and Venice-styled celebrations accompanied its increasing demonization and eventual prohibition (Ferreira 2004: 94–104). Some of the city's first registered *blocos carnavalescos* (a less organized variation of ranchos) incorporated the neighbourhood in its name, like the Guaranis da Cidade Nova.

As the city grew outward towards the suburbs and the first shanties that would form Rio's future favelas began to appear on the hillsides adjoining the Cidade Nova, the largely corresponding values of insalubrity and 'blackness' were increasingly associated to those zones of the city – although, as we have seen, they were quite racially diverse and would remain so. After Dom Pedro II's fall from power, São Cristovão was no longer the imperial neighbourhood and the Cidade Nova's geographical centrality faded. It became more clearly demarcated as a peripheral space in the lettered cartographies of the city. Although the city's cultural life was still marked by overlaps, mixtures, and circulation – or, perhaps, *because* of that – lettered representations tended to highlight polarization, often positioning writers and their audience on the side of refinement and superior tastes, as we saw with *Fritzmac*.[17]

In that context, from the perspective of the elites, the antipode to the Cidade Nova of Little Africa was Ouvidor Street, widely hailed in the press and among 'sophisticated' circles as Rio's most civilized and cosmopolitan street. Epicentre of the capital's more *chic* and prestigious commercial establishments, to which local elites aspired, it was there that Brazil's first cafés appeared. They witnessed the birth of several literary and political movements (Needell 1987: 186–7). An article in the *Jornal do Brasil*, recounting Rio's first cinematography exhibition in 1897, evidences the antagonistic but complementary relationship between both cultural spaces, leaving little doubt as to the role played by each:

> In a stupendous story, the Bible tells of Joshua stopping the sun. The cinema Super Lumière at the Paris-Rio, however, makes it dance the maxixe. Imagine the great star getting down with the over-the-top moves of our dance, like any rogue [turuna] from the Cidade Nova. Priceless![18]

Modern culture and the latest technological advances were showcased on the suggestively named Paris-Rio of Ouvidor Street. The excessive vulgarity of *our* dances belonged to the terrain of the *turunas* or rogues of the Cidade Nova. It is an association that cinema itself would reinforce, with Antônio Leal's film *Os Capadócios da Cidade Nova* (The Rogues from the Cidade Nova, 1908).[19] The turuna, synonym of capadócio (and precursor of the *malandro*) is neutralized in the newspaper article as a non-threatening caricature. The implication, however, is that it is him, or rather *they* at the Cidade Nova, who may keep *us* from being civilized like the Parisian. And the sun dancing the maxixe – what else! – represents not only the height of preposterousness but of the miraculous feats enabled by the new technology. As visual media begin to overpower the primacy of writing as modes of cultural transmission, we also see cinema's appropriation of the caboclo's magical abilities, displacing his house as the site of the supernatural.

Rio de Janeiro's (if not Brazil's) most prestigious publishing house, the Garnier, was also located on Ouvidor Street. Among its most important authors was Machado de Assis, a protégé of Manuel Antônio de Almeida as a young apprentice in the National Typography, and eventual literary giant. The founder and first president of the Academia Brasileira de Letras (Brazilian Academy of Letters) mentions the celebrated street more than any other in his newspaper *crônicas*.[20] The same can very likely be said of most of his contemporaries. From reading the accounts of travellers to Rio, one sometimes gets a sense of unease at the inflated pride felt by locals over the hyped street.[21] On the other hand, despite Dom Obá's ability to circulate among the nobility and to write in Rio's newspapers, the city's Little Africa would seldom appear in the literature of the period, except as a foil. To invert a well-known expression to those who study Latin America, as José Miguel Wisnik does in a different context, it is as if the Cidade Nova were a 'lugar-fora-das-idéias': not an 'out of place idea', the norm among Latin America's lettered cities, but a 'place outside of ideas'.[22]

Perhaps surprisingly, then, one finds the most relevant and revealing exceptions in the literature of Machado de Assis. The son of a Portuguese washerwoman with a mulato housepainter descended from freed slaves, he was born between the Cidade Nova and the port in the Livramento Hill, part of what we have been considering Little Africa. In a few instances, especially in earlier texts from his more romanticist phase, the neighbourhood appears in Machado's fiction rather predictably, confirming readers' expectations and social realities of the area. It is portrayed as a place of cheap rents and dwellers of modest means, though never with the mocking undertones of newspapers and revues, of which Machado was a vocal critic. One such example can be found in the short story 'O Rei dos Caiporas' (The King of Caiporas, 1870), where we learn of João das Mercês, a character followed by such bad luck that even his suicide attempt fails.[23] Eventually, he catches a break after living in the streets through poverty:

> The young fellow managed to find a job with which he could eek a living. He rented a little house in the Cidade Nova, and a few months went by. One day he noticed that on the other side of the street lived an old woman who did not fail to smile when he entered or left the house. João das Mercês greeted her courteously, but did not think much of the smiles. The old woman's house was the best in the street, and she could come across as rich.

Besides the interplay between new and old, the implication seems to be that there were a few, lingering wealthier residents in the Cidade Nova. João das Mercês would marry this one, but she would die right before naming him in her will, justifying his title as the king of the 'caiporas', the unluckiest of men.

Six years later, when *Helena* comes out (1976), we read another passing but meaningful reference: 'Fever kept me in bed for three days, in a poor bed rented in a terrible lodging of the Cidade Nova'. The novel presents a fairly conventional narrative, and the description of the neighbourhood offers no great surprise. It arrives through a story told by Salvador, the real father of Helena, who reappears after many years. He tells of returning to Rio after a visit to his ailing father in the southern province of Rio Grande. Upon returning, he finds Helena's mother, Angela, living with another companion in an 'elegant house' in São Cristovão, still the imperial neighbourhood. Salvador, shocked by the news, falls sick. Angela's wealthy new partner, setting off the novel's action, leaves his properties to Helena in a will.

Through specific spatial references (streets, neighbourhoods), here we already have Machado subtly but carefully plotting the social landscape of Rio de Janeiro. Salvador, the man once reduced to spending three days in a 'terrible lodging' of the Cidade Nova, had held several of the mid- to lower-level professions common to its residents: 'I was a pedlar, court staff member, bookkeeper, farm labourer, factory worker, innkeeper, registry clerk; for some weeks I made a living from making copies of plays for the theatre'. By then, it seems clear, the area's association to poor living conditions had sedimented even further, reflecting those changes we have described earlier.

In yet another work of fiction, *Casa Velha* (Old House), published in ten short chapters in *A Estação* during 1885 and 1886, Machado adopts a procedure common to his stories, setting them in earlier periods. This one takes place in 1839, when the narrator, a thirty-two-year-old priest, decides to write a book, 'a political work' on the history of Dom Pedro I's reign. To do so he must gain access to the old house of the title, where the widow of a minister of the empire conserves valuable documents, books, newspapers, and manuscripts. Machado reveals the location of the house by omitting it, something that became more and more common in his writing: 'The house, of which it is unnecessary to say the location and address [...]'. The aside naturally implies that when his narrators do choose to divulge an address, it is not irrelevant. Here, this rare omission gives the house a certain mythic, atemporal quality.

The priest penetrates the intimacy of the widow's family and is introduced to Lalau, a seventeen-year-old orphan living in the house as an *agregada*. The institution of *agregados* partly attenuated socio-economic distances, and can be interpreted as one of the factors lending a porous quality to social relations within nineteenth-century Rio de Janeiro and Brazil.[24] Machado de Assis himself came from such a family. In this case, after realizing something is in the air, the priest attempts to bring together in marriage Lalau and Félix, the widow's son. As much as she has affection for Lalau, and despite the girl's education, the matriarch opposes the union, unable to get over her modest origins. During a conversation with the narrator, the enchanting Lalau nostalgically recalls those origins by speaking of her late mother:

> – Oh! I would give anything to have her at my feet, in our little house of the Cidade Nova! The house was like this – she proceeded to lift her hands, opened in front of her face to mark the extension of a palm – I still remember well, it was nothing, almost nothing – there were no carpets nor anything golden there, but mother was so good! So good! Poor mom!

Written in the 1880s, the passage refers to a memory of the Cidade Nova as the place of a lost childhood, but also of humbler, happier residents. And it works towards reinforcing the 'social distance' between Félix, son of a minister from the empire, and Lalau, daughter of parents from the peripheries. Her mother was the 'daughter of a clerk from the countryside' and the father 'exercised a mechanical trade'. The story gets more complicated through a web of incestuous suspicions and mistaken identities, and we need not get into its vicissitudes.[25]

III

Machado de Assis, whose own origins were as humble as some of the characters we have discussed here, until this time appears to participate in the flattened notion of a divided Rio de Janeiro. As he matured, however, it became clearer that much more would be at play in his texts than in those of contemporaries, and they give us incomparable access to a more dynamic and complex understanding of the city.

Let us begin with a more detailed reading of a later work, 'Conto de Escola' (A Schoolboy's Story). First published in the *Gazeta de Notícias* (1894), it is another short story narrated in the first person and set in the historical period before Dom Pedro II's *maioridade*, or age of majority.[26] The narrative, also a recollection, opens with a precise location and date: 'The school was in the Rua do Costa, a little two-storey house with wooden railings. The year was 1840'. The Rua do Costa was certainly familiar to the author, and, we can imagine, had some personal significance to him. It was at the bottom of the Livramento Hill, on the Cidade Nova side, where Machado was born in 1839 and where his family lived as agregados. The story continues:

> That day – a Monday in May – I lingered for a moment in the Rua da Princesa to where I might go and play that morning. I hesitated between Diogo Hill and the Campo de Sant'ana, which wasn't yet the polite park it is today, but a more or less infinite rustic space, full of washerwomen, grass and loose donkeys. The hill or the Campo? That was the problem.

At Princesa Street, which intersected Costa Street, the narrator had pondered whether to play in the Campo de Santana or the mostly still uninhabited São Diogo Hill, at the edge of the Cidade Nova swamps. The contrast between the Campo of Machado's childhood and the Campo 'today' was drawn in stark terms. The memory of a more or less 'infinite', endless space evokes childhood impressions, before one's experience of the world becomes codified by measurements and defined by a sense of material proportion. At the same time, the Campo's dimensions did shrink during Machado's lifetime, its borders increasingly well-defined against the growing city. The 'polite park' ('construção de *gentleman*') refers to reforms begun in 1873 and inaugurated in 1880, on the anniversary of Brazil's independence (Santos

1907: 383). They were based on a project by Auguste François Marie Glaziou (1828–1906), who also proposed an ambitious, 164-foot-wide tree-lined boulevard parallel to the Mangue, one of the unbuilt plans for the Cidade Nova that circulated during the empire.[27] Glaziou's Campo de Santana was altered almost beyond recognition, urbanized and landscaped in the English Romantic style.

Between the still rustic Campo and the hill, the narrator opted for the school. A week earlier, he explains, his father had punished him with a beating over a couple of 'days off', and fear of being caught kept him from the more attractive initial options. From the classroom, full of regret for not playing with the other 'idle kids', 'the cream of the neighbourhood and of the human race', to his despair he spots a kite flying above Livramento Hill. The father, an old employee of the Arsenal, had high hopes that his son would ascend socially, a plan that excluded flying kites and neighbourhood kids: 'He dreamed of an important position in commerce for me, and wanted me to get the elements of bookkeeping, reading, writing and arithmetic, so I could get work as a cashier. He cited names of rich men who had begun serving behind the counter'.

At school, Raimundo, a classmate and the teacher's son, discreetly tells the narrator, Pilar, that he wishes to speak to him. The story quickly establishes a comparison between the intellect of both characters. Raimundo was hardworking but a slow learner. Pilar, modesty aside, confesses to his superior intelligence relative to his colleagues. The narrative draws another contrast: Raimundo was 'pallid', Pilar 'had a good complexion' ('tinha boas cores'). We should prudently assume 'boas cores' here has no other intention than to give an impression of vitality and good health, and indeed Raimundo is characterized as sickly. It is worthwhile to ask, nonetheless, whether Pilar could be a mulato. If the text does not authorize us to arrive at that conclusion, it is certainly not far-fetched given the story's autobiographical echoes and geographical location. In a school in all likelihood attended by children from the Livramento Hill or from the nearby Cidade Nova and port areas, the percentage of students of mixed race would be significant.[28]

Machado de Assis, for a long time read as only focusing on the elites, and skirting race, has been accused of being 'viscerally elitist'.[29] That he was attuned to issues of skin colour and social class seems difficult to ignore, as a description from the aforementioned *Casa Velha* attests, to mention but one instance: 'Some people from the neighbourhood began to enter the church, in general poor people, of all ages and colours'. He is never oblivious to racial relations – but, rather, often discreet. We are thus in some cases left with mild suspicions, where it is impossible to ascertain whether a character is a mulato – which in itself speaks to the slipperiness of racial classifications in a deeply miscegenated society. Nonetheless, there has been a recent critical reassessment of the role of race in his works with publications like the anthology *Machado de Assis afro-descendente* (Assis 2007).[30] Despite stories with direct references to slaves and their descendants, some of those most compelling to us contain mere hints (intentional or not), often reinforced by spatial references that have lost their meanings to readers today, and through which we may better map social relations and cultural spaces both within his literature and within the city.

In any case, mulato or not – and there seem to be no obvious consequences to the plot of 'Conto de Escola' either way – Raimundo offers a silver coin from 'when the Portuguese king lived in Rio' to the narrator in exchange for help with 'a passage in the syntax lesson'.[31] Pilar passes over the explanations on pieces of paper as the master reads the day's newspapers 'with fury and indignation' (552), completely indifferent to the students. A classmate named Curvelo denounces the arrangement and they are caught by the teacher, whose presumed duty it was to teach. The master's accusation of the narrator ironically spells out his own job, which he so plainly neglected: 'So you receive money to teach the lessons to others?' In a grand gesture, he takes Pilar's coin and throws it out of the window, punishing both students with a 'palmatória' ('a piece of wood with holes drilled in its flat, round end'), accompanied by insults which highlight even further the irony of the situation: he calls theirs 'a base, unworthy, vile act, a villainy' and accuses them of being 'shameless, insolent [...] Swine! crooks! cowards!'.

The next day Pilar goes looking for the coin, but instead runs into a marching battalion and finds himself seduced by its drums. The narrator follows them, misses school and later goes back home 'with no silver coin in the pockets and no resentment in the soul'. The story concludes: 'Still, the coin was pretty, and it was they, Raimundo and Curvelo, who gave me my first taste of corruption in one case, of betrayal in the other; but the beat of that drum ...'. The narrator's attraction to the military drums would not be out of place in the republic during which the story was published. At the same time, a dialectic reminiscent of *Memórias de um sargento de milícias* seems to be at work here, at least in what appears to be the final lesson: morals are relative, if not in this world, certainly in this city.

In his next volume of short stories, *Páginas recolhidas* (Collected Pages, 1899), Machado again places at the centre of the narrative cultural spaces identified in Rio de Janeiro's lettered cartographies as peripheral – and revisits the issue of a narrator who, while a student, draws his lessons from outside of school. Like the previous story, 'Um erradio' (An Errant Man) looks back at an episode from a character's youth. Although introduced in the third person, most of the narrative consists of Tosta explaining to his newlywed wife the identity of a man she finds pictured in an old photograph. An artefact of the recent invention sets off a series of memories of his years as a student, when he resided in the Rua do Lavradio. The street, which to this day preserves neoclassical facades from the nineteenth century, was one of the first residential addresses of the city's centre. In the text, the narrator, more bourgeois than bohemian, recalls his more bohemian than bourgeois youth, living in a 'simple room, sublet by a tailor, who lived at the rear of the house with his family'. With him 'lived five young fellows, but others showed up, and everyone was everything: students, translators, proofreaders, ladies' men, and they even found time to write a political and literary paper, published on Saturdays'. Despite not being wealthy or powerful, they are all legitimate members of the lettered city.

Elisiário, the protagonist and photographed, in contrast, lived towards the Gamboa, already notorious as a home of freed slaves and their descendants.[32] The narrator suggestively describes him as *moreno*, a common variation in Brazil for a light-skinned mulato, for which it is also often employed as a cautious euphemism. He recalls asking his peers: 'Where did he [Elisiário] live? I was told, vaguely, towards the Gamboa area [lá para os lados da Gamboa], but he never invited me over there, nor did anyone know with certainty where it was'. Their uncertainty seems emblematic of the lettered city's relation to marginal spaces: neighbourhoods like the Gamboa and the Cidade Nova are vague, distant, almost indistinguishable, in sharp contrast to the precision of references to the Old City, like the address in Lavradio Street.

'Latin teacher and explainer [explicador] of mathematics' – recalling the young Pilar from the previous story – the erudite Elisiário was not the product of a formal education, 'he had no degrees in anything'. According to the narrator, 'he would have been a good prose writer, had he been capable of writing for twenty minutes straight; he was a poet of improvisation, he did not write his verses'. Elisiário, more counterpoint than antithesis to the lettered narrator and his friends, shows up at the house in Lavradio Street with his *opa* and his irreverence: '– Only the opa come in', jokes one of the students, referring to the armless mantle that he wore, typically used by religious brotherhoods during ceremonies. Another room-mate proposes the challenge: '– No, the opa can't, only Elisiário comes in, but first, let's hear some improvised verses [há de glosar um mote]. Who's giving the theme?'. Soon enough someone does, and Elisiário 'recites verses, improvised', marvelling those present with his talent. Elisiário, though Tosta describes him as serious, makes proposals worthy of Almeida's Leonardo, representative of the logic of a *malandro* – a rogue-like character often idealized in Brazilian popular culture. First, he suggests that they sell Chico, a 'good looking black' ('bonito crioulo') as a slave, even though he is a freedman. As a result, the ruse would allow the students to pay him a salary. Next, he chastises Chico for handing out a receipt after collecting money from a subscription to one of their literary magazines. Had he not done that, the subscriber could be charged again, Elisiário concludes in jest.

Elisiário, in his mid-thirties, takes to the eighteen-year-old Tosta, also somewhat of an outsider in that house, having been sent by his father from the north-east province of Ceará to study in the capital. Elisiário declares he will 'make Tosta a man', and decides to help him with his studies. As the former student and narrator reminisces with his wife, we start to discover the extent to which that errant man made a deep impression on him. One day Tosta met him in São José Street and said that he was going to the top of the Castelo Hill to visit the Jesuit Church, where he had never been.[33] Elisiário accompanies his young friend, and with the 'evocative imagination' of a novelist added to the knowledge of a historian, makes Old Rio come alive. A flâneur who 'went everywhere' and could be found in the neighbourhoods most distant from each other, Elisiário defines himself as someone in perpetual motion, a type of Orpheus, ecstatic in the metropolis, to borrow the title of another book (Sevcenko 1992): 'I am an errant. The day that I settle down, you better bet that I am dead'.

On another occasion, Tosta ran into Elisiário in a fine arts exhibition. He recalls being stunned with Elisiário's classical knowledge, and with his ability not merely to explain but to incarnate the culture of ancient Greece:

> The types of things that he told me regarding the Venus de Milo [...] He spoke of aesthetics, of the great artists, of Greek life, of Greek marble, of the Greek soul. He was a Greek, a pure Greek who appeared in front of me and transported me from a narrow street to the Parthenon. His opa transformed into a chlamys [a Greek cloak], the tongue must have been from Hellas [...]. What a sorcerer, that damn man.

The transfiguration could only be rendered in close to supernatural terms, and the reference to him as a 'sorcerer' ('feiticeiro') although tongue-in-cheek, cannot help but bring to mind the semantic fields we have associated to the caboclo. The term would often be applied to central figures of Afro-Brazilian religions.

Following that experience, Tosta and Elisiário went for a walk, in an unusual itinerary for the former and a familiar one for the latter, as we will discover.

> We left; we went to the Acclamation Field, that did not yet possess

today's park, nor did it have any police other than the nature that made its grass sprout, and the washerwomen, who lathered and cleaned clothes in front of the barracks.

Attuned to the palimpsestic quality of the cityscape, Machado's narrative recovers submerged layers of its past. The description refers to some of the same differences between the Campo before and after Glaziou's reform as those evoked in 'Conto de Escola'. The fountain and tanks used by the washerwomen, where slaves congregated, were demolished in 1873 (Coaracy 1965: 233). Unlike the later 'park' of the interlocutor and the readers' time, when Tosta and Elisiário took their walk back in 1866, the Campo was still closer to the space we read about in Almeida – and may imagine from representations like Augustus Earle's watercolour of a 'Negro Fandango Scene at Campo de St Anna' (*c.*1822).

Beyond the scope of the police and of the ordered, manicured natural features introduced in the 1870s, the Campo here remained a type of frontier where 'civilized' central Rio turned into the 'exotic' Cidade Nova. Tosta uses the official nomenclature, Acclamation Field, while the narrator of 'Conto de Escola' had preferred the more colloquial, prior name, Campo de Santana, implying greater intimacy with the place. Elisiário later in the story also refers to the Campo by its former, unofficial name. In these apparently insignificant details, Machado's texts help us establish the divergent relationships between each of his characters and narrators to the city. By doing so, they allow us to uncover and explore how his fiction often functions in dialectic tension within competing cartographies of both the lettered city (of newspapers and its implied readers) and of Rio de Janeiro's ordinary dwellers – a process that besides enriching our understanding of his literature informs the city's history.

Able to circulate from Little Africa to the Academy of Fine Arts, Elisiário escapes the possibilities of a cartographer's map – he cannot be pinned down, and in fact draws his vitality and creative power from being an errant, a type of vagabond. It is, as we will find out at the story's end, analogous to how the inspiration and vigour of his poetry cannot be separated from his unwillingness to commit it to writing, paradoxical as it may seem. As Tosta accompanies Elisiário on this walk, we have a revelatory chance encounter:

I went along, consumed by Elisiário's speech [on the Greeks], by his side, as he carried on with a lowered head and pensive eyes. All of a sudden, I heard someone say in a low voice [baixinho]:

– Hello, mister! [Adeus, Ioiô!]

It was a street vendor of sweets, a Bahian black woman [crioula baiana], which I gathered from the embroideries of her skirt and shirt. She came from the Cidade Nova and was going across the fields. Elisiário responded to the greeting:

– Hello, Zeferina.

Why did the *quitandeira* or vendor from the Cidade Nova salute Elisiário in a low voice? Did she not want to interrupt Elisiário's conversation, or was she afraid that he might decline the salute, embarrassed to admit knowing her? Did she imagine her acquaintance might lower his station? To the contrary, Elisiário salutes her by name. The narrator is taken back, and Elisiário's response positions him as a true cosmopolite, one who does not subjugate the local to the 'universal', the Afro-Brazilian to the European.

He halted and looked at me, laughing without laughter, and a few seconds later:

– Don't be frightened, kid. There are many types of Venus. What no one can say is that this one lacks arms; and he continued to look at the vendor's arms, even blacker due to the contrast with the short sleeves of the white shirt.

The enigmatic exchange with the Bahian Venus may be read in the context of an erotic relationship, but at any rate Tosta's reaction reveals – codified in his 'discretion' – certain prejudices he probably shared with his housemates and many of Machado's readers:

Me, being embarrassed, I couldn't find a response. I didn't tell anyone about this episode at Lavradio Street; they could give Elisiário a hard time, and I didn't want to seem indiscreet.

The apparently unpretentious episode strikes as even more relevant because Machado's Elisiário proposes his 'many types of Venus' criterion not only in 1866, when the story is set, but also in 1896 when it is published – precisely when discourses of scientific racism had deeply taken hold in Brazilian society, particularly among the elites, and a ruthless hierarchy had been internalized whereas most things black were held as not only inferior but as a corrupting influence.[34] In that context, Elisiário, mulato or not, becomes a type of counterpart to Dom Obá, who presented himself above all as a poet, and whose verses occasionally espoused the value of blackness: 'It is not a defect to be the color black / It is sad that envy should rob it of its worth' (Silva 1993: 130).

On a different occasion, after leaving the theatre early because the 'erradio' could not stay put for a play's last two acts, the two friends sit at a bar near by. After a conversation where Elisiário 'planned a thousand journeys to the backlands of all Brazil', where he would 'harvest everything, plants, legends, songs, expressions', Tosta hears the following pitch: 'Would you be capable of going from here to São Cristovão, by foot, right now?'. The student replies with a tepid 'sure', which Elisiário interprets as a decline justified by tiredness, and goes off alone. Tosta decides to follow him: 'I caught him at Ciganos Street. He went slowly, with his cane under the arm, and hands sometimes behind the back, sometimes in his pockets. He crossed the Acclamation Field, entered São Pedro Street, and went down the Landfill Road'.

The date in which Machado sets the story prompts another digression here. This peripatetic plot preceded by a couple of years what to the urban geographer Maurício de Abreu constituted a watershed in Rio de Janeiro's evolution during the nineteenth century: the increase of train service to the suburbs, and the implementation of reliable *bonde*, or streetcar, lines after 1868 (1988: 37).[35] European travellers seemed impressed with the city's services: the Count d'Ursel in 1873 saw in them 'the most democratic equality' (Taunay 1947: 74), and a decade later Hastings C. Dent – who otherwise had much to complain about his year in Brazil – found that 'the ubiquitous system of tramways [...] is so excellent that it would be easier to suggest improvement in the means of locomotion which exist in London than in those of Rio' (1886: 235). Their role in real estate speculation, privileging the future South Zone, has been documented (Abreu 1988: 41–50). The extent to which Rio's inhabitants came to rely on the streetcars, at the same time, explains why in 1880 a 10 per cent rise in their prices was met with violent public uproar, a reaction later known as the Revolta do Vintém, or Tuppenny Revolt (Silva 1993: 68–9). Besides the city's socio-economic cartography, reliance on streetcars for mobility also altered an individual's experience of space. Passive streetcar riders might have less need to rely on the cognitive maps through which pedestrians can plot their itineraries or find their way in an urban environment.[36]

Streetcars attracted enough attention from Machado de Assis to warrant a recent anthology of his writings related to the matter.[37] Deeming them 'essentially democratic' in an 1883 *crônica* (Assis 2001: 9), in another text, from 1889, only a few years before publication of 'Um erradio', he reveals a habit and ethos close to Elisiário's: 'It is my habit, when I have nothing to do at home, to go about this world of Christ, if we can call the city of São Sebastião [do Rio de Janeiro] that, in order to kill time. I know of no better thing to do [...] especially if we make it to eccentric neighbourhoods'. As if a prescription to his readers, he adds, not without a metonymic nod to the lettered city: 'Naturally, once my legs are tired, I take the first bonde, which can bring me home or to Ouvidor Street, which is where we all live' (15). The reduced time it took to travel from one place to another might have led to a certain democratization of Rio's urban spaces, or at least to bring the Cidade Nova even closer to the Centro. It can perhaps help us make sense of Tosta's hesitation, as he follows Elisiário, once he reaches the border with that neighbourhood: 'At the Campo, I wanted to leave, but curiosity made me keep walking'.[38]

Would the thought not have occurred were there already a system of streetcars in place? Or was the desire to turn back motivated more by a fear of crossing the imaginary line, of going past the border where the familiar, civilized city ended? Whatever the answer, Tosta's decision to keep following is not met with any cataclysmic events. Elisiário's walk turns out to lack a utilitarian motive, much like Machado's. After traversing the entire Cidade Nova, Elisiário reaches a little church by the sea, and takes a boat back to the Campo, where he spends the night at an inn, as he would tell Tosta the next day. Tosta, however, is left without familiar coordinates: 'I found myself lost, far from the city and exhausted'. The 'city' here refers specifically to the Centro, in a metonymic displacement that remains in usage to this day. But even before streetcars Tosta would have had no trouble finding a tilbury, and make his way back to Lavradio Street.

Machado de Assis, who at the time he wrote the story lived in the bucolic neighbourhood of Cosme Velho, unlike Tosta, and much like Elisiário, had the custom of circulating in the city's less prestigious areas, and perhaps counted the Cidade Nova among those 'eccentric' places. On at least one occasion we find him walking around the stigmatized neighbourhood with an attentive mind and a sympathetic spirit. In a chronicle from 1 May 1892, after protesting against an enclosing that a private company placed around a fountain of the Largo da Carioca, he concludes with the following lesson: 'Sometimes, from where you don't expect much, that's where it comes from. Days ago, I found a new verb on a sign in a store of the Cidade Nova: '*We opaque glass*'. Tell me in which dictionary one could find a word so appropriate to the circumstance' (Assis 1996: 53).

IV

Machado de Assis adopts the procedure of setting a plot in the past in yet another short story relevant to our discussions. The device, which Wisnik calls Machado's 'technique of counterpoints' and recurs in much of his fiction, was the object of a systematic study by John Gledson (1986). It is related to our methodology here, of exploring toponymic references in the attempt to articulate how a writer's (or a text's) particular mapping of a social or a cultural space fits into, pushes against, elaborates on, or even subverts not only the cartographer's representation of a city's physical features but also the cartographies of a lettered city, with their (at times unbeknownst) biases, prejudices, and agendas. If both cartographers and writers tend to share perceptions coloured by a conscience of producing from the centre of a city – albeit the periphery of a capitalist world order, an awareness all too present in the case of turn of the century Latin American intellectuals – Machado developed the capacity to reorder Rio de Janeiro according to the experience of characters hailing from the city's peripheries, and who were sometimes quite different from his presumed readers.[39] The effort to recover or recreate associations elicited by places which have lost their meaning to today's reader seems particularly productive in the case of 'Uns braços' (A Pair of Arms), a celebrated narrative that can and has been read as unfolding between four walls, restricted to a domestic and private sphere.[40]

'Uns braços' opens at the dinner table, and we are immediately confronted with a gallery of not too literary insults thrown by the lawyer Borges at Inácio: 'layabout [malandro], daydreamer, idiot, nutcase'. Inácio, the supposed 'malandro', is a fifteen-year-old taken by his father to work as 'an agent, scribe, clerk, or something of the sort with Borges the lawyer'. The narrator explains: Inácio's father, not unlike the father of 'Conto de Escola', had hopes that 'he would rise in the world, because he thought barristers got a lot of money'. The text supplies the following details: 'His father's a barber in the Cidade Nova'. The lawyer Borges, along with D. Severina, the owner of the arms in the title, with whom he lived 'maritally', inhabited Lapa Street. The story takes place in 1870.

Gledson highlights the date's importance – the end of the height of the period known in Brazilian history as the Segundo Reinado, or Second Reign (1840–89) – not only to the country's social reality but also to Machado's fiction. Besides 'Um erradio', as we have seen, it serves as the backdrop to the novel *Quincas Borba* and to the main episodes of *Dom Casmurro*. To Gledson it is 'the period of crisis that most fascinated Machado [...] the end of the 1860s and beginning of the 1870s, when for the first time it could be seen that slavery was going to end, with a new commercial class tied to international capital representing a threat to the power of the traditional dominating class – or at least to its confidence' (1986: 19). The years around 1870, he reminds us, witnessed a number of critical events to Brazil's history: 'the Paraguayan War, the Law of the Free Womb, and the foundation of the Republican Party' (20).[41] They also represented, as we have begun to see, a turning point for the development of cities both locally and globally.[42]

Part of the fascination of 'Uns braços' comes from the fact that its characters are not those that, by representing the extremes of the population, tend to be featured: slaves and the ruling elites. Borges, D. Severina, and Inácio belong to the vast intermediate ranks that would be equally affected by all the changes occurring. At the same time, already in the first paragraph, the narrator subtly positions Inácio, 'badly dressed' and the son of a barber from the Cidade Nova, in an inferior socio-economic class relative to the lawyer, a resident of Lapa Street. The contrast between the two addresses would not go unnoticed by a contemporary reader, and deserves some consideration. Adjacent to the Passeio Público, an elegant and aristocratic public space, the Rua da Lapa maintained a certain prestige at the time. The profession of Inácio's anonymous father, added to his affiliation with the Cidade Nova, allows for further speculative interpretations: barbers in Imperial Brazil were most likely to be blacks or mulatos.[43]

We are not dealing here, however, with an insurmountable social abyss: the young man, after all, was sent by his father to work with the lawyer because he held on to the aspiration (or illusion) that his son could enter a career in law and 'move up' in life. Borges, a bailiff, was not exactly a wealthy man: Severina exposed those famous arms not 'to show off' but because 'she'd already worn out all her long-sleeved dresses' and, we presume, did not have the money to replace them. Later in the story, the lawyer refuses a visit to some good friends, justifying it with how he worked 'like a black man'. The implication, in other words, is that Borges was barely ahead of blacks in the social scale.

In a dynamic common to Machado's fiction (and not unusual in human relations), exploitation generates further exploitation. The 'terrible Borges' submits Inácio to a regimen of intensive and abusive work. The story opens with the bailiff's insults because of Inácio's apparent heavy sleep and constant 'dozing', leading to the threat: 'Leave it to me; tomorrow I'll wake him with a broomstick!' Faced with a desolating routine, Dona Severina's arms become 'the tents where he took his repose'. The young man 'put up with all the work in town [...] all his boss's rude abuse, just for the reward of seeing, three times a day, the famous pair of arms'. Borges goes on 'firing off threats' against Inácio, but the narrator exempts him from any great blame: he was 'incapable of carrying them out, for he was more of a loudmouth than a truly nasty man'.

From the very beginning, the story accentuates a contrast between Dona Severina and Borges. When he 'spat out' insults at Inácio, threatening physical punishment, she protectively 'prodded Borges gently with her foot, as if asking him to stop'. Severina's unstated compassion extends itself throughout the text, eventually expanding into a mixture of maternal and erotic (sensual more than sexual) sentiments towards Inácio. This climaxes when she is led to 'leave him a kiss on the mouth' while he slept. 'Here the dream coincided with reality', declares the narrator. For Inácio, described earlier as having 'dreamy' eyes, the kiss and Lapa Street were just that ('And it was a dream! No more than a dream!'), ending without the fulfilment of his father's own dreams of seeing him as a prosecutor. The boy has to leave the house. And, for Dona Severina, self-censorship after the act re-transfigures feelings that had been born pure: 'A child! she said to herself, in that wordless language we all have within us'.[44]

The scene seems to address what Gledson calls 'the recurrent theme in Machado of love cutting across class barriers' (19). Machado touches on Inácio's subaltern condition with all of his narrator's suggestive powers when Severina becomes aware of the young man's admiration for her: 'She saw it was true, she was loved and feared, with an adolescent, virginal love, held back by social ties and a feeling of inferiority which prevented him from understanding himself'. While the age disparity between the two acts as a factor, it is in the latent class distinctions that we encounter the socio-cultural tensions of the author's Rio de Janeiro.

It is indisputable, after all, that Inácio found himself in a subordinate social position in relation not only to the couple but also to the contemporary reader. The real transgression of 'Uns braços', in other words, may be to cross social borders between characters and public. We know the *implied reader* of the First Republic to be restricted – the number of those who were literate was relatively small. Machado's writings were in great part consumed by elites that we may presume not to have been necessarily preoccupied with a drama between four walls where the protagonist hails from the popular masses. 'Uns braços', in a sense, attempts to bridge not only the divide between the Cidade Nova and Lapa Street, but also to the prestigious Ouvidor Street of so much of his public, not to mention his publishing house. He seems to act as a mediator, then, between the stigmatized and those who stigmatized.

If in 1870 the associations between the Cidade Nova and a universe of insalubrity, barbarous African practices, and swarming tenements were in the process of being formed, by 1896 – when the story was published – that identity had taken hold in the minds of the reading public of the First Republic, as the next chapter will make clear. The attributes that the Cidade Nova became known for were precisely those that city administrators and politicians wanted driven out of the capital's centre.[45] The early republican regimes, then, of which Machado de Assis was a vocal critic, exacerbated an era of authoritarian urban policies that reached their pinnacle through demolitions to give place to a monumental new avenue. The *bota-abaixo* ('put down') carried out by Pereira Passos, an engineer appointed as mayor of the

Federal District and as the architect of the ambitious reforms (1902–6), has become a much-discussed turning point in the city's history – another topic for the pages ahead.

Already before publication of 'Uns braços', however, to cite two examples of great repercussion in 1893, the popular kiosks of central Rio were condemned to be razed, and hundreds were evicted from the Cabeça-de-Porco (Pig-Head), a famous cortiço in Cidade Nova street where Dom Obá last lived. Some of those who witnessed the demolition of their residences appear to have used discarded materials to build makeshift homes on the adjoining hillsides – not far from the birthplace of Machado de Assis. Thus began to be formed the communities eventually known as favelas.[46] And, just as significantly, the episode was also foundational to the rhetoric of urban reforms as a war on the 'uncivilized', or a cure against the threat of 'dangerous classes' that were increasingly equated with the poor.[47]

In the interval between when 'Uns braços' and 'Um erradio' are set and when they are published (and most likely were written), we observe an intensification of efforts to segregate the city socially. The poorer are pushed to the peripheries and further marginalized, goals that would be articulated in rather explicit terms in planning projects of the early twentieth century. These urban interventions were frequently in tandem with or inspired by changes abroad, particularly the renovation of Paris under Haussmann, which a young Pereira Passos had experienced first-hand while living in the French capital between 1857 and 1860 (Benchimol 1999: 192). At the same time as they responded to global shifts in ideas about how cities should function, the measures enacted in Rio during the First Republic also sought to undermine very local forms of spatial porosity. Much of this naturally does not surface in Machado de Assis's fiction, which precedes their execution. But in the case of broader and incipient developments related to the goals of these reforms it is possible that he adopted that well-known strategy of writing about the past to criticize the present. In 'Uns braços', for example, one can detect a conspicuous association between the lawyer Borges and ideals identified with the new regime.

Intentionally or intuitively, the story seems to unmask the nature of certain political projects that gained force under the republic, like the propagation of a type of blind faith in the virtues of literacy. Machado ironically makes the uncouth Borges a spokesperson in defence of schooling. The narrator resorts to the device known as free indirect speech to make the lawyer's thoughts known:

> he attacked [their good friend] Fortunata, her husband, and their son, who wasn't going to school, at the age of ten! He, Borges, when he

was ten, already knew how to read, write and do his sums, not very well, it's true, but at least he knew. Ten! He'd come to a good end: a good-for-nothing, he'd be press-ganged in no time. Life in the army would teach him a lesson.

The reference to military life reinforces the alignment of Borges with technocratic and positivist principles of the republic – installed through a military coup – and which professed the equation of literacy with prosperity, and of formal education with progress.[48] This mentality, or at least an acritical implementation of its tenets, seems to be a target of irony in 'Uns braços'. Borges's conduct as exploiter and his condition as exploited, to say the least, exposes the hypocrisy in the defence of literacy alone as an instrument of liberation rather than social conditioning. The same critique appears embodied in the schoolteacher of 'Conto de Escola', perhaps a sign that Machado increasingly placed value on Rio's *erradios*, if not on 'that wordless language we all have within us' of Dona Severina.

Wisnik comments on how the Machado de Assis of the 1870s identified himself with his readers' presumed attitudes on the superiority of written culture (2004: 24). By the time he wrote stories like 'Conto de Escola', 'Um erradio', and 'Uns braços', Machado had developed a more reflective sense of belonging in a lettered city, something that echoes in how his representations of the Cidade Nova altered over time. By positioning a critical eye on the compulsive apologist of literacy, Machado's fiction anticipates forces that would be channelled by reformist projects that were still in their infancy in the 1870s.

Machado de Assis seemed to share with Baudelaire and others in what Marshall Berman calls the 'first great wave of writers and thinkers about modernity', an 'instinctive feeling' for the 'intimate unity of the modern self and the modern environment' (1982: 132). In a context where the sense of a mostly homogenous, stable, lettered city begins to pulverize amidst a series of political, economic, and technological developments, Machado charts a city that no longer merely matches or reproduces the mental maps of an elitist contemporary public. His writings capture social relations with a precision and subtlety that recognize what the experience of Rio's spaces must have been like from a variety of perspectives, not just those of colleagues from Ouvidor Street. His cartographies of Rio de Janeiro's social relations, in fact, prefigure transformations that would take shape with the authoritarian, modernizing urban reforms brought about in the first decade of the twentieth century. When writing the short stories we read here, during the 1890s, Machado de Assis projected an imperilled porosity to a Rio de Janeiro of the recent past. Certain practices and situations portrayed in that recent past – the time periods when those narratives are set – had not coincidentally entered a process of becoming residual, or were becoming increasingly confined to spaces like the Cidade Nova.

Notes

1 See Tinhorão 1998. Among the most notable early examples of the convergence between erudite and popular musical traditions are the works of Anacleto de Medeiros and Ernesto Nazareth, born in the Cidade Nova's Morro do Nheco (or de São Diogo), now known as the Morro do Pinto. On Medeiros, see Diniz 2007. On Nazareth, see Machado 2007.

2 Maxixe, played and danced in a fast 2/4 rhythm, absorbs elements from European polkas, the more African-based *lundus*, and Cuban *habaneras*. It influenced the later instrumental choro, which remains one of Brazil's most popular music styles. Terms like maxixe, polca, tango, and lundu were often interchangeable or applied to related genres in the nineteenth century. See Livingston-Isenhour, Elena, and Garcia 2005.

3 The title alludes to Roberto Schwarz's seminal *A Master on the Periphery of Capitalism* (2001), which examines how Machado's literary form internalizes and reveals ambiguities and tensions in Brazil's social relations. The book was first published in Brazil in 1990.

4 In 1885, the Italian doctor A. Lomonaco, for example, found pianos 'even in houses of lesser means': 'if the number of pianists could provide a test to evaluate the musical tendencies of a people, then Brazil should be considered a land of most passionate and fierce musicomaniacs' (Taunay 1947: 228).

5 Some early historians of Brazilian music claim that choro originated in the Cidade Nova during the mid-1900s. See, for example, Almeida (1942: 122). In Gonçalves Pinto's first-hand account of Rio's choro scene after 1870 (1936), the Cidade Nova indeed figures prominently. Addresses of musicians and gathering sites, however, were fairly spread out. There was clearly a great deal of circulation. Several of the over 300 musicians mentioned held day jobs as public servants. A musician's compensation often consisted of food and drinks only, aside from the sheer pleasure of playing for a party.

6 That was a position of the São Paulo Republican Party, largely formed by conservative coffee oligarchs and a major force of the so-called First Republic (1889–1930), also known as 'the oligarchic republic'. For a study of the transition to the republic that accounts for its unfulfilled promises and elitist nature, see Carvalho 1987. Obá experienced extreme difficulties after 1889, related to no longer being paid tributes, and to a context where 'there was no space for the old political loyalties' (Silva 1993: 160).

7 Also known as the Paraguayan War, the conflict lasted from 1864 until 1870. See Whigham 2002.

8 This quote is translated from the Brazilian edition of Silva's book (1997: 144). It seems to replace a similar quote from the English edition (1993: 132). Silva quotes from the pages of *O Carbonário*, 8 September 1882, p. 4.

9 Silva (whose calculations are cited above) notes that the increase in the percentage of whites coincided with the formation of an 'ideology of whitening' (1993: 57).

The census may reveal desires for a 'whiter' Brazil. As Wilson Martins remarks, the country's censuses offer 'psychological truths besides statistical truths' (1976: 145).

10 Although the classification of residence types was notoriously unreliable, scholars have made useful data available. See Lobo 1989 on the location of *cortiços* and *estalagens* (59); on conditions (62); on density (151).

11 Parish lines did not reflect neighbourhood boundaries, but we will again consider the Santana parish as representative. It was still the city's most populated, with 67,385 inhabitants, 28 per cent of whom were foreigners (second only to the adjacent Sacramento, 33 per cent), and 52 per cent of whom were illiterate (compared to 48 per cent for the entire city).

12 In the Santana parish, the racial breakdown according to the 1890 census was: 66.4 per cent white, 19.5 per cent *mestiço* (mixed), 11.8 per cent black, and 2.2 per cent caboclo. Among parishes of the Old City, the percentages of whites were: Sacramento 76.6 per cent, São José 74 per cent, and Candelária 88.7 per cent. The ratio of blacks to mixed was roughly 1 to 2. The exception was the parish of Santa Rita, which included the port area: blacks comprised 14.3 per cent and mestiços 22.6 per cent of the population. Owing to the preponderance of men among immigrants, they constituted 56 per cent of the city, close to the 56.7 per cent in the Santana parish.

13 Music was composed by Leocádio Rayol. Musical scores listing the show as Frotzmac can be found in the Biblioteca Nacional in Rio de Janeiro. A *revista de ano* or year-end revue, it was first staged at the Teatro Variedades Dramáticas. On the relationship of revistas de ano to the city's history, see Süssekind 1986. On the teatro de revista, see Paiva 1991.

14 Also called Clubes Carnavalescos, or simply Sociedades, they were the closest in Rio's carnival to the French model of masked balls, and in the 1850s incorporated street parades with expensive and often imported costumes. The Sociedades were in a sense the upper-class response to the more popular, anarchic, and sometimes violent *entrudos* of Portuguese origin. See Eneida 1987; Cunha 2001; and Ferreira 2004.

15 For a discussion of the Progressistas da Cidade Nova relative to other Grandes Sociedades, see Pereira (1994: 109–67), a study of the relationships between literature and carnival in nineteenth-century Rio de Janeiro.

16 Perhaps Brazil's first national dance and music, the lundu originates from practices of Banto slaves and incorporated elements of various Iberian traditions like the Spanish *fandango*. The lundu's syncopated rhythm and flirtatious dance, related to the umbigada, influenced the formation of the maxixe. The term has appeared in records at least since 1780, and its various uses render any definition insufficient. For a discussion of its history, and association to eighteenth-century modinhas sung in Brazil and Portugal, see Tinhorão's (2004) study of the poet Domingos Caldas Barbosa.

17 Other examples can be found in the *Folhetins* of França Junior (1838–90), in their fourth edition by 1926.

18 Cited at Velloso 1996: 48. The session showcased the omniographer, a precursor of cinema. Velloso's study offers a valuable portrait of the city's café culture (35–86), reminding us of how cinema shows were accompanied by music from some of Rio's choro players. On how new technologies altered literary techniques,

see Süssekind 1997. On cinema, literature and modernity in Rio, also see Conde 2012.

19 The musical featuring João Barbosa, João de Deus, Eduardo Leite, and Antônio Serra was released on 26 June 1908. A summary in the *Jornal do Brasil* that day claims that the film 'will be shown with all the required "mis-en-scène" [...] an acclaimed troubadour with a guitar, singing the most popular modinhas'.

20 According to the index of place names included in volume 3 of his *Obra Completa* (Assis 1962: 1168).

21 Longchamps, for example, in 1872, was not impressed by its imitative French-ness (Taunay 1947: 66), and Aimard in 1880 fails to understand why it was a source of pride for local elites (147).

22 See Roberto Schwarz's 'As idéias fora do lugar', first published in 1972. It provides a sophisticated analysis of how, due to slavery, European political economy principles and liberal ideologies, which presupposed free labor, were out of place amidst Brazil's social reality (Schwarz 1977).

23 The term caipora, meaning 'forest dweller' in Tupi, denotes one followed by bad luck and misfortune. All Machado quotes have been translated from his *Obra Completa* (1962), unless otherwise noted.

24 Agregados of a house could be servants, associates, lodgers, orphans, or members of a family – for all or most intents and purposes. This other form of spatial porosity – people of different social classes under the same roof – must be contrasted to how this institution, by giving an illusion of social mobility, in fact might serve to reinforce social stratification. The agregados of Machado's literature are central to much of Schwarz's critical work. Perhaps the most memorable of these characters is José Dias, from the novel *Dom Casmurro* (1900). Sheltered in a wealthy family lacking a patriarch, he develops complicity both with the character of the title and with his mother.

25 For an analysis of *Casa Velha* in the context of Machado's other works and Brazilian history, see Gledson 1986: 26–57.

26 In 1840, at the age of fourteen, Dom Pedro II was recognized as an adult fit to govern. For a reading of the short story that highlights its historical dimension, see Gledson 2006: 91–102. The story was reproduced in the collection *Várias histórias* (1896). I rely on Gledson's translations of Machado's short stories (Assis 2008), but do not always quote them verbatim.

27 The French landscape designer and botanist came to Brazil at Dom Pedro II's invitation, becoming the director of parks and gardens. His 1874 project for a boulevard (*Embelezamento do Rio de Janeiro*) would extend from the Praia dos Mineiros to the Andaraí Grande, passing between the Campo and the Central Station, avoiding the Praça Onze. The original can be found in the Cartography Division of the Biblioteca Nacional in Rio de Janeiro.

28 As we have seen, the Santa Rita parish where the Livramento was located had a significant population of mestiços and blacks. Indeed, it is probable that the racial diversity of an average Brazilian school would have been greater than a century later, after the institution of educational reforms in the early twentieth century disqualified black teachers and segregated schools racially. On these changes under the republic, see Rodrigues 2008 and Dávila 2003.

29 Tristão de Athayde uses the expression in an article published in the *Jornal do Brasil* (1983), reprinted at Barreto 1997: 508.

30 There were prior studies focusing on the role of slaves in his fiction, like Sayers 1956: 201–32.

31 The 'moeda do tempo do rei' cannot help but resonate with the opening of Almeida's novel, though we can imagine the expression was commonly used to refer to the period of Dom João VI.

32 On the neighbourhood, see Bueno 2002.

33 In the first chapter of the novel *Esaú e Jacó* (1904), we find a passage – describing two wealthy women going to a fortune-telling cabocla – that seems to underline the importance Machado gave to the excursion: 'It was the first time that the two had gone to Morro do Castelo hill. They began the ascent from the Rua do Carmo. There are many people of the city of Rio de Janeiro who have never been there, indeed many will die and many more will be born and die who will never set foot there. Not everyone can claim to know an entire city' (Assis 2000: 3, translated by Elizabeth Lowe). The Castelo Hill would begin to be levelled around the time of the book's publication, a process that reached its completion in 1922.

34 For a study of racial discourses between 1870 and 1930 in Brazil, there is no better source than Schwarcz 1999.

35 The first lines were by animal traction, and the term bonde most likely originated from the coupons (*bonds*) that were used to deal with problems caused by lack of change (Abreu 1988: 44). To give an idea of their impact, the Rio de Janeiro Railway Company, formerly Companhia São Cristóvão, transported more than three million passengers in 1871 (Laemmert 1872: 72–3).

36 Akerman makes an analogous point, although his edited volume is more concerned with cartographies of travel at much broader geographic scales, exploring for instance the impact of railroad lines (2006: 2).

37 See *Machado de Assis: crônicas de bond* (2001).

38 An alternative explanation of how 'Um erradio' might have been different were it set after 1892 – when the electric bondes took over the streets – can be found in Sevcenko 1998. He suggests that Machado captured how, after the advent of electric streetcars, one took to the street with a spirit of 'caution' and 'alarm' (549). It was a new spirit that would most likely threaten the story's flânerie, which of course preceded a change that contemporary readers were experiencing right then.

39 The idea of a geographic centre equating with power can be traced back to the Renaissance (Rama 1984: 5). The relative nature and limitations of centre/periphery constructions will be addressed in the following chapter.

40 See, for example, Junqueira 2008. 'Uns braços' appears in the collection *Várias histórias* (1896), along with 'Conto de Escola'. It was also translated by Gledson (Assis 2008).

41 The children of slaves born after the Law of the Free Womb were considered free. In a study concerned with intersections between Machado and historical changes, Chalhoub discusses how the author became deeply involved in the law's application while working at the Ministry of Agriculture (2003: 138–9).

42 Those pivotal years, described by some historians as the 'take-off' of the Second Industrial Revolution, ushered a series of innovations – from electricity to new metallurgic techniques – that would irrevocably alter the life of cities. See Sevcenko 1998: 7–48.

43 Almeida describes barbers as usually black, a point echoed by recent scholars (Fryer 2000: 140).

44 Quite a bit remains to be said of Severina, who appears to be yet another Machado character of ambiguous ethnic background: we can imagine her too as a mulata. The narrator writes that her arms 'lost none of their color' ('não perdiam a cor'). On her hard-to-subdue ('revoltos') hair, we read: 'She smoothed, gathered, and tied and fixed it on top of her head with the tortoiseshell comb her mother had left her'. The detail of a tortoiseshell comb left by her mother, apparently gratuitous, may be related to Oxum, an orixá associated to the artefact. If indeed we imagine her so, as an object of seduction without being 'faceira' (coquettish), we would have in Severina a woman who resists literary stereotypes of the sly mulata.

45 Chalhoub (1996: 33–4) discusses the shift of focus on the location – rather than the condition – of cortiços: in 1873, their construction was forbidden in central areas of the city, including the zone between the Praça Tiradentes and the Praça Onze. Similar policies gained force after 1889 (35). Although, as often noted, the classification of cortiços lacked objective criteria – resting on the eyes of the beholder, one might say – forcing them further out sometimes constituted an 'out-of-sight, out-of-mind' approach. Other plans were explicit in their desire of building housing for the poor in the Cidade Nova, like the *Proposta de Felíssimo Vieira de Almeida Dr. Lourenço Ferreira, da Silva e Antônio José Roiz de Araújo* (1884) found in the Arquivo Geral da Cidade do Rio de Janeiro.

46 On the relationship between the Cabeça-de-Porco and the origins of favelas, see Vaz 2002: 54–7. Newspaper estimates of the number of residents at the time of its razing range from 400 to 2,000, with speculation that up to 4,000 had once lived there (Chalhoub 1996: 15).

47 See Chalhoub 1996: 20–8. After leading the demolition of the Cabeça-de-Porco, Barata Ribeiro, a despotic mayor and protégé of the 'Iron Marshal' Floriano Peixoto (Brazil's second president), was celebrated in the press for ridding Rio of 'filth' and 'troublemakers' (18–19).

48 Especially during its initial years, competing ideological currents marked the republican transition. See Carvalho 1990, especially the chapter on positivists (129–40).

CHAPTER THREE

Beyond the Belle Époque: On the Border of a 'Divided City'

A boundary is not that at which something stops but, as the Greeks recognized, the boundary [*peras*] is that from which something *begins its presencing.*

Martin Heidegger, 'Building, Dwelling, Thinking'

I

In 1890, Aluísio Azevedo published the now classic *O Cortiço*, a mark of naturalism in Brazilian literature.[1] The novel constitutes a microcosm of Rio de Janeiro's society: the cast of characters includes the bourgeoisie, an ambitious vendor, exploited workers, vagabonds, and musicians. It concentrates on the portrayal of life in the precarious lodging of the title, inhabited by scores of Portuguese and Italian immigrants, mulatos, and freed-persons, often presented in the zoomorphic descriptions common to the naturalist aesthetic. In the novel's opening sentence, Azevedo locates it in the South Zone neighbourhood of Botafogo, where João Romão becomes the owner of a small shop that would propel the development of his formidable cortiço, in great part due to the toil of Bertoleza, a slave who lives as Romão's partner and who he ultimately betrays in a tragic ending.

As the plot unfolds, we are introduced to another of the protagonists, Jerônimo, a hard-working and skilled Portuguese labourer who convinces Romão to hire his services at a higher than usual rate, to do work in a quarry behind the property. When Romão inquires whether he would move to his cortiço, Jerônimo replies: 'Of course! Why should I stay in Cidade Nova if I'm going to work here?' Jerônimo is an honest man, dedicated to his family, and who devotes most of his time to work. He has social ambitions, which Azevedo illustrates by how sometimes on weekends, along with his wife, they stroll in the Passeio Público wearing their best clothes. Like the fathers of Machado de Assis's short stories, Jerônimo wants his daughter to do better than he ever could:

When they were still living in Cidade Nova and before Jerônimo had begun to earn more money, he had joined a religious society and tried to save a bit each month. He enrolled his daughter in a school, saying 'I want her to know more than I do, because my parents never taught me anything.' Their house had been the cleanest, most respected, and most comfortable in the neighbourhood. (2000: 39)

In an expected deterministic twist, having been seduced by Rita Baiana, a mulata from Bahia, Jerônimo quickly abandons his previous ways and gives in to the irresistible temptations of the tropics. As to the text's clues to mapping, other than revealing details about Jerônimo's immediate past, the brief mentions of the Cidade Nova are notable precisely for their seeming unimportance. Unlike in Azevedo's *Fritzmac*, here the reference appears as no more than a plausible alternative address for a cortiço. In that sense, then, it functions in the novel as a cultural space more or less equivalent to the South Zone neighbourhood of Botafogo, the actual site of the narrative.

The fact strikes one as relevant simply because of how that scenario would have lost in verisimilitude within only a few years. The Pereira Passos reforms (1902–6) helped to create the conditions that would enable the South Zone's emergence and consolidation as the city's wealthiest area. At a time when the number of Rio's licensed cars had not reached double digits, a major avenue – the Avenida Beira-Mar (Seafront Avenue), advertising proximity to the ocean in its very name – led from the Centro to Botafogo.[2] Likewise, granted with 'dictatorial dispensations' (Needell 1987: 34), Passos built a controversial tunnel, the Túnel Novo, to allow electric streetcars from Botafogo to reach the then remote marshes of Copacabana. He also drew an avenue along Copacabana's seafront, the aptly named Avenida Atlântica, one of the city's main tourist destinations today. As the use of *bonde* lines as a referential for real estate speculation reached new heights (Sevcenko 1998: 548), these neighbourhoods were endowed with unparalleled infrastructure, becoming increasingly privileged by the upper classes.

The Rodrigues Alves administration's most dramatic gesture, however, was reserved for the Old City. Rio de Janeiro at the start of the century was the third major port of the Americas, behind New York and Buenos Aires. The reform entailed a drastic modernization of Rio's ports, coupled with sanitation measures and the construction of the monumental Avenida Central. There were prior projects for a major avenue to cut across the centre's colonial streets, and the direction chosen for the Central Avenue holds significance, as it led precisely to the South Zone (Needell 1987: 44). Besides easing the circulation of merchandise out of the port, which Old Rio's tortuous and narrow lanes complicated, the avenue aimed to signify the republic's ushering of Brazil into a new era of modernity and civilization. We can certainly interpret it as an effort to actualize the country's positivist slogan, printed on the flag: Ordem e Progresso, Order and Progress. Not accidentally, the Avenue was inaugurated on 15 November 1905, in a grandiose ceremony timed to coincide with the anniversary of the Proclamation of the Republic.

The reform's objectives, its relation to republican ideals and capitalist pressures, as well as the popular resistance and far-reaching consequences, have all been documented and discussed in a vast historiographic production. Over the past two decades works like Jeffrey Needell's *A Tropical Belle Epoque* (1987), Teresa Meade's *'Civilizing' Rio* (1997), and Jaime Benchimol's *Pereira Passos* (1999) have approached the subject from different critical perspectives, and historians like Nicolau Sevcenko and Sidney Chalhoub have also made it central to their writings on Rio. As a result, today we better understand how the demolition of almost 600 central buildings, in what became known as the bota-abaixo, led to a worsening of living conditions for a great number of people and remains deeply interconnected to the growth of favelas. We have gained a clearer sense of the extent to which Brazil's elites equated the notion of civilization to France; and, as Needell puts it, how 'to civilize' meant to leave behind, leading to the persecution and repression of popular practices considered anachronistic, particularly those of African origin or related to immigrant groups, and especially in the public sphere (1987: 48). We have also learned how these reforms and the often heavy-handed vaccination campaigns that accompanied them were met with popular uprisings and protests.

In the period between 1890 and 1906, Rio de Janeiro's population kept expanding at a rapid pace, growing from 522,651 to 805,335.[3] By that time, it had one of the world's most extensive urban areas, occupying a surface that was more than twice larger than that of much more populated cities like Paris, New York, and Berlin – all of which were considerably denser.[4] During the Pereira Passos reforms, approximately one-tenth of the Old City's residents were forcibly evicted (Needell 1987: 256). Efforts to modernize the city also clearly imposed a spatial redistribution of its population – mimicking the Haussmannization of Paris. We may say that it was a large-scale and unprecedented urban intervention to a great degree predicated on the elimination or reduction of the contact between social classes and racial groups, forcing those who did not fit the desired 'civilized' and 'modern' mould into the city's outskirts and favelas.

These changes are reflected in the uneven dynamics of the city's growth. While 52.7 per cent of the city resided in the central areas (including the Cidade Nova) in 1890, that percentage declined to 27.8 thirty years later. In the same period, the North Zone's percentage of the population increased from 22.8 to 33.6 per cent, and the suburbs' surged from 16.6 per cent to 30.9 per cent. The South Zone, however, retained a stable proportion of the city's residents: 7.7 per cent in 1890 and 7.5 per cent in 1920 (Meade 1997: 124). As the industrial expansion was driven to the north and west after the Pereira Passos reforms, both the suburbs and the North Zone absorbed a disproportionate amount of the city's growth. While the outskirts – developing along the rail lines – concentrated the poor and the working classes, the northern districts contained a more heterogeneous combination of upper-, middle-, and lower-class areas: mixtures accentuated by the favelas that were beginning to appear throughout the city.[5]

True to its in-between status, the Cidade Nova seemed to follow neither pattern. Though at a lower pace than the suburbs, the Santana district experienced population growth at a much higher rate than other central areas, as it partly offset the housing shortage catalyzed by demolitions in the Old City.[6] In a report on the city's 'popular housing', authored by the engineer Everardo Backheuser and published in 1906, the streets of the Cidade Nova – along with those of the Gamboa and Saúde – are deemed to be those most sought after by the poor. Painting a scenario of 'horrifying promiscuity', the report describes 'vagabond Italians' living alongside 'oily haired black women', singing modinhas while washing clothes (Backheuser 1906: 108). The area had not remained unaffected by the Pereira Passos reforms: the Mangue Canal and the Praça Onze were revamped, for example.[7] The neighbourhood, however, was undergoing transformations not only in terms of its infrastructure but also in the roles that it would acquire in both local and national imaginaries.

II

Another important factor behind the urban reforms was the preoccupation with Brazil's image abroad, and as its showcase Rio was remodelled to project a new national capital, one that could compete with the Parisian-inspired reforms of other Latin American metropolises, particularly Buenos Aires (Needell 1987: 33). Travellers at the start of the century remained unimpressed by the capital's crowded and dirty streets, besides being terrified of yellow fever, since immigrants and foreigners died more frequently (Damazio 1996: 76). In comparison with imperial Rio, when the Cidade Nova had been an obligatory route of passage for those visiting Dom Pedro II in São Cristovão, after the republic's establishment foreigners no longer had as compelling a reason to explore the city beyond the Campo de Santana.

One of the exceptions was João Chagas (1863–1925), a journalist and writer descended from a family of liberals forced to abandon Brazil for political reasons. Born in Rio, he left for Portugal at an early age. An active republican in Lisbon and Porto – the Portuguese Republic was not declared until 1910 – Chagas faced imprisonment on more than one occasion. From his exile in Angola, he travelled to Rio in 1895 to meet with a minister and other public figures (Teixeira Barbosa 2003: 15). That trip inspired a short book written almost in diary form: *De bond: alguns aspectos da civilisação brazileira* (By Streetcar: Some Aspects of the Brazilian Civilization). It came out in 1897 and was never again reprinted, despite the fact that João Pinheiro Chagas – as he became known to history – would go on to become the first prime minister of the Republic of Portugal.[8]

De bond constitutes one of the last portrayals of Rio de Janeiro prior to the Passos reforms, but it captures a moment of profound changes in the urban fabric, with the proliferation of electric streetcars after 1892 – alluded to in the very title. If this period of intensified technological innovation affected people's notions of time and space, Chagas's narrative becomes a good starting point to the question of how these perceptual shifts transpire in literary texts. His itinerary begins, rather predictably, at Ouvidor Street: 'It was around 2 p.m. in this autumnal September day that I suddenly found myself in this famous Ouvidor street' (Chagas 1897: 41). The contrast with Lisbon, then a city of around 350,000, strikes him: 'To me, coming from the monotony of Lisbon life, this seems to be an absolute party [...] a talkative and boisterous crowd' (42). As if predicting the impending reforms, Chagas finds the Ouvidor crowd 'impatient to civilize itself' (42). After describing his walk across the narrow lane, interspersed with enthusiastic comments on the women – 'I heard that Brazil is the paradise for women' – and observations about its 'luxurious establishments', Chagas looks back once he reaches the end of the Ouvidor: 'in more tranquility, free from bumping into others and from the hubbub, I consider with bemusement this alley without lights, and ask myself for what reason the population of such a beautiful city chose such a sad and ugly place to promenade, to see and be seen, and to chatter about' (50).

Chagas hops on a tilbury to reach his removed boarding house, and as he left the old city 'he wanted to see no more' (51). He closes his eyes and, as if in a blink, opens them in the next chapter, and we find him in the Mangue of the Cidade Nova. It is as if, as Franco Moretti claims, 'the metropolis [...] calls for a change not so much of space as of the *flow of time*' (1998: 109). Unlike the walker Elisiário, Chagas experiences the urban space from a carriage in motion, and its consequences are articulated in temporal terms, exaggerated for dramatic effect: 'When I opened my eyes the carriage was going along a canal of dark and greasy water, lined with slender palm trees, and which seemed to me the most fetid' (53). Besides the palm trees, little seems recognizable from what had been one of the empire's proudest urban interventions. This was now a neglected part of town, and Chagas offers not only the fresh perspective of an independent and newly arrived traveller but also the testimony of his coachman.

Albeit filtered through the journalist's memory, it is a rare non-literary voice of one who we can imagine came into contact with the Cidade Nova routinely, and at the same time retained knowledge of the area's recent history. As the coachman spoke of its swampy past, Chagas inquires about yellow fever, suggesting that such a filthy canal at the centre of a populous neighbourhood must be a permanent source of infection. The coachman interrupts him with a smile, asserting that, to the contrary, the canal was 'excellent for the health'. Though we cannot discard the possibility that Chagas misinterpreted a sarcastic remark, the length and detail of the response points to an earnest exchange. Runoff from the nearby gas factory, the local explains, had the power of purifying the atmosphere.

Apart from the likely gap between the side-effects of runoff from a gas factory, and the popular belief of its benefits, the coachman's comments are significant for suggesting how discourses associating the Cidade Nova and unhealthy conditions seemed to have been disseminated from the top down. In fact, when the traveller insists – whether based on hearsay or not – that the area would have been prone to yellow fever, the reply again surprises:

> I thought that such a place must have been terrible during the time of the fever, because the recently arrived always inquires about the fever, but the coachman [...] answered simply by saying: 'It is where the fewest people die.' It seemed to me extraordinary! (54)

Regardless of whether the coachman's assessment was correct, the exchange signals the dissonance between, on the one hand, hygienist discourses and republican sanitation measures that targeted poor areas of the town, holding the Mangue as one of its prime suspects, and, on the other hand, popular perception that the area of the canal was actually the city's safest.[9] The disjunction can help to explain some of the city's least understood historical events, like the 1904 Revolta da Vacina (Vaccine Rebellion) which erupted in the vicinity of the Mangue, in the Campo de Santana, when many of its residents rebelled against a mandatory vaccination campaign during the Pereira Passos reforms.[10]

That latent disconnect between the lettered elites and everyday life in the city's outskirts gains more explicit form as Chagas traverses the Cidade Nova. His descriptions establish an implicit contrast with the hustle-bustle and attempts at being *civilisé* of Ouvidor Street:

Down the long street we were going, at each moment open tramways
went by, as well as transport carts pulled by three mules. The movement
of pedestrians lessened. At the doors of grocer shops, barefooted
blacks, sitting on the sidewalks, seemed to doze off. At the doors of
houses, garnished with blinds, women and children loomed without
the least concern [em desleixo]. It could be said that the city ended here,
and that another city would begin. (55)

Even before the Pereira Passos reforms, we begin to identify the appearance
of the idea – or at least the hypothesis – that there are 'two Rios de Janeiro'
(Sevcenko 1998: 543). In accounts earlier in the century, the Campo de
Santana had constantly served as a border between the Old and New City.
Now the Cidade Nova was the border itself, between Rio the capital of Brazil
and 'another city' altogether, a semi-suburban milieu of barefooted blacks
and of a more morose, unhurried rhythm. It provided scenes unbecoming
of a metropolis, and if mid-nineteenth-century travellers noted the Cidade
Nova's streets were well paved, now they are neglected, as if authorities
merely hoped or expected no foreigner would ever see them: 'the streets were
poorly paved', Chagas quips, 'yet those that we were going down weren't
simply poorly paved, they were in the most complete state of abandonment'
(55).

After resting at his pension, in a bucolic and unnamed setting by the
mountains, Chagas decides to return to the Centro to experience Rio's
nightlife. He gets there through the bonde of the title, bypassing the same
streets seen during the day. Of those same 'peaceful outskirts', he notes:

Inside the grocer's shops, leaning against the counter, groups of blacks
smoked; in many, billiard tables installed in ground-level rooms, with
windows to the street, the game was played to the yellowish light of
gas jets; at the gardens by the door, children dressed in white played,
and behind the curtains of certain rich residences one could glimpse
at the living rooms inside, where people and their guests sat around
talking. It could be deemed a neighbourhood from a provincial town
[dir-se-ia um bairro de província]. (66)

Chagas's text emerges to us as the inverse of Machado's, where landscapes
are rarely described and their content remains latent, signified by the
internal relations between place names buried within a plot. Here, we have
descriptions void of specific references, and the reader must guess the
author's itinerary, although one is not necessarily expected to care. Aboard
the tilbury, earlier, Chagas writes of how, leaving the road along the Mangue,
they 'penetrated a poor outer neighbourhood, lined with tram tracks, but

almost deserted' (55). We cannot plot his trajectory in a map, but we can infer that to him the Mangue remained a part of the centre, as the border where the city's outskirt ('arrabalde') announced itself.

The descriptions of children playing outdoors and of indoor scenes of a nonetheless public character, coupled with that final insinuation, *dir-se-ia um bairro de província*, allow us to reflect upon a distinction drawn by Moretti: 'if we compare city life to other types of communities the significance [of the "public sphere" or the action of "being in the street"] appears to have enormously *diminished*'. In that regard the Cidade Nova of Chagas's account resembles more a village or province where 'the near-totality of life occurred in the road, or in places of work, or even in homes which were normally exposed to the eye of the passer-by'. Moretti goes on: 'But then, compared to the village, the city has certainly given full value to the street as a channel of communication (and also of communication of information, that is, of stimuli) – but it has drastically and irreparably devalued it *as a place of social experience* [...] simply, because in the city experience is had *elsewhere*' (1998: 127).

Chagas has no trouble encountering the *stimuli*: in the vicinity of the Praça da Constituição, former Campo dos Ciganos and Rio's theatre district, 'everything was activity, animation, noise'. It seemed 'that some party had attracted the population from the outskirts to the centre of the city, but it wasn't so. Brazilians greatly enjoy having a good time and that movement of people arriving [...] is normal in Rio, every night after dinner' (67–8). But the aesthetic quality of the *social experience* leads him to regret leaving his beautiful pension, as a visit to three theatres turned out deeply to disappoint. Rio, after all, had not undergone the types of transformations implicit in Moretti's comments – or at least not fully or organically. In a telling sign, well into the twentieth century the city's theatre scene remained mostly mediocre and imitative, and much of its most vibrant and even theatrical cultural life – notably the carnival – never left the public sphere, despite the efforts of those first republican regimes.

If in Moretti's terms and Chagas's description the Cidade Nova maintained characteristics of a village, proximity to the centre of the nation's capital meant that it could not escape the vigilance of a state eager to assert its control over the public sphere. This was particularly the case during and after the Pereira Passos reforms, when there were attempts to repress the maxixe, and those not dressed 'decently' were prohibited from circulating in central areas (Sevcenko 1998: 623). Customs inherited from the nineteenth century were likewise rendered illegal, from hawking food on the streets to the wild and sometimes violent entrudo during carnival (Needell 1987: 136). Besides measures to regulate the popular processions of ranchos and *cordões*, the government began to organize more 'civilized' initiatives that were easier to control, like a parade of vehicles decorated with flowers, held at the Campo de Santana and inspired by the *Bataille des Fleurs* (Battle of Flowers) from carnival in Nice (Santucci 2008: 138).

The functions of streets as sites of social experience, however, were too deeply entrenched in everyday life to be so easily erased and remade. Several 'barbarian' carnival traditions persisted, informal economies continued to subsist in public spaces, and some recent phenomena even flourished, like the *jogo do bicho* or 'animal game', a lottery that remains popular – albeit illegal – on Rio's street corners (Chazkel 2011). Nonetheless, the impact of the changes associated with the belle époque should not be underestimated. In a city with a substantial population of Afro-Brazilians, practices associated with them – reminiscent of those found in the Campo de Santana only a few decades earlier – became increasingly persecuted and forced inside.[11] In this context, the houses of the *tias baianas* of Little Africa, centred on the Praça Onze, emerged as sanctuaries where Afro-Brazilian culture was able to thrive, and had to adapt to new conditions. In the Cidade Nova, surrounded by the formal financial and political centre, by the suburbs, favelas, and port area, among uprooted immigrants from various parts, Rio de Janeiro's more porous cultural practices found a fertile ground. There, where Chagas had noticed in neighbouring buildings well-off folks entertaining guests and grocer's shops with blacks socializing over a smoke, the houses of these Bahian women, affectionately known as *tias* or 'aunts', became bastions of Afro-Brazilian spiritual, cultural, and social life.

Like Dom Obá, the tias frequently came to Rio from the state of Bahia, most of Yoruba descent, and were able to amass social status in their immediate communities, due to their role both in Afro-Brazilian religions and in creating networks between black Brazilians. As a great deal of competition arose between them, their prestige often hinged on the quality of parties that attracted people from afar. With income from activities like religious rituals and selling sweets in the streets, they maintained enough of a prestige to escape law-enforcers. In fact, some were married to policemen or public functionaries with a certain pull among authorities, while others received protection from congressmen and even senators who frequented their houses. Of these tias, one would acquire mythical status among later modernist writers and musicians, receiving great attention from current scholars: the Tia Ciata, Hilária Batista de Almeida (1854–1924), who came to Rio de Janeiro at the age of twenty-two. Her house in the Praça Onze became a meeting ground for pioneering samba musicians like Sinhô, Pixinguinha, Donga (1890–1974), and João da Baiana (1887–1974). The anthropologist Roberto Moura has written our main reference for that milieu in a book entitled *Tia Ciata e a Pequena África no Rio de Janeiro* (Tia Ciata and Little Africa in Rio de Janeiro, 1995) based in part on interviews with descendants of Hilária.[12] His book popularized the expression Little Africa. Yet the best contemporary sources come from the work of João do Rio, pseudonym of Paulo Barreto (1881–1921).

III

Most of the prominent authors of the belle époque – names like the 'prince of poets' Olavo Bilac and Coelho Neto – were enthusiasts of the ideals espoused by the Passos reforms and welcomed the changes that ensued, hailing Rio de Janeiro as the 'Marvellous City' and declaring that, at last, 'Rio civilizes itself' ('o Rio civiliza-se'). Few, like Manuel Antônio de Almeida and Machado de Assis, were willing to venture to the 'undesired' and 'uncivilized' quarters of the Cidade Nova. Chief among these was the chronicler João do Rio. João do Rio had the curiosity of an investigative journalist and the ability to mediate between the upper-class public of his newspapers and the subjects of his prose, both as chronicler and as a writer of fiction. In 1902, he had been 'diplomatically' rejected from foreign service at the Itamaraty by the Baron of Rio Branco for being 'fat, mulato, and homosexual' (Gomes 1996: 114), not an auspicious beginning for a career. In the following year, he began to write for the *Gazeta de Notícias*, where he remained for over a decade. In 1920, João do Rio started the newspaper *A Pátria* and in a Lusophobic climate became a victim of several attacks for his defence of the Portuguese colony (he had lived in Portugal). He died in 1921, and more than 100,000 admirers attended his funeral, according to estimates in the press (O'Donnell 2008: 13).

Somewhat neglected after his death, João do Rio's work has met a major revival since the 1990s, inspiring a number of re-editions, books, and dissertations.[13] In her study, Julia O'Donnell reads him as an ethnographer, and scholars repeatedly stress his 'flâneur gaze', deeming him as the chronicler *par excellence* of the so-called tropical belle époque.[14] Part of the fascination that he exerts on readers of our time, however, derives precisely from how his narrative uncovers the flip side of the era's rapid development, often lingering over the archaic and miserable in Rio de Janeiro's urban life.[15] At the same time, unlike a modern ethnographer or the flâneur, as one of the first Brazilian writers to make a living as a journalist, João do Rio dealt with the pressures of the marketplace on a daily basis: on some level, the need to sell books or help to sell newspapers must have borne impact on his approach to writing.

As such, João do Rio's ventures into the Cidade Nova – and to the incipient morros – should be approached with some caution. In his narratives, one can never be too certain where the reporting gives place to dissimulation or irony. João do Rio's chameleonic abilities and acumen, nonetheless, put him in the position of being intimately attuned to the city's cultural cartography and to the cognitive maps of his readers – including their racial prejudices, of which several of his own observations were not immune. In at least one text, 'A rua' (The Street), published as the introduction to *A alma encantadora das ruas* (The Enchanting Soul of the Streets) in 1906, he gives the dimension of the biases against the Cidade Nova and its inhabitants:[16]

> In the big cities the street creates its own type; it moulds the morale of its inhabitants and mysteriously imbues them with tastes, customs, habits, manners and political opinions. All of you must have heard or said something like this: 'How those girls smell of the Cidade Nova!'
> (69)

Although claiming in somewhat Taine-like fashion that milieu creates certain types ('Oh yes! The street makes the individual; we know it all too well'), João do Rio seemed equally aware that the pen too can induce, highlight, or perpetuate certain associations. In that same year, for example, the author was capable of celebrating the role of the Cidade Nova and of the nearby port neighbourhoods in the preservation and renewal of those practices largely condemned by intellectual or governing elites as barbarian, outdated, and unsanitary, if not dangerous:

> Carnival would have disappeared, it would today mean less than the Glória festivities or the 'bumba-meu-boi' were it not for the enthusiasm of groups from Gamboa, the Saco, the Saúde, the S. Diogo and the Cidade Nova – this ardent enthusiasm that months before the three days [of Carnival] starts to burn like small bonfires to end up in the total and formidable flame that involves and entangles the entire city.
> (114)

The comment ascribes to the listed locales an 'ardent enthusiasm' that diverges from the city's cosmopolitan and refined aspirations, yet it is spun as something positive. These are, after all, some of the syncretic traditions – drawing from rural Portuguese and Afro-Brazilian expressions – which would later be incorporated (or co-opted) as integral components of national identity and 'folklore'.[17]

That judgement above initially appears in the words of a man João do Rio claims to have accompanied him in the city's streets during carnival, in a dialogue included in a *crônica* entitled 'Elogio dos Cordões' (In Praise of Cordões), published in a February 1906 edition of the upscale *Kósmos* magazine. It opens by situating the reader in a familiar place: 'It was right on the Ouvidor Street' (114). In the prestigious venue, the writer paints a scene of pandemonium amidst the parading of a cordão.[18] Uncomfortable with the overwhelming sights, smells, and sounds, he searches for shelter from the crowd under a door, when his 'companion' asks: 'Why are you running away?' (116). The narrator does not hesitate to explain: 'Oh! These cordões! I hate the cordão!' The unnamed interlocutor replies by proclaiming the cordões as the primitive lifeblood of Rio's most important festival: 'But what are you thinking? The cordão is carnival, the cordão is the delirious life, the cordão is the last link to pagan religions.' This exchange sets off an impassioned and eloquent defence: 'and all of them, more than two hundred groups, are unconsciously the portable sanctuaries of a religious tradition of dance, of a historic custom and a habit infiltrated throughout Brazil' (117).

At a point when two separate groups run into each other, and an advance of the parading crowds follows a sudden loss of momentum, our chronicler becomes swept along with the multitude: 'My friend and I fell into the imperious flow' (123). The writer, initially suspicious of his feverish companion, now calls him a friend. And not only does he cave in to the appeal of cordões, but the previous 'hatred' towards them transforms into a paroxysmal acceptance – long before it was fashionable to do so – of that popular form of carnival as the most authentic and deepest manifestation of the country's spirit:

> Oh! Yes! He was right! The cordão is carnival, it is the last link to pagan religions, it is indeed the preserver of the sacred day of ritual mockery and debauchery; the cordão is our ardent soul, lascivious, sad, a tad enslaved and unruly, drooling lust for women and wanting to marvel. (124)

The text concludes with João do Rio joining the 'triumph and fury' of the procession, having completely surrendered his prior resistance. It is of course conceivable that the experience was indeed transformational, but we have good reason to suspect of a made-up interlocutor. Keenly aware that regarding the cordões with such fervour might not befit a writer of the elitist *Kósmos*, the author arrives at the suggestion of an equivalence between carnival and the Brazilian condition through what appears to have been a carefully constructed narrative. Independent of the extent to which the story was based on an actual event, he renders the dialogue through a stylized and literary language. And by deliberately using an anonymous friend's voice to introduce positions that would have been anything but palatable to the lettered sensibilities (or aspirations) of his contemporaries, João do Rio at first aligns himself with the views of unsympathetic readers – a strategy that would serve to entice rather than alienate them.[19]

This type of two-step strategy, of partly acceding to a reader's expectations while being faithful to his own experiences and impressions, is not unlike what we have already observed with Almeida and Machado de Assis. It also defines much of the writing in *As religiões do Rio* (The Religions of Rio), the wildly successful series of reports published in the *Gazeta de Notícias* between February and March 1904. Edited in book form the following year by the prestigious Garnier publishing house, João do Rio's collection of articles on the city's less visible religions would go on to sell around 8,000 copies before the end of the decade, a record at the time (O'Donnell 2008: 103).

The entire account of Rio's religious *bas-fond* plays with the notion of two worlds, far apart, yet occupying the same city. In those months between the texts' serial appearance in newspapers and publication as a book, Rio's central areas were in the process of being irrevocably changed by the Pereira Passos reforms. Accentuation of the contrast between the city of his readers and that of his subjects might have further contributed to the editorial triumph of *As religiões do Rio*. Although João do Rio did not seem to have timed his project with the reforms, he nonetheless demonstrates an ability to manipulate the reader's presumed lack of knowledge of the city's extra-Catholic religious life. In the preface to the book he claims that Rio does not stand out among other urban areas: 'Rio, like every city in these irreverent times, has in each of its streets a temple and in each of its men a different creed' (15). Painting the city as similar to other places as well as full of dissimilar faiths, the text predicates its appeal on the reader's ignorance of this plurality, and the author's journey would seek to shatter their preconceived ideas about religion in contemporary urban life.

He attributes these misplaced expectations to the lettered city in rather explicit terms. They are produced by newspapers, whose version of the country dissipates upon a closer and active look not only by a writer, but by any reader or city dweller. All it takes is willingness to jump out of one's complacency and routine rhythms, to observe the everyday, to *inquire* the city's street corners, as he puts it. João do Rio's vehicle to communicate the results of his own inquiries and to shake up those unaware of Rio's vibrant and diverse religions remains, naturally, the written word of newspapers. He arrives at his methods, though – at least according to the introduction – not through literary sources but through personal experience:[20]

By reading the major dailies, we imagine that we are in an essentially Catholic country, where some mathematicians are positivists. However, the city swarms with religions. All you have to do is stop at any street corner, and ask around. The diversity of cults will astonish you.

Imbued with the naturalist's taxonomic impulse but freed from the comprehensive aspirations of the enlightenment, João do Rio finds himself able to roam from one place of worship to another, a mixture of flâneur and. detective. He infiltrates the 'exotic' and distant-seeming circles of Swendenborgians, blood drinkers and *babalâos* from Lagos, displaying marvel at how such religions could be found in the central streets of a 'civilized' city. João do Rio's accounts, nonetheless, prove to be more than just sensationalist. They in fact come close to celebrating this 'Babel of creeds' (35), and perceive differences and tensions between, for example, Islamic Africans and those who assimilate Christian elements. In fact, *As religiões no Rio* has become an important source for scholars of Afro-Brazilian religions (Rodrigues 1996: 10). However inaccurate its details might be, the text catalogues different divinities, languages, religious hierarchies, internal disputes, and social relations between peoples and traditions originating from various parts of Africa, and arriving in Brazil's capital through different paths.

On the one hand, there is every reason to believe that João do Rio chose to report what was more likely to cause a stir in the reader's imagination and prior images of the city – without skirting embellishments and exaggeration. As if to lend credibility to his narratives, on the other hand, he frequently gives the precise address of places visited. In an introduction to a recent edition of the book, his biographer João Carlos Rodrigues writes of a certain unrest among followers of Afro-Brazilian religions at the time, as many feared repression after specific names and locales were divulged in the press. Although the republican constitutions assured freedom of worship to all creeds, the penal code forbade commercial use of superstitions and the exploitation of 'public credulity'. On those grounds, the religions João do Rio describes were sometimes framed by the police as illegal (Rodrigues 1996: 10). The book did not seem to have motivated a surge in those cases, although it does suggest the extent to which these rituals involved a number of financial transactions and constituted part of the informal economy. Unlike in the nineteenth century, when, as we have seen, certain public spaces served as sites for umbigadas and other rituals, now only during specific festivals like carnival were the streets and squares taken over by such manifestations – which were otherwise largely driven into private houses. In the very first of his twenty-three investigative profiles, João do Rio introduces us to his guide into the secluded world of Rio's African religions: he names him Antônio, most likely a fictional character and a composite of various informants. The fact that he needs an escort lends an adventurous air to the writer's enterprise, but he at once undermines Antônio and renders him in familiar, demystified terms: 'he only respects paper money and port wine' (19). With help from the expert, though, he came to know 'the houses from the streets of São Diogo, Barão de São Felix, Hospício, Núncio and América, where the Candomblés take place and where the pais-de-santo live. And I thanked the lord, because there certainly isn't, anywhere in the city, a milieu as interesting' (19–20).[21] *Pais-de-santo*, literally fathers-of-saint, and *mães-de-santo* or 'mothers-of-saint', are translations of the Yoruban *babalorixá* and *ialorixá*, titles given to priests and priestesses (Silva 1993: 147).

Of the five streets singled out by João do Rio, one is at the heart of the Cidade Nova, two lead into it from the port area, one connects the Campo de Santana to the Old City, and another is the closest parallel to the Campo on its south side. Although in that first decade of the century the Cidade Nova continued to receive little attention from intellectuals, a large number of the city's more unique religious institutions were located there – beyond the *terreiros*, the generic term for places of Afro-Brazilian worship. In the same Barão de São Felix mentioned above, where Dom Obá last resided and the infamous Cabeça de Porco tenement was located until its destruction in 1893, João do Rio meets a famous *alufá* – a Moslem leader of African origin (27).[22] The neighbourhood also hosted temples of the *fisiólatras*, 'who have passed through several houses of the Cidade Nova' (122), a system of beliefs founded by a descendant of Icelanders; a Presbyterian (143) and a Baptist church (161); a YMCA (173); a number of *sacerdotizas do futuro* or priestesses of the future, fortune-tellers loosely connected to Gypsies, who one of those interviewed dismisses as swindlers (230–1); as well as some of the 'thousands' of centres of *exploradores*, reputed to be fraudulent practitioners of Spiritism.

João do Rio's scepticism in general comes down harsher on those religions associated with the lower classes. He interestingly directs his venom towards those figures whose influence would be perpetuated in Rio's oral histories, and whose names would enter Brazil's cultural heritage – presumably because they commanded greater respect in circles that the author viewed with cynicism. He refers with an ironic tone to the 'celebrated João Alabá, a rich black man and know-it-all from the Barão de São Felix Street, 76' (83), and speaks of the Tia Ciata (he writes Assiata), who came from Alabá's terreiro, as a 'presumptuous' and 'short black woman' (65). Despite João do Rio's mixture of fascination and dismissive attitude towards these rituals – much like Almeida's towards the caboclo – they nonetheless emerge as a persistent space of mixture in an increasingly segregated city. João do Rio seems to take pleasure at recounting in his chronicles how he often ran into well-known members of the *high life* in these disreputable Afro-Brazilian places of worship. The insinuation is that these rituals – such as one requested by a society girl pleading for a wedding with a lawyer – were costly for the visitors, and a major source of income for the leaders of terreiros. At one point we read:

> I saw ladies in high positions hopping out of carriages, covertly, as if in a feuilleton novel, to run to these house, faces hidden behind thick veils; I saw sessions during which glove-wearing hands took bills and bills out of rich wallets, to the screams of ill-bred blacks who demanded: – Put money in here! (61)

João do Rio most likely included these accounts to pique the curiosity of his readers, who were accustomed to similar scenes in contemporary novels, and doubtless wondered at the identities of these ladies, willing to subject themselves to such treatment at the hands of rude black men.[23] Yet the text also unwittingly reveals one of the mechanisms through which some Afro-Brazilians were able to fend for themselves and preserve the integrity of their socio-cultural life amidst a very hostile environment.

Asymmetrical as these inter-class and inter-racial exchanges may have been, establishing a relationship with a politician could provide a valuable shield against police repression and ensure one's ability to circulate freely in the city. João da Baiana (1887–1974), a grandson of slaves who worked as street vendors and a habitué of Tia Ciata's house, tells of his youth as a carpenter and percussionist in a samba group. At the time, it was 'frowned upon', but already accepted enough that they were invited to play at the *palacete* of Pinheiro Machado (1851–1915), a powerful senator during much of the First Republic. Once there, the senator immediately asked about the boy, and it was explained that the police had confiscated and broken João da Baiana's instrument, the *pandeiro*, a type of tambourine. As a result, according to the story, Pinheiro Machado invited him to the Senate the following day, giving him a new pandeiro with a dedicatory that was sure to keep the police from ever confiscating it again.[24]

João do Rio himself mentions a mãe-de-santo, Xica de Vavá, who had 'political protection' (24). Even more remarkable, and with far-reaching consequences, was the event narrated by another *sambista*, or samba practitioner, Bucy Moreira (1909–82), a grandson of Tia Ciata, during an interview. As the story goes, president Venceslau Brás (1868–1966) had an eruption in his leg that doctors did not know how to cure. Indeed, during his term from 1914 to 1918, Brás left office for a month in 1917 due to illness. His chauffeur, a policeman named Bispo, then suggested the services of the Tia Ciata, and after her herbal treatments the president's ailment was cured. As a reward, Venceslau Brás appointed her husband to the cabinet of the police chief, a position that would have given Tia Ciata and her numerous family a certain amount of financial stability and social prestige.[25] And although she became more famous than other tias, Ciata was certainly not the only one to have achieved stature. Several other matriarchs are mentioned in subsequent interviews with sambistas.[26]

Amidst the Pereira Passos reforms, João do Rio's *As religiões no Rio* does not explicitly demarcate the Cidade Nova and its Praça Onze as the centre of the city's Afro-Brazilian milieu: in fact, despite its several Candomblé houses, we still find that addresses mentioned in the text are fairly spread out. Perhaps it was the later role Tia Ciata's house played in carnival parades that led to the identification of the area as Rio's Little Africa.[27] Or, more likely, since João do Rio's book precedes the full effects of the rearrangement provoked by the urban interventions, it seems that the reforms themselves led to an even greater concentration of terreiros and immigrants from Bahia around the Praça Onze. Besides the construction of the Avenida Central, which eliminated cortiços and forced lower-class residents out of the centre, the modernization of the port exerted similar pressures in another area long inhabited by Bahians and blacks in general. The trajectory of Tia Ciata itself exemplifies that process: João do Rio finds her in the more central Alfândega Street (44), and not in the house later made famous as the site where the 'first' samba was created in 1917, in the Praça Onze.[28] There are other examples –Cipriano Abedé's Candomblé house transferred from the Propósito Street, near the port in the Gamboa neighbourhood, to the João Caetano Street, near the Central do Brasil train station (Moura 1995: 99).

In any case, only a few years after the Pereira Passos reforms, the area surrounding the Praça Onze would enter the memory of one of its more illustrious residents as an 'África em miniatura', a miniature Africa, or a Little Africa in the phrase later made prevalent (Sodré 1979: 21). The phrase is attributed to Heitor dos Prazeres (1898–1966), a samba composer, singer, handyman, and self-taught painter, born near the Praça Onze from Bahian parents, in a house that like so many others, he says, had a piano.[29] In the decades to come, several scholars would 'highlight the existence, during the beginning of the twentieth century, of tight connections between the tradition of ranchos and the celebrations and rituals of the Bahians who fixed residence in the Cidade Nova neighbourhood, establishing in that part of Rio de Janeiro a haven of Afro-Brazilian culture' (Cunha 2006: 39).

More than a neighbourhood in any conventional sense, the Cidade Nova acquired a symbolic significance that would echo beyond the confines of its geographical spaces. In a plot indebted to João do Rio's incursions into Little Africa – but freed from his prejudices and incomprehension – the

Afro-Brazilian musician and intellectual Nei Lopes returns to this setting in a recent novel, *Mandingas da mulata velha na cidade nova* (Sorceries of the Old Mulata in the Cidade Nova, 2009). But let us not place the cart before the horse. What cannot be disputed, and should not be played down, is that as new musical forms emerge their development remains inextricably tied to the Afro-Brazilian social and religious practices found in the environment of the Praça Onze.

IV

Under the republic, music and military service continued to provide some of the few possibilities for social ascension in Carioca society. Yet, if the cards were stacked against recent immigrants, blacks, and the lower classes, it was also not uncomplicated for someone from a well-off background to integrate the ranks of popular musicians: particularly in the case of a woman. Francisca Gonzaga (1847–1935), later known as Chiquinha Gonzaga, was born to a mulata mother and a father with aristocratic pretensions, who held a position as a military officer. Married at sixteen to a man who forbade her from pursuing a musical career, she cut ties with both husband and father. Gonzaga would become one of the country's most prolific composers and pianists. A long-time frequenter of lundus and umbigadas, she reputedly authored close to 2,000 compositions, ranging from waltzes, polkas, maxixes, choros, and tangos, to now standards like the *marcha-rancho* 'Ó Abre Alas', credited as the first Brazilian song written specifically for carnival.[30]

Although from a relatively affluent background and having received an erudite start, like some of her contemporaries from Little Africa she circulated from modest houses of the Cidade Nova to the salons of Rio's elites.[31] In fact, Gonzaga is sometimes likened to Princesa Isabel – who signed the Golden Law of 1888, ending slavery in the country – for her role in 'freeing' Brazil's popular music. In 1914, Chiquinha Gonzaga involuntarily provoked a scandal of national proportions when her 'Corta-Jaca' was executed at the Palácio do Catete – the presidential palace (Diniz 1984: 195–207).[32] The following day, the prominent jurist Rui Barbosa reacted in a virulent Senate speech: 'before the finest of Rio de Janeiro's society, those who ought to set an example to the country of the most distinguished manners and the most reserved customs, elevated the corta-jaca to the level of a social institution [...] the lowest, most base, the most vulgar of all the savage dances, the twin sister of the batuque, the cateretê, and the samba'.[33]

Not content with that litany, Barbosa uses Gonzaga's composition to disqualify the presidency, and his conclusions give an idea of the intense resistance faced by popular musicians: 'But at presidential receptions, the corta-jaca is executed with all the honours of Wagner's music, and yet we expect the conscience of this country not to revolt, that our faces not redden [with shame]!' If any doubt could yet remain, it had now become clear that the sensual – sometimes licentious – sounds and dance of the maxixe no longer belonged only inside the Cidade Nova; and Rui Barbosa was not alone in his crusade against the popular genre's dissemination.[34]

Since that episode, Chiquinha Gonzaga has become an icon not only of Brazilian music but also of female emancipation: through her courage to separate from a controlling and adulterous husband, because of her active participation in the fight for abolitionism, and for her struggles over protecting authors' rights.[35] In her own days, however, she probably became best known to the wider public after the resounding success of *Forrobodó*, a play named after an expression meaning something like a spree of revelry. It premiered in June 1912 and continued to be staged for 1,500 consecutive nights. Two young and inexperienced authors, Carlos Bettencourt, a police reporter, and Luiz Peixoto, a caricaturist, were responsible for the text, and Chiquinha Gonzaga created the musical numbers.[36]

Although Gonzaga should be understood as one of those in-between figures at the heart of Rio's processes of cultural formation – a mediator between social classes and musical genres – the *Forrobodó* in effect reflects a growing notion of the Cidade Nova as possessing a static identity. It was a place celebrated for, or reduced to, its dance clubs and carnival. In the city's lettered and cultural cartographies, the neighbourhood was increasingly the site of maxixe and carnival.[37] The association had already appeared in the theatre in *Fritzmac*, and now we have an entire hit show dedicated to it.

The play's plot was secondary, as dance and music constituted the main ingredients. It concerns the theft of chicken, a dance club owner's failed attempts to get members to pay their dues, a seductive mulata who gets her way, and a score of good and bad malandros. Rather than 'correct' written grammar, informal speech marks the dialogue, anticipating a feature of modernist aesthetics. All the tension unwinds into a great ruckus, and the play ends with everyone in the ballroom dancing maxixe. This setting garnered significant attention from the press and in many ways defined the play's comic appeal. A review from the 18 June edition of the *Correio da Manhã* takes interest in how 'she made a very well done study of our humble outskirts, as the plot unwinds in a Carnival club', and shows surprise at all the interest generated by the topic: 'Who knew that a forrobodó from the Cidade Nova could take so many to the theatre' (Diniz 1984: 208). The play became known, incidentally, as the *Forrobodó da Cidade Nova*.

Another reviewer, in the *Jornal do Brasil*, approximates the practices of neighbourhoods by the port with those of *all* the Cidade Nova: 'The play mirrors the customs of the Gamboa, Saco do Alferes, and of all the Cidade Nova; all of the choros, forrobodós and sambas of those destinations are treated with truth' (Diniz 1984: 208). Once again, the spaces of the so-called Little Africa are grouped together in the lettered imaginary. And reference to the musical gatherings of *those destinations* denotes both a familiarity with that scene and a vague sense of geographic distance. Like João do Rio's account of the city's non-hegemonic religions, *Forrobodó* provided a window for theatregoers into the supposed lives of Rio's lower classes.

As the city became more spatially segregated, a fascination with how 'the other half' lived appears to have grown[38] – and, along with it, so did the possibilities or the taste for caricatured and flat portrayals. Despite the newspaper assessments of its putative realism, the play in fact presents largely predictable characters: the indolent, corrupt, and womanizing guard, the irresistible but perilous mulata ('dengosa feiticeira'), and the pretentious type whose naive attempts to imitate the elites render him ridiculous. The dialogue indeed replicates the everyday language of the streets with apparent accuracy, but the errors are grossly exaggerated for comic effect. By locating the object of its satire in a relatively known and near-by neighbourhood, the authors assured that the parodies were familiar enough to entertain, yet targeted enough at an 'other' that they did not produce discomfort in the audiences.

While we may say that *Forrobodó*, akin to João do Rio's narrative, explored the Cidade Nova's 'exotic' appeal to the theatre-going public, at least one contemporary author, rather than entice the readers with tendentious or typecast portrayals of that space, chastised their lack of knowledge of what lay so close. Lima Barreto (1881–1922) was probably the most active critic of the First Republic and of the Pereira Passos reforms among Brazil's writers. He denounced the hypocrisies of the belle époque, evoking it as no more than a facade symbolized by the construction of the Central Avenue, after which to him Rio de Janeiro became another city (Sevcenko 1998: 645). As one of the few authors who incorporated settings and characters from Rio's poorer suburbs – where he indeed lived through most of his life – Lima Barreto could be listed as yet another to integrate the gallery of mulatos acting as mediators in Carioca society, circulating from centre to periphery. It is a title, however, that we must imagine he would reproach.[39]

As a matter of fact, Lima Barreto's works and biography serve as a lesson not only on the relative nature of concepts like 'exotic' but also on the inadequacy and unstableness of worn-out centre-periphery binaries. A resident of the suburbs, he eventually had his works published by the prestigious Garnier of Ouvidor Street, while struggling with feeling like an outsider in the literary circles centred there. João do Rio, for example, despite being occasionally attacked by important contemporaries like Monteiro Lobato, sometimes with racial and homophobic overtones, was accepted by the venerated and mostly conservative Brazilian Academy of Letters in 1910. Lima Barreto's relationship with the literary establishment, on the contrary, was far more turbulent: he was thrice rejected by the Academy, and was often accused of being a 'bad writer' due to his colloquial prose.[40]

A particularly poignant passage of his journal, written while in a psychiatric ward between 1919 and 1920, gives certain clues as to the complicated dynamic of his ambivalent sense of belonging within the lettered city: 'No one reaches out to me. It used to be that I was sought out. I am very esteemed at the Rua do Ouvidor; but over there [aí], who isn't?' (78).[41] The comment appears to unearth a lingering pride over the part he had once played in the city's literary and socio-political circles. It may be interpreted as revealing a mixture of irony and deep resentment when he interpolates a subject presumed to be located 'aí', *there where he is not*, both physically and by means of feeling excluded.

Lima Barreto's writings from the stay at a mental hospital are marked by their fragmentation, a trait that critic Beatriz Resende identifies as defining his experience and representation of the city in a landmark study for the author's gradual critical rehabilitation.[42] He perceives a shift during the First Republic that would find resonance in later discourses of Rio de Janeiro as a broken or divided city, where social inequality reflects in the city's lettered cartographies and cultural geography. Resende argues that 'the antagonism that Lima Barreto establishes between his writing versus "[writing] to make toasts over desert, for the satisfaction of the ultra-rich", corresponds to the growing antagonism between the "aristocratic", "civilized" neighbourhoods of the "refined", and the suburbs with their petty bourgeois and working class'. In that reading, these were the folks 'that the clan-like, self-serving upper classes [...] had kicked out in the name of progress, towards peripheries neglected by the state, away from their "postcard" scenario' (25).

Reflections about the spatial manifestations of social condition permeate Lima Barreto's work. The attention that he pays to the city's peripheries, a peculiarity in the literature of the period, becomes one of the major reasons for his high regard among literary critics and cultural, social, or urban historians. While overtly placing the marginalized at the centre of his literature, however, the author sought to dialogue not with the urban poor but – often combatively – with lettered elites. Resende herself tempers what she calls the 'myths' of Lima Barreto as above all concerned with suburban residents. The Centro most likely represents an even greater preoccupation in Lima Barreto's literature.

Awareness of readers' cognitive mappings and the place of his narratives within them transpire throughout his work, as in the now canonical *Triste fim de Policarpo Quaresma* (The Sad End of Policarpo Quaresma). It was published serially in the *Jornal do Commercio* in 1911, and as a book in 1915.[43] In a mention of the Cidade Nova, the novel refers to the neighbourhood's precarious housing and evokes Almeida's earlier description of the Mangue: 'The barracks were still installed way out there [lá para as bandas] in the Cidade Nova in an old tenement house that had been condemned by the Sanitary Authorities'. The Cidade Nova might be *way out there* like the caboclo's Mangue, and Lima Barreto's novel might operate in a dialectic mode like *Memórias de um sargento de milícias*, but there is no equivalent notion of writing from a centre, reflecting the outlook of a lettered city. Especially towards the end of his life, Lima Barreto frequently seems to be writing against it, attempting to articulate the perspective of those who paid a heavy price for modernization projects, but who reaped few of the benefits. The author, despite all his literary ambitions, sided with the populations kept at the margins of 'civilization': in juxtaposition to the 'ideal city' desired by intellectuals like the Parnassian poet and Academy of Letters member Olavo Bilac, he would focus on the 'real city' to be found beyond the Campo de Santana, away from the Centro and the South-side neighbourhoods.[44] He wanted, for example, to name one of his prose collections *Marginália*, and to create a magazine with the same name (Resende 1993: 68).

Amidst this antagonism between the 'two Rios' in Lima Barreto's vision, where do we find the Cidade Nova? He provides an eloquent response in the novel *Numa e a Ninfa*. The narrative asserts that this is no longer the early nineteenth-century Cidade Nova of Almeida's militia sergeant, and projects onto its spaces a conception of what constitutes Brazil itself. If João do Rio positions himself carefully as an outsider when visiting the neighbourhood, in order to facilitate a sense of complicity with the reader-voyeur, in Lima Barreto's fiction we for the first time see it not only placed at the centre of a narrative but as its subject.

Published during 1915 in an opposition newspaper, *Numa e a Ninfa* is a political satire *à clef*, where the names of Brazil's cities and states are changed, but not those of Rio de Janeiro's streets.[45] The novel recreates the environment of Ouvidor Street, where the news of the day has quick repercussions and where the elites still go to trade information, to see and be seen. The plot involves a fraudulent congressman, Numa, whose speeches are written by his wife Ninfa. Another major character is Lucrécio Barba-de-Bode (Lucrécio Goatee), a mulato who 'wasn't exactly a politician, but took part in politics and had the role of connecting it to the popular classes' (43), by which the narrator means a professional agitator – part of what Lima Barreto calls the 'industry of demonstrations'.

Halfway through the third chapter the narrator launches into a description that takes up several pages, and is worth quoting at length. It leaves one with the clear sense that an authorial intervention shifts the text to a non-fictional, journalistic mode, where the third-person voice positions itself as an authority on the Cidade Nova's daily life, history, and symbolic importance. It opens with the following lines:

> Lucrécio lived in the Cidade Nova, in that sad part of the city, of long and almost straight streets, old houses with latticework, door and window; that one-time marsh, landfilled with detritus and sediments of the hills that compress it, a neighborhood almost in the heart of the city, curious in more ways than one. (64)

Almost in the city's heart because Rio de Janeiro's geography, he suggests, does not allow for a centre: 'Irregular as Rio is, it cannot be said that [the Cidade Nova] rests at the center of the city; it is, nonetheless, an obligatory point of passage to Tijuca and environs, São Cristovão and suburbs'. On the one hand, Lima Barreto sticks to the physical and geographical attributes of the neighbourhood. On the other, it is as if he wishes to remind the Ouvidor Street elites that though peripheral and distant to them the Cidade Nova is a central space to a vast number of suburbanites: people who like him arrive in the Central Station, traversing the neighbourhood to arrive at jobs or commitments in the Centro. Rio de Janeiro, after all, might have become increasingly depicted as 'divided', but to the majority of its residents it was still experienced – sometimes gleefully, often painfully – as one interconnected whole, where opportunities and rights are not distributed equally.[46]

The narrator continues to gloss over the geography and history of 'that sad part of the city', mentioning Dom João's landfill, the Mangue, and the occasional devastating floods. In the process, the Cidade Nova becomes gradually anthropomorphized, and the author identifies with its predicament:

> The Cidade Nova did not have time to fully rise out of the marsh that it was; time was not given for the waters to bring from up above the necessary quantity of sediment: it ended up instead as the deposit of the nascent city's detritus, of the races that people us and have been brought to these lands by the slaves ships, by the ships of immigrants, forcefully or of their own accord.

Amidst the metaphors suggested in these seemingly unremarkable comments, a subtle and vital switch takes place in the voice of the narrator: he adopts the third-person plural when referring to the multiple races that people *us*. Comparing the mixture of races to the mixture of debris through which the city advanced into the swamps can hardly be called celebratory. This is not, therefore, an early expression of the cult of miscegenation which a few decades later became an integral component of Brazil's racial discourses. Lima Barreto's image conveys something else: an implicit *we*, the peoples of *these lands* emerge out of the excluded, the dejected, the discarded.

Lima Barreto does not introduce the idea of a collectivity born out of racial mixtures as an abstraction. Instead, his narrator locates it in the spaces of a particular neighbourhood in Rio de Janeiro, as he specifies, inhabited by recently arrived European immigrants and by the descendants of slaves. In a country still under the process of being formed, the writer proposes that an authentic Brazil was to be encountered not in the new Parisian-like boulevard of the city centre, but in the Cidade Nova – and, by extension, other places where similar mixtures occurred. The neighbourhood had not functioned, until then, as a metonymy for the nation in lettered imaginaries. And in a context where tensions between European immigrant workers and black-controlled unions were not uncommon, the narrative approximates different ethnic groups:[47]

> Misery united them or embedded them there; and there they flourish in evidence. It undid many dreams that left Italy and Portugal in search of wealth; and to balance it out, many fortunes were made there, to continue to feed and excite those dreams.

By adding nuance and psychological depth to its populations, the text challenges the usual representations of the Cidade Nova in the press and in the theatre. Here, there is the recognition of a solidarity arising from necessity, shared hardships and the prospect of better days.

The passage proceeds explicitly to contest the distorted perception of the neighbourhood in lettered cartographies: 'to the copy-cats, in the yearly revues and in the newspapers, the population of the Cidade Nova is almost entirely of colour; as in everything else that follows, they are mistaken'. His is an effort to de-exoticize the neighbourhood, to demystify it as a site of blackness – which he claims not as inaccurate but outdated. As we have seen elsewhere, the neighbourhood had in fact been racially diverse from the very beginning, and census data indicates that it continued to be inhabited by a disproportionately high number of European immigrants relative to the entire city.[48]

In *Numa e a Ninfa* and elsewhere, like so many among the great authors of urban modernity, Lima Barreto rewrites the city with a very personal sensibility while being faithful to broader realities. His conscience of writing in the city – of the spaces which literature occupies in a certain geography, close to what Maurice Blanchot called *l'espace littéraire* (1982) – extends to an understanding of the city in writing, of the narrated city. To put it more directly, lettered representations of a neighbourhood do not merely reflect something about the place itself or about the respective author, they can also play a role in its construction, its perception by those in power, and even in its treatment by authorities. Lima Barreto exposed how the discourses and 'myths' surrounding the Cidade Nova, then, were in their own ways as 'real' as census data, since they directly influenced its everyday life by producing or perpetuating biases. At a time when the intellectual milieu still sought rationalization for social processes in scientific racial hierarchies, he offers a sociological explanation that cuts across race, and that would also apply to the expansion of favelas:

> The same reasons that led the colored, free population [to the Cidade Nova] sixty years ago, led the white impoverished immigrant population and its descendants to inhabit it as well. In general, the population of color was and still is composed of people of reduced economic means, who [...] have, therefore, to seek cheap housing, near the places where they work.

Lima Barreto, in touch with both the material conditions of the neighbourhood's residents and the economic interests of his readers, suggests that those apparently 'fragile' houses in those 'poor streets' could be a good investment for the capitalist: 'Because they are not so cheap those humble houses, and on-time payment is the general rule'.

At every turn, the prose avoids a romanticizing portrayal, but the writer does not remain immune to his own prejudices and predilections. A significant portion of this *crônica* inside a novel is dedicated to disprove the increasingly persistent associations between the Cidade Nova, samba, and maxixe. Yet, while proceeding to counter accusations that its dance balls were 'licentious', Lima Barreto internalizes the criteria by which they were considered inferior and less refined. In his defence of the neighbourhood, he perpetuates some of those ingrained animosities of the epoch, so well represented by Rui Barbosa's senate speech condemnation of Gonzaga's 'Corta-Jaca'. We read that the Cidade Nova 'truly loves' and asks not for the rural-tinged cateretê but for 'French-style or American-style dancing to the piano', as if to illustrate its residents are more sophisticated than readers would assume.

In the process, nonetheless, Lima Barreto registers the enormous diversity of musical genres found in the neighbourhood, from 'friorituras' to schottisch, modinha, waltzes, and polkas. And we cannot help but imagine, as many have, that the new urban rhythms of maxixe and samba emerged as a synthesis of all these encounters and intersections. Ironically, then, in the increasingly divided Rio of the belle époque, it is precisely in the neighbourhood where the Brazil desired by dominating elites began to end, that the Brazil imagined and celebrated by a next generation of modernist artists *begins its presencing*.

Notes

1 It has been translated into English both as *A Brazilian Tenement* (1926) and more recently as *The Slum: A Novel* (2000). I have relied on the translations from this more recent edition. Cortiço literally means beehive.

2 In 1903 there were only five cars registered in the city, a number that grew to 143 by the time that the Beira-Mar Avenue was inaugurated in 1906, and to 208 the following year (Santos 1907: 301).

3 After abolition in 1888, Rio grew at a rate of 2.9 per year: from 266,831 residents in 1872, its population would reach 1,124,572 in 1920 (Meade 1997: 47).

4 According to the *Recenseamento do Rio de Janeiro*, Paris and Berlin were around fifty and forty times denser, respectively, if we consider the totality of Rio de Janeiro, much of which remained undeveloped (1907: 30).

5 The most comprehensive source for these demographic shifts remains Abreu 1988. For representations of the Zona Sul as picturesque and desirable in magazines, see Oliveira 2010: 137–61. It should be noted that the terms Zona Sul and Zona Norte have been used here even though they were not yet current at the time. If what later corresponded to the Zona Norte included relatively affluent neighbourhoods – such as Tijuca and Vila Isabel – the oceanfront southern districts were home to tenements and to precarious hillside settlements.

6 The district's population reached 79,315 (1906), now the second largest after the Engenho Velho, corresponding to the 'Grande Tijuca'. While the Santana district had grown 17.45 per cent since 1890, the central Candelária district lost over half of its population.

7 The gardens of the square were reformed (Santos 1907: 47), and the Mangue was extended until the ocean. Gamboa and Saúde were also significantly altered through landfills and the construction of the Avenida do Cais, future Rodrigues Alves Avenue.

8 He headed the Portuguese state for a little over two months in 1911, following the provisional government of Teófilo Braga.

9 Although data to verify the claim is not readily available, at least according to statistics from 1870, the number of deaths by yellow fever in the Santana parish did not significantly diverge from the city's average (Souza 2009). Likewise, a *Cartogramma do Cholera-Morbus* (1895–6) shows that cholera was fairly evenly distributed throughout the city. The map is available at the Cartography Division of the Biblioteca Nacional in Rio de Janeiro.

10 Much has been written about the episode. See Sevcenko 1984, Chalhoub 1996:
    97–101, Pereira 2002 and Santucci 2008: 94–137.

11 The 1906 census did not collect information pertaining to race, but Needell
    speculates that more than half of Rio's population might have been of African
    descent (1987: 49). Several sources discuss how Afro-Brazilians and practices
    linked to African origins were targeted under the republic. See, among others,
    Needell 1987: 45–51; Holloway 1993: 8; Benchimol 1999: 277–85; Cunha 2001:
    337; and Sevcenko 2003: 49 et passim.

12 Moura 1995 serves as the starting point of several discussions of the tias. Ciata
    appears to have been a lyakekerê, an important ritual officer. In English, see
    Chasteen 2004: 33–49. See also, among others, Velloso 1988: 14–16; Silva 1997:
    60–3; Galvão 2000: 117–22; Lírio 2003: 47. For an analysis focusing on issues of
    gender and race in popular song during the three decades following abolition,
    see Abreu 2005.

13 On scholarship dedicated to João do Rio, see O'Donnell 2008, particularly the
    introduction. Also see Green 1999: 51–61, which pays special attention to the
    author's sexuality and the reactions it generated.

14 See, for example, Rodrigues 2010.

15 At least in an initial phase of his career. João do Rio's journalism would later
    became much more concerned with the lives of the elites, as Needell argues (1987:
    208–9).

16 The book has been translated as *The Enchanting Soul of the Streets* by Mark Carlyon.
    I quote from this bilingual edition.

17 The *bumba-meu-boi* is a musical-theatrical folk tradition that often involves
    dramatizing a bull brought back to life. Its characteristics have great regional
    variation, and festivities and rituals around it remain popular in parts of rural
    Brazil, and in the north and north-east of the country. Unlike the *festa* in the
    Glória church, to which he also refers, the Festa da Penha in the Zona Norte was
    the only other manifestation capable of rivaling carnival in its popular appeal
    (Moura 1995: 108–15). See Velloso 1988, and the first chapter of Soihet 2008.

18 The cordões, like the ranchos, blocos, clubes, e sociedades, were groups that took
    over the streets during carnival: João do Rio's text refers to hundreds of them,
    and in 1902 alone around 200 were licensed by the police. Cordões frequently
    came from the city's outskirts, and incorporated costumes and songs created
    specifically for the occasion (Gonçalves 1936: 64). For a social history of Rio's
    carnival from 1880 to 1920 that accounts for differences between these categories,
    see Cunha 2001.

19 In the pages of that same magazine, Olavo Bilac frequently derided traditions
    like carnival as an embarrassment to 'civilization' (Cunha 2001: 32–3). On one
    occasion he wrote of the cordões: 'I believe [...] that, of all civilized cities, Rio de
    Janeiro is the only one that tolerates this shameful exhibition ... it is revolting
    that these orgies spill out onto the streets, in erotic processions'. 'Chronica',
    Kósmos, March 1904 (cited at Needell 1987: 49).

20 His writing was of course not free of literary influences: the pseudonym João
    do Rio seems to have been inspired by Jean de Paris, a writer from *Le Figaro*
    (Faria 1988: 86) and he later translated works by Jean Lorrain, Paul Alexandre
    Martin Duval, and Oscar Wilde (Broca 1960: 219). On his influences, particularly

in fiction, see Antelo 1989. It is possible, as has been noted, that a series by Jules de Bois, *Les Petites religions de Paris*, published by *Le Figaro* in 1898, served as inspiration for João do Rio's project, although he credits the idea to Victor Viana, a friend and publicist.

21 Recent research by Juliana Barreto Farias explores how the press covered the negative reception of João do Rio's chronicles among practitioners of Afro-Brazilian religions. Based on articles published in the *Gazeta de Notícias* in March of 1904, she writes of a meeting among concerned feiticeiros and mães-de-santa to uncover the identity of João do Rio's source, responsible for exposing the secrets of their rituals. I am grateful to Lilia Schwarcz for bringing this unpublished material to my attention.

22 Known as *malês* in Bahia, Moslem slaves – in general literate and better educated than their masters –were behind a major nineteenth-century rebellion in that state. See Reis 2003.

23 We might recall the aforementioned opening scene of Machado's *Esau e Jacó* (1904), where two upper-class women pay a visit to a cabocla in the Morro do Castelo.

24 See Moura 1995: 83. João da Baiana recounts the story in an interview recorded at the MIS in Rio de Janeiro (24 August 1966). He adds that the senator, along with others like Hermes da Fonseca (president from 1910 to 1914) frequented the houses of the baianas, and knew his grandparents through connections to the freemason Grande Oriente.

25 The interview was given to Moura (1995: 97). The veracity of details is complicated by the date given for the death of Tia Ciata's husband, João Batista da Silva, in 1910 (101).

26 João da Baiana, for example, mentions the Tias Prisciliana, Nélia, Tomásia, Carmen, and Rosaré. Donga, in his own testimony to the MIS (24 June 1966), displays annoyance at the interviewer's insistence on asking about Tia Ciata, taking the side of her rival Hilário.

27 One observer writes that it was obligatory for ranchos to parade in front of her house – or else 'they might as well have not gone out' (Guimarães 1933: 117).

28 Her house was in Visconde de Itaúna Street. 'Pelo Telefone', considered the first recorded samba, was registered by Donga (with lyrics by Mauro de Almeida), a habitué of Tia Ciata's house, where it was reportedly conceived (Moura 1995: 116–27). The claim has generated controversy among musicians and historians. See Hertzman 2008.

29 Heitor dos Prazeres, interview at the MIS (1 September 1966).

30 The number is most likely exaggerated. Her biographer accounts for 282 compositions, but we can only speculate as to how many were either wrongly attributed or lost (Diniz 1984).

31 See Diniz 1984: 31. On the role of salons in Carioca society under the empire and the First Republic, see Needell 1987: 82–115.

32 The song was deemed a 'tango brasileiro', a rhythm closely related to the maxixe. President Hermes da Fonseca's wife Nair de Teffé was responsible for the innovation, including it in a recital. The original title was 'Gaúcho', a word that denotes a native of Rio Grande do Sul, and thus as a further aggravation alluded to that state's senator Pinheiro Machado, at the time a political rival of the president.

33 Cited from the *Diário do Congresso Nacional*, 11 August 1914, p. 2789 (Rodrigues 1996: 172).

34 For a study of the dance's journey from clandestine Cidade Nova clubs to the French capital – and on the resistance and persecution it faced – see Jota Efegê 1974.

35 She helped to establish the Sociedade Brasileira de Autores Teatrais (SBAT), when no such institution was in existence. See Hertzman 2008.

36 It premiered at the São José Theatre, in the Praça Tiradentes. There were several stagings of the play. Related material – including different versions of the script – can be consulted at the Instituto Moreira Salles in Rio de Janeiro.

37 In a revue from 1886, Gonzaga included a section called 'O Maxixe na Cidade Nova' (Diniz 1984: 120). Most scholars locate the maxixe's origins in the neighbourhood. See, for example, Jota Efegê 1974: 23; Schreiner 1993: 88; Moura 1995: 54; Tinhorão 1997: 81; Chasteen 2004: 21; and especially Sandroni 2001: 62–83. Between 1901 and 1910, over 40 per cent of the city's carnival clubs – and almost half of the cordões – were located in the parishes of Santana, Santa Rita, and Espírito Santo (Cunha 2001: 166).

38 Something similar can be identified in the success of Jacob Riis's *How the Other Half Lives* (1890), a pioneering work of photojournalism depicting the living conditions in New York City's crowded tenements.

39 Lima had an ambivalent and complicated relationship to being of African descent. He harshly rejected scientific racism and suffered greatly for his skin colour, prevented from graduation in Rio's positivist Escola Politécnica owing to the prejudices of a professor (Needell 1987: 221). In a lecture delivered at Princeton University (8 February 2010), Lilia Schwarcz argued that Lima Barreto was the first Brazilian author to recognize and define himself as black.

40 For an analysis of his desire to enter the institution, and his awareness that lack of social position made it impossible, see Needell 1987: 223–4.

41 His writings while at the Hospício Nacional in the Praia Vermelha were published posthumously in a two-part volume, *Diário do hospício* and *O cemitério dos vivos*. The quotes are from the latter (Barreto 1988).

42 See Resende 1993. Francisco de Assis Barbosa's biography (1964) had a major role in that process, followed by works like Sevcenko 1983.

43 The novel has been translated by Scott-Buccleuch as *The Patriot* (1978). I have relied on this edition, modifying it when appropriate.

44 For an analysis of Lima's simultaneous reproduction and deconstructing of these dichotomies, one that adopts the notion of an 'ideal' versus a 'real' city, see Velloso 1988: 39–51.

45 He dedicates the novel to Irineu Marinho, who founded *A Noite* in 1911. From the very beginning, the newspaper adopted a stance against president Hermes da Fonseca and Pinheiro Machado (Magalhães Júnior 1978: 166) – the senator who replaced João da Baiana's pandeiro. They are some of the targets of *Numa e a Ninfa*, a novel written at the newspaper's request. After 1915, Lima Barreto increasingly adhered to more radical politics and wrote in the emerging leftist press (Needell 1987: 224).

46 On representations of the city that highlighted putative divisions between its neighbourhoods, see Velloso's discussion of a cartoon by Raul Pederneiras (1988: 49). Musical scenes of three regions of Rio are drawn: the most *chic* belonged in

Botafogo, Copacabana, and other southern districts; in between, São Cristovão, Vila Isabel, and other northern neighbourhoods; and in the Cidade Nova and port areas we find a rather wretched group, where most are made out not to look white, and accompanied by a guitar instead of the former's piano.

47 Moura (1995: 71) addresses some of the conflicts related to jobs in the ports, where blacks had held a monopoly and began to face competition from Portuguese immigrants. These disputes were sometimes carried on to unions. For diverging views of the roles of ethnicity and nationality, see Maram 1979: 31 and Chalboub 1986: 109.

48 The census from 1920, like the preceding one, does not provide information on race. In 1906, 37.31 per cent of the Santana parish was composed of foreigners, compared to 25.94 for the whole city – the vast majority of which were European, mostly from Portugal. In 1920, when the percentage of Rio's foreigners dropped to 20.8, they were 38.1 per cent of the Santana residents.

CHAPTER FOUR

Afro-Jewish Quarter and Modernist Landmark

De fato este salão de sangues misturados parece o Brasil ...
Há até a fração incipiente amarela
Na figura de um japonês.
O japonês também dança maxixe:
Acugêlê banzai!

[In fact this dance hall of mixed bloods resembles Brazil ... /
There is even the incipient yellow fraction / In the figure of a
Japanese. / The Japanese also dances *maxixe*: / Acugêlê banzai!]

Manuel Bandeira, 'Não sei dançar' (I Can't Dance), Libertinagem

I

In 1930, George Gershwin introduced a book on Tin Pan Alley by stating that 'in a word, [it] is a unique phenomenon, and there is nothing in any other country of the world to compare with it' (Goldberg 1930: vii). The great composer and pianist, né Jacob Gershowitz, was quite correct when one considers the number of music publishers and the financial sums circulating in the Manhattan district.[1] At the same time, something comparable though less widely known could be found in Brazil's capital, centred on the Cidade Nova's main public square, the Praça Onze. If Tin Pan Alley represented a pinnacle of the impressive synthesis between Jewish musicians and producers with the Afro-American inflected sounds of cakewalk, ragtime, jazz, and blues, one could say that in Rio de Janeiro it is as if frequenters of New Orleans's Congo Square and New York City's Jewish or Italian immigrants all shared the same buildings, public meeting places, occasions to dance.

Lima Barreto's *Numa e a Ninfa* goes to great lengths to portray a Cidade Nova inhabited not only by blacks but by newly arrived Europeans, above all Italians ('valiant Neapolitans'), yet also Portuguese and Russians. The 'doctor', Bogóloff, a Russian émigré, is one of the novel's major characters, living with Lucrécio in his modest Cidade Nova house and rising in the ranks of Brazil's republican technocracy on account of his pseudo-scientific projects and appearance. To be white suffices, implies Lima Barreto. His mulato protagonist, on the other hand, hints at the arrival of a new immigrant group that would add yet another layer to the socio-cultural landscape of the neighbourhood. Upon hearing from his wife, that Mr Antunes, owner of the nearby small general store, would no longer sell to them on credit due to unpaid debts, Lucrécio loses his temper. In a fit, he exclaims to his mulata wife and son, 'You don't know what it is like being mulato!', takes money from his pockets and sends off the young Lúcio: '– Go pay that Jew!' (72).

During the 1920s, the same Praça Onze of the Tia Ciata and of Rio's popular street carnival became home to thousands of Jewish newcomers, primarily from Eastern Europe.[2] Ashkenazi Jews began arriving in Brazil in significant numbers during the late nineteenth century, fleeing czarist regimes.[3] Since at least 1910, they congregated on the Praça Onze and the surrounding area (Fridman 2007: 46). In 1916, the first synagogues opened, the Beit Yaakov and the Beith Israel, and by the mid-20s, the public square could be considered the 'nevralgic centre of Ashkenazi life' (Malamud 1988: 14). It was in the vicinity of the Praça that most of their civil and religious institutions were located, and where several different Jewish newspapers circulated, at least three of them in Yiddish. In July 1917, one of these publications, *A Columna*, ran a poll to decide whether it would adopt Yiddish or Hebrew as its language. That particular newspaper never ceased to circulate in the Portuguese language, but, according to Samuel Malamud's memoir, Yiddish was the 'language that predominated in the environment' of the 'Jewish neighbourhood' (17).[4] It should be noted here that Praça Onze and Mangue, often used to designate the Cidade Nova, after that decade became the most common ways of referring to the neighbourhood.[5]

Though frequently referred to as a community in the historiography and memories of its former residents, the Ashkenazi milieu of Rio de Janeiro concentrated several of the political currents and tensions that enveloped Jewish life elsewhere. A variety of ideological tendencies – religious traditionalists, leftists, socialist Zionists, revisionist Zionists, and assimilationists, for example – were represented by different institutions found near the Praça. In a city where, by 1940, the first time the census accounts for religion, Jews comprised a mere 1.1 per cent of the total population, they were 9.7 per cent of the residents of the New City's Santana parish.[6] Some interviews conducted with former residents give the impression of an almost exclusively Jewish neighbourhood, suggesting a degree of insularity: we hear that 'there were few Brazilians, the majority were of Jews' or that 'practically [...] there were only Jews' (Ribeiro 2008: 145–7). Likewise, there seem to be no records of Afro-Brazilian musicians speaking about the Jewish immigrants that also laid a claim to the Praça Onze as the focal point of their community.

Here and there one finds inklings of a *convivencia*, of the intersections and interactions perhaps inevitably produced by close contact and shared public spaces. Malamud remarks, 'the neighbourhood of the Praça Onze also counted with a numerous population of Italian and Portuguese immigrants, besides the natives that immortalized the neighbourhood in their popular poetry' (18). Recalling Jewish-owned commercial establishments, he writes of how 'everyone admired the coloured employee who since he was young worked at a garment factory and spoke fluent Yiddish' (30). The gallery of eccentric and memorable characters who were influential or cherished among the Praça Onze Jews includes but one 'gentile'. 'Dr' Jacarandá, 'spiritually cultured' though 'unbalanced', was a perpetual candidate to any electoral office. A man of 'very dark skin, kinky hair [cabelo caracolado]', he 'was everyday at the tavern that could be found at the centre of the Praça Onze, under the Israelite Youth Club [Clube Juventude Israelita]' (92).

Other former residents of the areas' several 'vilas' speak of Jews, blacks, Portuguese, Italians, and 'paus-de-arara' (migrants from the Northeast) living side-by-side in relative harmony.[7] In one of the few remaining of these villas, the so-called 'last Jew of the Praça Onze', the aforementioned Pinduca declares in a newspaper interview that 'here there was no prejudice'.[8] Another resident suggests there might not have been distancing based on colour as all were more or less of the same social condition (Ribeiro 2008: 246), echoing Lima Barreto's image of solidarity in poverty. The majority of Eastern European Jews who migrated to Rio were indeed poor and lacked technical skills. The most common profession of the newly arrived was *klientelshik*, or peddling. Fridman estimates that it employed around 30 per cent of Jews who arrived in Brazil without a defined occupation (45).

In the introduction to Malamud's memoir, without drawing socio-ethnic distinctions, the historian Elias Lipiner evokes the rich tapestry of profiles one encounters among the Praça's regulars: 'The popular mass was composed of silent types and don-quixotes, homeless bohemians and well-situated vendors, bozos and sharp-tongued jokers, professional comedians and art amateurs, eternal beginner writers and naive poets, and mainly, of peoples full of goodwill and anger, solicitous and envious, puritan and decadent' (10). When asked about whether there were more whites, more mulatos, or more blacks in the early samba circles of the square, a slightly aggravated João da Baiana responds: 'Everything. The whites at that time liked samba

[...] There were whites in capoeira, singing samba, composing, drumming and all else. There was no race classification, no [...] everything was mixed'.⁹

On the basis of somewhat scant or anecdotal historical documentation, one must resist the temptation to paint an idyllic haven of multicultural ethnic pluralism. Little remains recorded of Afro-Jewish relations during the 1920s in the Cidade Nova, yet faced with a lack of evidence of serious conflicts, one may imagine there was never a parallel to the gang violence along ethnic lines experienced in New York City, for example.¹⁰ We do know that a number of industries – including the Brahma brewery, founded by a Swiss Jew in the Cidade Nova – employed workers of various races and provenances.¹¹ But, if anything, there seems to have been as much competition within particular social groups as between them. Rio de Janeiro, at any rate, differed from other American metropolises that received large number of immigrants, like New York, Buenos Aires, and São Paulo, in that it did not have neighbourhoods associated with a single ethnic group.¹²

Unlike other major cities, where a street address often served as a marker of ethnic or national background, in the Cidade Nova there seems to have been a considerable degree of overlap in how physical spaces were occupied – a greater porosity, we might say. Not far from Tia Ciata's address, at Visconde de Itaúna 117, one found the Iuguend Bund – the Israelite Youth Club, started in 1919 – at no. 203, the boarding house of Sarah and Jaime Verger at no. 151, the printers Horowitz e Cia. Ltda. at no. 78, the Morris Wintschevsky Workers' Center – which in the mid-1920s hosted an amateur theatre group – at no. 155, and the Zionist Tiferet Tizón Carioca Organization, in the street since 1913 (number unknown) – to mention but a few of the dozens of synagogues, social clubs, political and philanthropic organizations, schools and restaurants located alongside important sites of Little Africa.¹³

And in what may seem like the most unusual of combinations, on the other side of the Praça Onze, at Senador Eusébio street, the Jewish Bialik Library shared a multi-storey house with a legendary *gafieira*, or ballroom dance hall, the Kananga do Japão, where people like Sinhô – then known as the 'King of Samba' – were a constant presence (Alencar 1981: 5).¹⁴ Amidst the area's large number of gafieiras, bars, bowling alleys, and pool halls (21 in 1926) (Fridman 2007: 61), the Kananga had special importance due to its origins in a cordão and its connection to the group of musicians that congregated at Tia Ciata's house. After 1917, the Grupo de Caxangá, which included among its members Donga, Pixinguinha, and João Pernambuco, rehearsed at the club (Cabral 1996: 40). Their repertoire, besides many of the musical genres that we have already mentioned, also incorporated song forms and rhythms from Brazil's north-east.

Through the suggestion of a Ukrainian Jew, Adolpho Bloch, the Kananga do Japão became the title and subject of a major television production in 1989. Adolfo Bloch (1908–95) arrived in Rio as a teenager and became a frequenter of the dance hall. He eventually founded and headed the Rede Manchete media conglomerate, and suggested to the writer Carlos Heitor Cony that he write a soap opera, set in the 1920s and 30s, revolving around the Kananga do Japão.[15] Within its 208 episodes, mixing historical and fictional events, there are appearances by Sinhô (played by Paulo Barbosa) and the pai-de-santo João Alabá (played by Antônio Pompeu). Along with the Candomblé priest, there is also the minor character of a rabbi, played by Jitman Vibranovsky.

Amidst presumably many other undocumented encounters, what were the consequences of this 'Afro-Jewish' space to the formation of Rio de Janeiro's culture? The answers must remain to some extent speculatory. There are no equivalent musicological studies in Brazil to those undertaken in the United States, tracing contributions of Yiddish and synagogue music to Tin Pan Alley.[16] Nonetheless, we do know the Jews of the Cidade Nova cultivated a lively cultural scene, beyond those activities directly related to religious practices. Besides several local amateur theatre groups, plays, melodramas, and musical comedies were staged throughout the early 1920s at the Cinema Centenário, where professional artists like Eva Polanski and the Lustil couple performed. Samuel Malamud's memory of Jewish notables includes 'one of the most popular figures of the 20s', Zisman, a musician who both interpreted traditional Eastern European melodies on the violin or clarinet and led an orchestra, which made him 'an integral part of the environment of the Praça Onze' (Malamud 1988: 89).

Though potential musical exchanges have yet to be studied, Malamud himself recalls nostalgically the 'extraordinary revelry' of the Praça Onze carnival. And one finds several examples of that Carioca institution penetrating Jewish life: in 1928, a group of leftist dissidents from the Israelite Youth Club attempted to form a parallel entity, and fundraised by organizing a carnival ball which Malamud describes as having been a success (63). That same year, the periodical *O Novo Mundo*, published almost entirely in Yiddish, announces in Portuguese a 'musical parody, humoristic and critical, utilizing Brazilian carnival music, related to the Jewish community'. A 1927 bulletin for the Centre for Israelite Young Women notes the animated nature of its carnival costumed ball.[17] Participating in the festivities seemed to be common among immigrant groups. The involvement of Italians from the Cidade Nova in carnival, for example, did not escape the attention of Jota Efegê: he mentions the Cruzeiro do Sul, with its headquarters two doors down from Tia Ciata's house, led by the Baroni brothers and known as 'the rancho of the Italians' (Jota Efegê 1982: 217).

The extent to which Jewish individuals and culture penetrated or influenced the daily life of the Cidade Nova at large seems a bit harder to ascertain, as it is not the type of question interviewers tended to pose to our only non-Jewish primary sources who lived there, the pioneering sambistas related to the Bahian diaspora. Among the very few samba lyrics to bring up Jews, two are by the celebrated and prolific Noel Rosa (1910–37). The composer, who we will return to in the next chapter, lived in the middle-class neighbourhood of Vila Isabel but was a fixture in musical circles throughout the city, including the São Carlos hill near the Praça Onze. In 'Cordiais Saudações' ('Cordial Greetings'), recorded in 1931, a rare almost spoken song of the 'samba de breque' genre, in the form of a letter, he mentions a Jew in passing and unflatteringly: 'I am pawned at the hands of a Jew'. Written for the theatre that same year, the humorous 'Quem dá mais?' ('Who pays more?') makes a similarly stereotypical reference to a Jew buying a damaged guitar at an auction, and selling it to a museum for twice the price. The relative absence of references, however, is counterbalanced by encounters between individuals that had far-reaching consequences to the development of Brazil's culture.

Once again, it is music that provides the arena of permeability in a society of deep inequalities: the convergence occurs be it through a foundational composer like Jacob do Bandolim (1918–69), or through a behind the scenes figure like Isaac Frankel. Jacob do Bandolim, né Pick Bittencourt to a Polish Jewish mother and a Brazilian father, mastered the Italian instrument that became part of his name, adapting it to the sounds of that early genre from Rio de Janeiro, the choro. Jacob, who had no musicians in his family and grew up in Lapa, came into music through quintessentially urban experiences: as a child, he would overhear a French neighbour playing violin, and a modinha singer who passed by in the street. Raquel Pick, his supportive mother, would sing along with her son after giving him a first instrument. Later in his adolescence, Jacob would accompany fado players from Portugal, and go to the Praça Onze to see the circles of *partido alto*, where sambistas would challenge each other with improvised rhymes, and things got so heated that sometimes the mounted police showed up. Although not a practising Jew, Jacob once planned a waltz for a violin orchestra, with Italian and Jewish musicians in mind, the 'kings of the bow'.[18]

Isaac Frankel, a lesser-known figure, was the manager of the Cine Palais who in 1919 created the Oito Batutas band and hired them to play in the lobby of the prestigious cinema, breaking with previous racial barriers. Leading this multiracial group were former members of the Grupo de Caxangá with links to the Kananga do Japão and the Bahian tias: Donga and Pixinguinha. When interviewed years later, Pixinguinha does not diminish the significance of the invitation to play in the Palais, in the central Rua Sete de Setembro: 'I was surprised, because invitations of this kind were usually only made to white musicians' (Sodré 1979: 63). These Oito Batutas would spend six months in Paris in 1922, when many African-American jazz musicians were also in the French capital (Shack 2001). They created a great sensation, capitalizing on the impact that Brazilian music had caused on composers like Darius Milhaud, whose 1920 surrealist ballet *Le bœuf sur le toit* (The Ox on the Roof), choreographed by Jean Cocteau, was named after a maxixe song.[19]

These examples and encounters may be too cursory, or too particular to music circles for one to speak of an Afro-Jewish quarter. Nonetheless, we can speak of at least one lasting union between Afro-Brazilians and Ashkenazi Jews – in a twenty-first-century relic of that unlikely milieu: the couple with which we opened this book, Celi and Pinduca, along with their descendants. And where did Celi and Pinduca meet? They will proudly recount: dancing, in one of the Praça Onze's many gafieiras.

II

Besides the Oito Batutas's stay in Paris, the year 1922 marks another watershed moment in the history of Brazilian culture. In February of that year, the burgeoning city of São Paulo hosted the Semana de Arte Moderna, or Modern Art Week, an event that has come to signify the inauguration of Brazil's modernist and avant-garde aesthetic movements. Held at the Municipal Theatre and sponsored by members of São Paulo's elite, it showcased some of the young writers, musicians, and painters that would go on to become leading voices in the country's artistic modernity.

What David Harvey in his *Paris, Capital of Modernity* (2003) calls the myth of modernity as 'a radical break with the past' applies to Brazil's now canonical modernism. Many of its participants carefully cultivated the notion that their innovations represented a rupture with the country's colonial past and the aesthetic preferences of Romanticism, Parnassianism, or Academicism. After studies like Nicolau Sevcenko's *Orfeu extático na metrópole: São Paulo, sociedade e cultura nos frementes anos 20* (Orpheus Ecstatic in the Metropolis: São Paulo, Society and Culture in the Roaring '20s, 1992), we can better comprehend the origins of the Modern Art Week and the artistic movements that sprung out of it in a wider socio-historic context.[20]

In the years following the event, the Cidade Nova would emerge as a privileged locus for a number of poets, novelists, and painters directly or indirectly involved in Brazil's modernism. If, as we have seen, a majority of turn-of-the-century intellectuals and artists mostly ignored or disparaged the neighbourhood, why did a new generation of modernists seem fascinated by it, some even embracing it as representative of a syncretic, more 'authentic' Brazil? Once the previously neglected diversity and complexity of the Cidade Nova reaches a sort of centre-stage for a number of authors and painters, we are faced with a new set of questions: how did this Brazilian artistic modernity – or perhaps its more Carioca offshoot – relate to the fast-paced modernization and urbanizing processes undergone by the city, and how did these artists engage cultural expressions and/or ethnic groups widely seen as antiquated, uncivilized, and a hindrance to the country's progress?

There are of course no simple answers, and to begin approaching the questions we must first seek to understand some often overlooked changes that took place during that decade. The Pereira Passos reforms, as we have seen, sought to take Rio's development elsewhere. One of the symbolic shifts of this definite reorientation happened in 1925, when the Senate was moved from the Conde dos Arcos Palace, on the Cidade Nova side of the Campo de Santana, to the Monroe Palace near the Central Avenue (by then already renamed Rio Branco Avenue). The palace, in the French eclectic style like much of the new avenue, was named after James Monroe (1758–1831), the US president behind the Monroe doctrine ostensibly opposing European influence in the Americas. A monument to the belle époque, it had served as Brazil's pavilion in the St Louis World's Fair of 1904 – formally the Louisiana Purchase Exposition – where it won the Great Prize of Architecture for foreign pavilions.[21]

During the administrations following Pereira Passos, public and private investments and urban interventions largely privileged the centre and the South Zone. Adjacent to the Rio Branco Avenue, the Castelo Hill was at last flattened to the ground in 1922, ridding the Centro of one of the last remnants of poverty and 'backwardness', besides freeing up valuable real estate.[22] The visit of King Albert and Queen Elizabeth of Belgium to Brazil's capital, in 1920, had presented mayor Carlos Sampaio with the opportunity to push for the completion of the hill's flattening (Caulfield 2000b: 236), and provided continuity to earlier projects of 'civilizing' Rio. As historian Sueann Caulfield demonstrates, the occasion engendered large-scale mobilizations, serving to showcase the country's progress and to 'illustrate the dawn of a new spirit of nationalistic optimism in post-World War I Brazil' (2000b: 61).

The reforms following the Pereira Passos 'bota abaixo', although more modest, did have unintended major consequences for the city's cultural life, and to the Cidade Nova in particular. In 1910, the demolition of the Senado Hill, begun in 1891, was finally completed. The avenue that took its place, the Mem de Sá, brought the Praça Onze closer to Lapa, then a bohemian district increasingly popular with artists. Previously separated by a hill, the two spaces were now a little over a mile apart, and connected by a direct streetcar line. Another new avenue, Avenida Salvador de Sá, would further integrate these two locales to another key neighbourhood in the city's music development, the Estácio, next to the Mangue. Though Lapa remains a vibrant and popular destination in the city, and perhaps for that reason still integrates the mental maps of residents and historians, its initial role in Rio's culture was inextricably tied to the Cidade Nova. Several of the writers, painters, and musicians associated with it in the 1920s and 30s were also frequenters of the Praça Onze – and, especially, of the Mangue.

During and after the Pereira Passos reforms, there were significant pressures to push prostitution houses out of the city's centre. The movement culminated during the visit of the Belgian monarchs, when authorities designated the Mangue – safely outside of their itinerary – as Rio's red-light district.[23] Whereas Lapa's cabarets were also notorious for prostitution, they were more upmarket than the Mangue, which became virtually synonymous with the red-light district. While one gained the reputation of a tropical Montmartre, the other's place in the collective imaginary became reduced to its prostitution houses. Many of the figures whose names are linked to the Lapa of the 1920s and 30s, however, were also more than familiar with the Mangue and the Praça Onze.[24] The singer, composer, and radio announcer Henrique Foréis, better known as Almirante, remarks in the biography of his friend Noel Rosa that the famous samba composer preferred the Mangue to Lapa. The painter Emiliano Di Cavalcanti (1897–1976), another whose name became associated to the latter, fondly remembers the former, writing of 'soirées in the Cidade Nova' (11) in his *Reminiscências líricas de um perfeito carioca* (Lyrical Reminiscences of a Perfect Carioca, 1964).

Just as authorities increasingly marginalized it, the Mangue emerges as a type of trope, entering the aesthetic imaginary and plotted in the cartographies of a generation of modernists who made it a setting or subject for a number of poems, novels, and paintings. Amidst the Jewish quarters and the 'African Carnival' of the nearby Praça Onze, it was the Mangue of prostitution houses that commanded the attention of major painters like Di Cavalcanti, Oswaldo Goeldi (1895–1961) and Lasar Segall (1891–1957). Prostitution was an important theme of modern artists worldwide, and representations of the Cidade Nova's red-light district flourished. Around the same time, Oswald de Andrade (1890–1954), one of the central figures behind the Modern Art Week in São Paulo, began to write his long dramatic poem *O Santeiro do Mangue* (The Saint-Maker of the Mangue) unpublished until 1991. Set in the Mangue, it contained a highly ideological attack on bourgeois values, the exploitation of women, and Catholic orthodoxies.

Before we proceed to the examination of specific works, it is prudent to put something else in perspective. In *Fin-de-siècle Vienna* (1981), Carl Schorske argues that unlike the case of Austria's capital, in cities like London, Paris, and Berlin the intellectuals of various communities barely knew each other. The Rio de Janeiro of the 1920s in that sense was certainly more comparable to Vienna – even if its peculiar ethnic and racial mixtures would be out of place there, as elsewhere in the European continent. The similarity, then, may be explained as a matter of scale. Rio's population had grown from 1,157,873 in 1920 to 1,764,141 in 1940. Vienna in 1923 was populated by close to 2 million, whereas urban centres like Berlin, Paris, New York City, and London had at least twice as many inhabitants.[25] Artists and writers cited in this chapter, at any rate, often had personal relationships with each other, knew each other's works, and frequently either collaborated or disagreed – sometimes competing vehemently.

This, which one may deem porosity or provincialism, to a certain degree extends to musicians of the lower classes. One of the contributions of Hermano Vianna's *O mistério do Samba* (*The Mystery of Samba*, 1995; trans. 1999) was to shed light on how contacts between upper-class intellectuals and popular musicians were not uncommon. The book's first chapter, 'The Encounter', recalls a meeting in 1926 between the then-young anthropologist Gilberto Freyre (1900–87), the historian Sérgio Buarque de Holanda (1902–82), district attorney and journalist Prudente de Moraes Neto (1904–77), and classical composers Heitor Villa-Lobos (1887–1959) and Luciano Gallet (1893–1931), with what Freyre – remembering the event in his book *Tempo morto e outros tempos* (Dead Time and Other Times, 1975) – describes as three 'true Brazilians': Pixinguinha, Patrício, and Donga (Vianna 1999: 5).

Of those present at that meeting, the first had studied at Columbia University under Franz Boas, and upon returning from a subsequent trip to Europe organized a Regionalist Conference in his native Recife, in the north-eastern state of Pernambuco. The next two founded and directed *Estética*, a modernist magazine, in 1924, while Sérgio Buarque de Holanda had also been denominated the representative in Rio de Janeiro of another modernist publication, the *Klaxon*, based in São Paulo and circulating in 1922–3.[26] Villa-Lobos, already a prominent musician, had headlined the last night of the Modern Art Week in São Paulo, and Gallet was a student of Darius Milhaud's when the French modernist composer was in Brazil in 1917. Among the other three, all illustrious representatives of Little Africa, two led the Oito Batutas band, back in Rio after their successful national and Parisian tour some four years earlier.[27]

Freyre's notion of three black sambistas as 'true Brazilians' gains special significance in the context of the intellectual debates and cultural shifts under way. Part of what animated what we may call the modernist project was the search for an 'authentic' Brazil, and the desire to set the country apart from its colonial past as well as from European influences. Paradoxically, the articulation of a 'true' Brazil was, to a degree, inspired or legitimized by the sensibilities of European artists. One way to understand the process might be to highlight the genesis of another trope of Brazilian modernists related to the Cidade Nova: Rio's favela. In the early 1920s, the term still largely referred to a specific hill, the Morro da Favela (Fig. 2), which, as we have seen, was initially settled by, among others, those evicted from one of the Cidade Nova's most populous cortiços.[28]

The hills scattered throughout the city – several surrounding the Cidade Nova – were increasingly populated in often precarious conditions. Along with many of the city's poorest, they also inherited the role reserved to tenements in the nineteenth century. In the binary categories that predominated in discourses of the press and among authorities – primitive, outdated, unsanitary, dangerous, poor, versus civilized, modern, ordered – favelas embodied the undesirable.[29] Amidst that dominant polarized framework, they also came to signify something positive in the representation of certain writers and artists: the favela was a source of a purer, primitive, and more authentic Brazil. In 1924, Oswald de Andrade opens his 'Manifesto da poesia pau-brasil' (Manifesto of Brazilwood Poetry) by enlisting the Morro da Favela among other national symbols in his pursuit of a sense of 'Brazilianness': 'Poetry exists in facts. The saffron and ochre shacks in the green of the favela under the Cabralian-blue sky, are aesthetic facts'.[30]

A year later, the avant-garde writer from São Paulo published a collection of poems entitled *Pau-Brasil*, where he attempts to put into practice the precepts laid out in the manifesto. Published in the French capital, it was prefaced by Paulo Prado, a member of the São Paulo coffee aristocracy and patron of the Modern Art Week. He declares that Oswald, 'in a trip to Paris, from an atelier of the Place Clichy – the world's belly button – discovered, dazzled, his own land'. The poet himself dedicates the book to the Swiss-born poet Blaise Cendrars (1887–1961), 'for the occasion of Brazil's discovery'.

In 1920 and again in 1923, a very talented painter, Tarsila do Amaral (1886–1973), went to study in Paris and ended up 'discovering' Brazil herself. Also from São Paulo, she developed a relationship with Oswald de Andrade that led to various collaborations and an eventual marriage in 1926. In the year of his 'Manifesto of Brazilwood Poetry', among other paintings of similar themes, she depicts the Morro da Favela as perhaps a foreigner might: it is colourful, idyllic, all its subjects are black. In France she had befriended Blaise Cendrars and Constantin Brancusi, two of the main promoters of black art on the Parisian scene.[31] Tarsila very acutely perceived

Figure 2   The Cidade Nova seen from the Favela Hill

that Paris was tired of Parisian art (as she puts it in a letter to her parents) and seems to have sought the exotic in her own country.[32] Her depictions of Carioca scenes, in the process, exaggerate the presence of Afro-Brazilians.[33] To Tarsila's credit she seems to have had no pretence of documenting the favela realistically, and achieves quite a bit in her representation of a place that Brazilians in her social class tended to be embarrassed by. In effect, the favela had become a centrepiece of her new-found tropical Utopia.

During the 1920s the Morro da Favela attracted the interest of some prominent visitors to the city, like Blaise Cendrars, who developed a friendship with Donga and whose interest in Afro-Brazilian culture has been widely explored. In a less discussed episode, the Italian futurist Marinetti (1876–1944) also went there during a trip to Rio in 1926.[34] And for the first time since the days of the empire – for very different purposes – the former Landfill Road, now the Mangue, again entered the itinerary of travellers. Stefan Zweig wrote about his experience in the red-light district in a passage of his 1936 diary that we will discuss in the next chapter, and the poet Vinicius de Moraes took his friend Waldo Frank there, an incident with consequences we will soon address. Neither the favela nor the Mangue, or anything beyond the Campo de Santana for that matter, appeared in maps of tourist guides being published at the time.[35]

Simultaneously, as carnival became an increasingly accepted expression of nationhood – Oswald de Andrade follows his evocation of the favela in his Manifesto of Brazilwood Poetry with the statement: 'Carnival in Rio is the religious event of [our] race' – the Praça Onze's street celebrations emerged as another 'congregator', a temporary enabler or stimulant of cultural interchanges. It attracted people like Samuel Malamud, favela residents, and Heitor Villa-Lobos, a constant presence in the *blocos de sujo*, rowdy and improvised groups of revellers that took over the Praça Onze on Mondays during carnival (Cunha 2001: 235–6). The square's carnival was painted by Alberto da Veiga Guignard (1896–1962), who included in his representation the Mangue's palm trees. By the early 1930s, it would become institutionalized in the country's festive calendar, an indelible presence in Rio's cultural cartography, and an attraction for foreigners visiting Brazil – other topics for the next chapter.

III

São Paulo ended the second decade of the twentieth century as one of the fastest growing cities in the world – a fact over which the local press exulted (Sevcenko 1992: 36–7). By 1928, it would reach a million inhabitants and be solidified as a political, industrial, and economic centre, fuelled in great part by a national economy reliant on coffee exports: that year, approximately 78 per cent of coffee production in the world originated in Brazil (Camargos 2007: 103). It is no surprise, then, that the city held the Modern Art Week, nor that its young writers were so fascinated by technology and so deeply affected by the breakneck pace of the changes experienced in their home town. Nonetheless, if São Paulo hosted what has become seen as modernism's catalyzing event, and if the new metropolis in many ways incarnated the forces behind the movement, the capital still acted as the country's de facto cultural centre and 'resonance chamber'. As such, it witnessed a confluence of strands of modernisms from several states: not just from São Paulo, as we have begun to see, but also from Minas Gerais and Pernambuco.

Rio was indeed a 'pan-Brazilian' city, as Gilberto Freyre put it. In a famous definition by the poet Manuel Bandeira, another Pernambuco native, the Carioca is 'someone born in [the state of] Espírito Santo or in Belém [capital of the state of] Pará' (1993: 465). Despite glaring social injustices and economic disparity, a powerful mythology and ethos of inclusion became part of Rio de Janeiro's identity. Looking back at those years of intense immigration, Di Cavalcanti's memoirs – which present him as a 'perfect Carioca' – echo some of the contradictions in how the city thinks itself. He protectively complains of the 'countless [...] Northeasterners, *gaúchos*, people from the West and from the Amazon, installed in this city, joined to the Jews, Arabs, Portuguese, Spaniards, Italians and many other foreigners, all stuck in an arrivisme that has nothing of the old virtues of the authentic Carioca' (15). But soon the city breaks down the outsiders' ambitions, giving place to the image of a generous, accepting *urbs*: 'This city that repeals nothing, receives everyone and to everyone gives a little corner'. In Rio, Di Cavalcanti suggests, all become Carioca, discarding their previous backgrounds: 'There will yet be a place to those who will arrive, each bringing a baggage to throw out' (17).

Given those considerations, let us now reformulate our question: how did the Cidade Nova enter the aesthetic imaginary and become plotted in the cognitive maps of a generation of modernists who were in relatively constant contact with each other, and who, although hailing from various parts of the country, to different extents felt at home in Rio de Janeiro?

One transplant who explores the city's raw intoxicating powers to overcome even the most refined expectations was the poet Murilo Mendes, whose 'Noite Carioca' (Carioca Night) declares that 'Everything loses the equilibrium in this night', where

> sonatas de Beethoven realejadas nos pianos dos bairros distintos
> não são mais obras importantes do gênio imortal,
> são valsas arrebentadas ...
> Perfume vira cheiro,
> as mulatas de brutas ancas dançam o maxixe nos criouléus
> suarentos.

> [sonatas by Beethoven played on the pianos of distinct
> neighbourhoods / are no longer important works of the
> immortal genius / they are smashed waltzes ... / Perfume turns
> into smell, / the mulatas of brute hips dance the maxixe in the
> sweaty criouléus]

The term *criouléus*, full of racial connotations, designated popular balls held in general on Saturdays and attended largely by Afro-Brazilians, predominantly by the lower classes.[36] At first glance, one might interpret the zoomorphic mulata of 'brute hips' as the poem partaking in scientific racist discourses. Likewise, the reference to the music of 'distinct' neighbourhoods – an adjective used not without irony – a degradation of the great Beethoven, can be read as the horrified stance of a 'guardian of civilization'. Yet these characteristics are no longer used to disqualify or disparage popular culture and black Brazilians: rather, they are precisely the attributes that seduce the poetic voice and call for the poem's celebratory tone. Rio's night, 'so delicious' to the poet, distinguishes the city like its bay, personified as 'camarada', receptive and friendly.

Murilo Mendes (1901–75) moved to the capital in 1920 from his native Minas Gerais, and later in the decade began collaborating on some of the first modernist magazines like *Terra roxa e outras terras*, *Verde*, and the *Revista de Antropofagia*. In 1930, his first book, *Poemas (1925–1929)*, received the prestigious Prêmio Graça Aranha from the Brazilian Academy of Letters. The fact that one of the institution's top prizes was awarded to a book of free verse shows the extent to which aesthetic criteria had changed since the belle époque. Form aside, Murilo Mendes's themes also diverged significantly from the urns and statuary of the Parnassian repertoire. That volume, along with 'Noite Carioca', includes a sequence of other poems that evoke the Cidade Nova, its population, and practices. The first to do so directly is 'Biografia de músico' (Biography of a Musician). A poem of twenty-one free verses and no punctuation other than the final stop, it tells of a boy from a favela who goes through all the steps to become an acclaimed musician but gets denied the Conservatory's top honour for lack of inside connections:

> O guri nasceu no morro aniquilado de sambas
> bebeu leite condensado
> soltou papagaio de tarde
> aprendeu o nome de todos os donatários de capitania
> esgotou os criouléus da Cidade Nova
> bocejou anos e anos no Conservatório
> não tirou medalha de ouro
> coitado
> porque não tinha pistolão (90)

> [The kid was born in the hills annihilated by sambas / drank condensed milk flew kites in the afternoon / learned the names of all the [colonial] captaincy donors / exhausted the criouléus of the Cidade Nova / yawned years and years in the Conservatory / he did not win a gold medal / poor guy / for lack of connections]

The poet's tone reads as more humorous than outraged, and all ends well as our nameless musician arrives in heaven to be greeted by angels whose ocarina concert makes him faint from emotion. Again, Murilo Mendes refers to the criouléus, this time situating them explicitly in the Cidade Nova.[37]

In 'Marinha' (Navy), the very next poem, named after one of the republic's prized institutions, we instead come upon another institution - carnival - disrupting military exercises on its way to acceptance as Brazil's most emblematic feature:

A esquadra não pôde seguir pros exercícios
porque estava nas vésperas do carnaval.
Os marinheiros caíram no parati
e nos braços roliços e cheirosos
de todas as mulatas que têm aí pela cidade. (91)

[The squadron could not follow through with the exercises /
because it was the eve of carnival. / The sailors got hooked on
the parati / and on the plump and fragrant arms / of all the
mulatas that there are throughout the city]

Along with the carnival, the stanza enlists the 'parati' (a synonym of the
sugar cane-based spirit cachaça) and 'mulatas', enough to contaminate the
Navy men. Even after carnival, 'the folks got hooked on the maxixe all of a
sudden' ('o pessoal caiu de repente no maxixe'). The Navy squadron ends up
sold to an English ambassador, and the government sends half the money
to 'Turkish orphans', using the other half to throw 'one hell of a ball' ('um
bruto baile'). A measure of irony in the carnivalesque episode would not
be lost on the contemporary reader, especially considering the still fresh
memory of what became known as the Revolta da Chibata (Revolt of the
Whip). In 1910, a sailor injured with a knife the corporal who denounced
him for bringing cachaça on board. The sailor's punishment, 250 'chibatadas'
(a form of whipping) in the presence of the troops and accompanied by
drums, far exceeded the norm and set off a mutiny. Eventually, more than
2,000 mostly black and mulato sailors rebelled against poor conditions and
the use of corporal punishment by the mostly white officials, threatening
to bomb the city.[38]

The power of carnival and popular music to provoke irrevocable change
is not limited to the poet, the 'kid' from the favela, or the navy men. In the
next poem, 'Família Russa no Brasil' (Russian Family in Brazil), it extends
to the new arrivals from faraway lands. 'Mr Naum', the poet notes, did not
set up his corner shop in one of those neighbourhoods where immigrants
ended up, choosing the more upscale Botafogo, 'the chic neighbourhood'.
After a year, the Russian is assimilated: Mr Naum 'already knows about
Rui Barbosa, Mangue, Lampião', he plays the local informal lottery every
day, and is saving up for carnival ('Seu Naum já sabe que tem Rui Barbosa,
Mangue, Lampião. / Joga no bicho todo dia, está ajuntando pro carnaval').
His daughters, likewise, 'settled into national life', they know how to dance
the maxixe and strike conversations with sergeants in a Brazilian tone
('as filhas dele instalaram-se na vida nacional. / Sabem dançar o maxixe
/ conversam com os sargentos em tom brasileiro'). We may imagine that,
like the young Adolpho Bloch, on Saturdays, 'all spiffed up', he goes to

the criouléu ('Nos sábados todo janota ele vai pro criouléu') and like Lima Barreto's Bogóloff he might ascend in the political world: 'Mr Naum might yet become a senator' ('Seu Naum inda é capaz de chegar a senador'). It is improbable, by inference, that those who were black at the criouléu could meet the same fate.

In 'Casamento' (Wedding), from the same collection, Murilo Mendes's lyric voice treats similar themes but adopts a more critical tone, of which 'Marinha' and 'Família Russa no Brasil' are not exempt:

> O povo deixa a revolução no meio
> e toca a dançar o maxixe,
> carnes morenas se esfregando pra darem poetas e operários,
> dança minha gente, no crioléu, na planície, na usina e no dancingue,
> que a música é gostosa, todas as mulheres saem pra rua
> e os homens vão bancar o estivador pras pequenas terem vestido de seda.

> [The people leave the revolution halfway through / and break out to dance the maxixe / dark-skinned flesh rubbing against each other to create poets and labourers / dance my people, at the crioléu, in the plains, at the factory and the open balls, / because the music is delicious, all the women take to the streets / and the men act as dockworkers so the girls can have silk dresses]

The 'delicious' nightlife of Rio de Janeiro, the enticing criouléus of the Cidade Nova, then, do not just belong in some mythic plane, in the realm of sensual pleasure or in the formation of a festive national identity. They have political consequences as well, and might have an alienating effect, though in the case of Murilo Mendes's poetry we are not left with too clear a sense of whether that should be read as something positive or negative.

It would not be far-fetched to suggest that the mostly white, middle-class artists of the modernist movement looked towards places such as these criouléus for the type of 'primitive' inspiration that Picasso found in African or Polynesian masks – and one could contend that a painter like Tarsila do Amaral did something along those lines, although her creative spirit and multifaceted talents certainly deserve more credit. Murilo Mendes's poetry, providing the voice of a spectator-participant able to become enveloped in the scents and sweat of dancing bodies, in effect evokes the musical scene of Rio de Janeiro's peripheries as somehow summoning social forces that were an integral part of an 'authentic' Brazilian experience. Murilo

Mendes's location (or finding) of this authenticity in popular culture, in the margins of Rio, not only anticipates a trope of the 1930s and 40s but it does so without seeking to advance an ideological programme of Brazil as a country free of racial tensions. At the same time, although in line with a few other contemporary writers' treatment of the Cidade Nova and of Rio's popular music scene, these representations entered into contradiction with those disseminated in the press and elsewhere, wherein those dance halls still embodied the barbarian, backwards, even violent aspects of the city. Signs of an increasingly fractured 'lettered city'.

Around the time of Murilo Mendes's *Poemas* (1925–1929), another writer with a deep interest in music, the aforementioned Mário de Andrade, situated in the Mangue a chapter of the experimental *Macunaíma, o herói sem nenhum caráter* (Macunaíma, the Hero without any Character) – which he called not a novel but a rhapsody, and which was published in 1928.[39] The São Paulo native had been one of the primary figures behind the Modern Art Week along with Oswald de Andrade, and remained an active participant in the modernist movement. He named the chapter 'Macumba', a generic designation for syncretic Afro-Brazilian religious ceremonies. In a text that famously suspends temporal confines and dissolves spatial limitations, the narrator plots the macumba rite rather precisely in the Mangue: 'The macumba took place over at the Mangue at the house of Aunt Ciata, a sorceress like no other, a Mother-of-Saints full of fame, and quite the singer at the guitar' (57). The protagonist Macunaíma attends the macumba out of his desire to take vengeance on the greedy giant who refuses to return his 'muiraquitã' – an amulet given to him by his lover Ci. Just as Leonardo appealed to the 'sorcerer' caboclo *way over there in the Mangue*, Macunaíma goes to the 'feiticeira' Tia Ciata *lá no Mangue*.

On a cartographer's map, the site of Tia Ciata's house was of course not in the Mangue but rather in the nearby Praça Onze. Perhaps as the Mangue became a modernist landmark the spaces were conflated in the cognitive maps of artists and writers. Or rather we may interpret the macumba's location in *Macunaíma* as a nod to *Memórias de um sargento de milícias*, a novel that Mário de Andrade admired and knew very well. In an introduction to the book, he deems it noteworthy that 'having to describe a witchcraft ceremony (feitiçaria), the novelist does not opt for Candomblés, forgets about blacks and searches for a caboclo in the swamps of the Cidade Nova' (1944: 12). Mário de Andrade, who would become a notable folklorist, prized Manuel Antônio de Almeida's capacity for 'folkloric observation' and his novel's 'documentation of national customs'. *Macunaíma*, itself owing many of its Amerindian mythological allusions to the work of the German ethnologist Theodor Koch-Grunberg, devotes the 'Macumba' chapter to 'document' those blacks which the nineteenth-century novelist had 'forgotten'. It paid careful attention to the details of the ceremony, oscillating between the folklorist's interest in the picturesque and a dose of self-parody. Using Pixinguinha as a source, Mário de Andrade reproduces the language of chants in verses full of Yoruban words, and specifies some of the customs: bringing a bottle of 'pinga' (cachaça), taking the shoes off, saluting the saints, sacrificing a goat.[40]

In a residual expression of the porosity apparent in Almeida's novel, the macumba scene in *Macunaíma* provides a microcosm of the city, uniting people of several backgrounds and professions. We find 'sailors joiners journalists fat cats sham engineers hussies public servants, many public servants!' and 'lawyers ship stewards healers poets the hero crooks, some Portuguese, senators, all these people dancing and singing the response in the prayers' (57). Two pages down we have 'doctors bakers engineers shysters policemen maids cub reporters murderers' and then 'sellers book-lovers down-and-outs academics bankers', all joined in dancing and singing Candomblé prayers (59). The narrator uses those seemingly random lists and occasional lack of commas to give a sense of the drunken, overwhelming atmosphere, filled with the smells of sweating bodies not unlike Murilo Mendes's 'Noite Carioca'. The device also serves for comic effect and satire. When you eliminate the comma between 'deputados' (congressmen) and 'gatunos' (crooks), for example, the latter can be read not only as a noun but also as an adjective: 'there were tons of people there, honest people, poor people, lawyers waiters construction workers congressmen crooks [or crooked congressmen]'.

To Mário de Andrade, then, Tia Ciata's macumba was by no means an exclusively Afro-Brazilian affair. Besides the 'portugas' and numerous professions that presupposed someone of European descent, at the centre of the 'zungu' we have a nude-dancing young Polish woman, a 'polaca' – a term also frequently denoting a prostitute.[41] This redheaded 'polaca' receives the orixá Exu, a entity with ambivalent roles in Afro-Brazilian religious practices. Regardless of the extent to which it documents a reality, the scene participates in the increasingly prevalent discourses of Brazil as a land of three races, an emergent trend that would echo in the ideology of 'racial democracy'.[42]

The chapter ends with one of the samba parties for which Tia Ciata's house was famous, naming some of those in attendance, a list of contemporary poets, artists, and friends of Mário de Andrade: 'And the macumba-participants. Macunaíma, Jaime Ovalle, Dodô, Manu Bandeira, Blaise Cendrars, Ascenso Ferreira, Raul Bopp, Antônio Bento, all these macumbeiros, went out into the dawn' (64). Among these we find a resident of Curvelo Street, close to Lapa, the poet Manuel Bandeira (1886–1968), who Mário de Andrade deemed the John the Baptist of Brazilian modernism.

The young poets of São Paulo read with enthusiasm Bandeira's second poetry volume, *Carnaval* (1919), and in many ways it is a precursor of the modernist generation. Averse to literary schools but indebted to tradition – including the Parnassian poetry frequently under attack by vanguardists – he chose not to participate in the Modern Art Week, although his satirical poem 'Os Sapos' (The Frogs) was read at the event. Bandeira's fourth book, *Libertinagem* (1930), constitutes a watershed in Brazilian literature, where he seems to free himself from a certain 'anxiety of influence' and more fully embraces the modernist aesthetic. The book included a poem with the title 'Mangue', originally called 'Cidade Nova' (Bandeira 1993: 19). In fifty-three free verses it evokes much of the neighbourhood's history, attentive to the cultural depth and human dimension palpitating beneath its worn-out, decadent, everyday landscape:

> Mangue mais Veneza americana do que o Recife
> Cargueiros atracados nas docas do Canal Grande
> O Morro do Pinto morre de espanto
> Passam estivadores de torso nu suando facas de ponta
> Café baixo
> Trapiches alfandegados
> Catraias de abacaxis e de bananas
> A Light fazendo crusvaldina com resíduos de coque
> Há macumbas no piche
> Eh cagira mia pai
> Eh cagira
> E o luar é uma coisa só
>
> Houve tempo em que a Cidade Nova era mais subúrbio do que
> todas as Meritis da Baixada
> Pátria amada idolatrada de empregadinhos de repartições
> públicas
> Gente que vive porque é teimosa
> Cartomantes da Rua Carmo Neto
> Cirurgiões-dentistas com raízes gregas nas tabuletas avulsivas
>
> [Mangue more American Venice than Recife / Cargo boats
> moored at the docks of the Great Canal / The Pinto Hill
> frightened to death / Dockworkers with naked torsos
> sweating knives pass by / Cheap coffee / Bonded warehouses
> / One-person boats loaded with pineapples and bananas / The

power company making creolin products from coal residues /
There are macumbas in tar / *Eh cagira mia pai* / *Eh cagira* / And
the moonlight is something else. // There was a time when
the Cidade Nova was more a suburb than all of the Meritis
of the Baixada / Beloved idolized fatherland of small-time
civil servants / People who live because they are stubborn /
Fortune-tellers from the Carmo Neto Street / Surgeon-dentists
with Greek roots in the avulsive signboards]

It is an urban scenario of simultaneity and multiplicity, seemingly only
apprehensible through lists as those of Walt Whitman's New York City
poetry. Yet Bandeira's poem presents a peculiar juxtaposition of nature
and technology, industry and idleness, in a type of harmony much unlike,
for example, the at once frenetic and melancholic São Paulo of Mário de
Andrade's 1922 *Paulicéia Desvairada* (*Hallucinated City*, 1968).

In the very first line we find an intersection of references to places.
Bandeira subverts the cliché of his native Recife as the Brazilian Venice,
claiming the Mangue more broadly as an American Venice rather than
merely a national one.[43] Given how his preface for Lasar Segall's album
Mangue (which we will get to in a moment) actually ridicules the Imperial
pretension to build a second Venice, we might imagine that the poem's
lyric voice salutes not the Mangue's single canal, less Venice-like than
those of Recife, but rather the quarter's cosmopolitan character. It is as if
Bandeira intuitively foresees that the Mangue and its neighbourhood would
remain the neglected cosmopolitan heart of the city's cultural life – rather
than the monumental, costly, and imitative avenues of the capital's centre.
This Cidade Nova of 'dockworkers', 'macumbas', 'small-time civil servants',
'fortune-tellers', and 'surgeon-dentists with Greek roots' are a parcel of a
Brazil which he invokes metonymically, and perhaps with a measure of irony,
by citing a line from the national anthem: 'Beloved idolized fatherland [...]'.

Luís Martins (1907–81), an enthusiast of Lapa and one of the outstanding
chroniclers of Rio's interwar bohemian circles, would elevate the Mangue
to a national symbol in an even more explicit manner in 'Canção do Exílio'
(Exile Song). It was his take on Gonçalves Dias's romanticist paean to the
nation, a nineteenth-century poem of the same title that several twentieth-
century writers attempted to rewrite, most as a parody. Here, Martins inserts
the Mangue's palm trees in between the initial iconic verses of the original:
'There are palm trees in my country, / there are the palm trees of the Mangue,
/ where the Sabiá bird sings' ('Minha terra tem palmeiras, / tem as palmeiras
do Mangue, / onde canta o sabiá'). Luís Martins's version, however, seems to
have him exiled not in Europe but in São Paulo, where the Carioca lived for

most of his life, much of it in the company of Tarsila do Amaral.[44] It is Rio de Janeiro that he longs for, in particular the city of his youth.

In a different spirit from those more festive verses, Bandeira's do not idealize the Mangue. He recognizes it is also a place of poverty and desolation. Those long-gone palm trees planted by Dom João VI, the poet writes, have committed suicide, and its people live on because they are stubborn. Besides citing a macumba chant in collage-like fashion, 'Mangue' also enlists the sambas of Tia Ciata. Bandeira dedicated a chronicle to Sinhô, upon his death at the age of forty-one in 1930.[45] He eulogizes the composer as the 'most expressive trace connecting poets, artists, cultured and refined society, to the deep layers of the urban rag-tags [ralé]'. That, to Bandeira, explained 'the fascination aroused in all people when he was taken to a salon' (1993: 453). When 'taken' to a salon, Sinhô was the skilled mediator between the upper class and the urban masses: a socio-economic distance translated in the implicit hierarchized categories of high and popular culture. From the opposite direction, Bandeira's 'Mangue' seems to seek a similar mediation, approximating formal poetry to the language of favelas and the Cidade Nova. The poem asks in a colloquial turn of phrase evocative of the rural, Bahian origins of her milieu: 'Where is Aunt Ciata?' ('Cadê mais Tia Ciata?'). And, rather than describe, it performs the syncretic roots of carnival processions, setting up a dialogue in a nativity play, the Christmas-time *cheganças*, an Iberian practice that might have been absorbed in present-day Angola and Congo even before Europeans and African slaves crossed the Atlantic.[46] In Brazil, these manifestations, celebrated as part of Christmas festivities, slowly evolved into twentieth-century modern carnival parades.[47]

The short fragmented dialogue of this nativity scene enacts the language of its participants with phonetic precision, disregarding orthographic rules in a procedure common in *Libertinagem* and in the writing of his contemporaries, including the Mário de Andrade of *Macunaíma*. Bandeira, as he put it in another celebrated poem of that collection, 'Evocação do Recife' (Evocation of Recife), sought the language that 'Came from the mouth of the people, the incorrect speech of the people / Correct speech of the people / Because it's the people who speak with gusto the Portuguese from Brazil' ('Vinha da boca do povo, na língua errada do povo/ Língua certa do povo/ Porque ele é que fala gostoso o português do Brasil').[48] We may say that in a full circle the lettered city now pays tribute to the spoken word over the written word – and begins to flirt with the sung word in new ways.

In a tone quite different from that of historians, musicologists, and musicians who polemicize about where exactly samba and carnival were born, in 'Mangue' the poet declares: 'It was here that the Choros of Rio's carnivals first wailed' ('Era aqui que choramingavam os primeiros choros dos carnavais cariocas').[49] Given prior literary representations of the area as *over there*, the adoption of the adverb 'here' deserves notice. Bandeira's poetic voice provides the antithesis to exoticizing portrayals of the Mangue: it establishes an intimacy with the surrounding, personified hills – the frightened Pinto Hill – and in an autobiographical reference to the author's health condition, with the 'little houses so grounded where so many times oh lord I was a civil servant married to an ugly woman and died of pulmonary tuberculosis' ('casinhas tão térreas onde tantas vezes meu deus fui funcionário público casado com mulher feia e morri de tuberculose pulmonar').

Manuel Bandeira did indeed know the place well, and the verse above most likely alludes to his first-hand experience of the area's prostitution houses. Prostitution was the primary theme of Lasar Segall's album *Mangue*, and Bandeira's accompanying text the only to address the subject. The series included three woodcuts (Fig. 3), one lithograph with hand additions, and forty-two line block reproductions. Most date from the 1920s, and the album was published in 1944 in an edition of only 135 copies, also including texts by Mário de Andrade and Jorge de Lima. The Pernambucan poet's 'O Mangue' opens with an overview of the area's early history as a swamp, and quotes a description of the 1860 inauguration of the canal. After mocking the failure of Venetian pretensions and recounting how the area was chosen as Rio's prostitution centre by a republican chief of police, Bandeira launches into a passage where he details the rich musical scene:

> The Mangue had its great epoch then. The initial years of prostitution were a party every night. It was a city inside the city, with much light, much movement, much joy, and whoever wanted to know Brazilian popular music found it at its best [...] Such choro groups appeared there, such flutes, such cavaquinhos, such tambourines! [...] The women had all the freedom: they showed themselves in short shirts and low collars in the wide-open doors.

Reminiscing on the 1920s, Bandeira suggests a space operating with its own internal rules, separated from the daily doldrums of the rest of the city by the permissiveness, the music, and the women. His recollections exhibit little apparent regard for the women's welfare, as a contemporary reader might demand.

The fate of those women was the main preoccupation of Lasar Segall. Bandeira, evoking the language of the sacred, understands the painter's motivations as different from most others': 'Lasar Segall also did the pilgrimage [...] but what attracted him there was not the picturesque of

Figure 3   Original Engraving from O Mangue

the customs, it was not the flavour of popular music first-hand, nor the formidable Dionysiac unrestrainedness'. In this passage, Bandeira refers to the Mangue as *ali*, there but close by, instead of *lá*, over there. He proceeds, shifting the tone: Segall, 'a serious and grave soul, went there to ponder over the most solitary and anguished souls of that world of perdition, as he had already pondered over the most solitary and anguished souls of the Jewish world, over the victims of pogroms, over the third-class compartments of luxury transatlantic ships'.

Segall's *Mangue*, whether he was aware of it or not, represents another place of convergence in Brazilian culture – though it does not join the chorus of praising the country's miscegenation and supposed racial harmony. Jewish and black themes were early interests of the Lithuanian native, and both – separately – have occupied the attention of scholars of his work.

Lasar Segall, who moved to Brazil in 1923, himself Jewish, superimposes conditions of abandonment and destitution as he depicts his female subjects of the Mangue. There seems to be an ethnic ambiguity to many of the black-and-white representations: several of the women could be identified as either mulatas or blacks, or as Eastern European Jews.

Prostitution in the Mangue was in fact a space of convergence between Afro-Brazilians and Ashkenazi Jews: another aspect of the quarter's porosity, and perhaps one easier to attest than musical or other cultural exchanges. According to police and public health statistics from 1923 to 1924, about a third of the Mangue prostitutes were foreigners, approximately 70 per cent of whom were from Eastern Europe, compared to 40 per cent for Lapa. And although police records did not account for race, during the same period, the report of Betty Rice, a nurse from the United States, classifies nearly half of Mangue prostitutes as blacks or of mixed race (mestiças and pardas).[50]

At the start of the century, in noting the diversity of Jewish communities in the capital, João do Rio had written of how the number of 'loose women and pimps grows and grows' (1976: 297). He finds 'these people' living in the vicinity of the former Gypsy Field, today's Tiradentes Square. In *Numa e a Ninfa*, upon arrival in Rio de Janeiro's port, the Russian character Bogóloff must confront suspiciousness that he is neither a pimp nor an anarchist, revealing the types of expectations officials had of Eastern European immigrants. More specifically, Malamud expresses his distress over how in the second half of the 1920s the Praça Onze gained 'unpleasant and disturbing neighbours', and laments that an expressive number of Jews acted in that 'underworld' (1988: 81). Fridman dedicates a section of her book to Jewish involvement in prostitution (2007: 62–65).

The historian Beatriz Kushnir documents the lives of some of these women through their associations of mutual assistance. Her *Baile de máscaras: mulheres judias e prostituição* (Masquerade Balls: Jewish Women and Prostitution, 1996) takes a comparative look at 'spaces of sociability' in Rio de Janeiro, São Paulo, Santos, Buenos Aires, and New York, arguing that despite being integrated into local life, so-called 'polacas' (Poles) cultivated Jewish practices and a sense of identity, never fully assimilating. Segall's representations of the red-light district, likewise, seem preoccupied with imagining or attempting to express their subjectivities: the women often stare back at the viewer, and are not represented as objects of desire. Some seem jaded, others are faceless, some maternal, others hidden behind shutters. He portrays a mostly de-eroticized human landscape, evoking a pathos that contrasts with the sensuous forms and colours of Di Cavalcanti's Mangue, for example.[51]

In the 1930s, prostitution and its dramas became a recurrent theme in Brazilian literature as well, starting with Otávio Tavares's aptly titled *Mangue*, from 1933 (Tinhorão 2000–2: 60). Other important visual artists like Oswaldo Goeldi had also represented the red-light district in the mid-1920s.[52] The renowned engraver produced sombre woodcuts to illustrate a book entitled *O Mangue* by the journalist Benjamin Costallat, which remains unpublished. Yet when Bandeira introduces Segall's *Mangue*, he compares it not to one of its many counterparts in the visual arts, but to a poem by Vinicius de Moraes (1913–80). As he put it, 'another spirit of equally fraternal humanity'. The at once lyrical and unsettling 'Balada do Mangue' (Mangue Ballad) begins:

> Pobres flores gonocócicas
> Que à noite despetalais
> As vossas pétalas tóxicas!
> Pobre de vós, pensas, murchas
> Orquídeas do despudor
> Não sois Lœlia tenebrosa
> Nem sois Vanda tricolor:
> Sois frágeis, desmilingüidas
> Dálias cortadas ao pé
> Corolas descoloridas
> Enclausuradas sem fé,
> Ah, jovens putas das tardes
> O que vos aconteceu
> Para assim envenenardes
> O pólen que Deus vos deu?

> [Poor gonococcal flowers / That at night de-petal / Thy toxic petals! / Ye poor, dried-up, withered / Orchids of the unchaste / Thou art not tenebrous Lœlia / Nor a tricolour Vanda; / Thou art fragile, shrivelled / Dahlias cut off at the feet / Discoloured corollas / Cloistered without faith, / Oh, young whores of the afternoon / What happened to ye / To poison in this way / The pollen that God gave thee?]

The poem closes on a dramatic note, asking the women why '[you] did not set fire to the vests / And launched thyselves as torches / Against these men worth nothing / In this no-man's land!' ('Não ateais fogo às vestes / e vos lançais como tochas / Contra esses homens de nada / Nessa terra de ninguém!'). In that way, to Bandeira, Vinicius 'avenged the women of their social neglect'.

The visit to the red-light district had a profound impact on the man who went on to pen 'Garota de Ipanema' (Girl from Ipanema). Long before writing Bossa Nova classics, Vinicius had been a rather conservative Christian neo-symbolist. In a conversation years later, he recounts taking Waldo Frank (1899–1967) to a favela during the author's tour of Latin America in 1929. The visit was followed by an experience in the Mangue that Vinicius placed at the centre of a political awakening – if not a spiritual conversion – which in many ways became the task of his lifetime:

> The Day of St. George (Shango by syncretism) is very important in Rio, and we spent it in the street of the fiercest prostitutes. I saw crime and sexual degradation and poverty for the first time. It was also the gestation of one of my best-known poems, 'Balada do Mangue'. Within thirty days I was no longer a boy, no longer a citizen of the Upper Middle Class prepared by their priesthood to be a good rightist. I swung full circle. My vision was never the same again.[53]

Unlike Murilo Mendes, and especially Mário de Andrade and Manuel Bandeira – in other words, against the grain of modernist aesthetics – Vinicius de Moraes does not poeticize the Mangue through a language that befits its frequenters and locals. 'Balada do Mangue' adopts a noble, erudite, and antiquated language, using the second-person plural – *vós* – normally reserved in Brazilian Portuguese for the most formal circumstances.[54] It thus de-familiarizes and elevates the women: their tragedy becomes comprehensible only in terms of antecedents, encapsulated in the archaic poetic form of the ballad. At the same time, the poem alternates the musicality of seven-syllable verses and expressions of affection with scientific and technical terms related to botany or pathologies. This produces a type of estrangement also found in Lasar Segall's and Oswaldo Goeldi's engravings of the Mangue. Combining expressionist traits with techniques of traditional woodcuts from the north-east of Brazil, the two visual artists lent a similar effect to illustrations for Jorge de Lima's *Poemas Negros* (Black Poems) – in Segall's case – and in Goeldi's, to the covers of several works of regionalist north-eastern literature, much of it in a social realist mode, denouncing the harsh living conditions of the country's poorest.

Besides serving as a stage for universal dramas of exploitation and human dignity in the face of misery, Vinicius's Mangue, like Lasar Segall's, captures a particular social reality. The national, ethnic, and racial plurality of the Cidade Nova's dance halls, bringing together Russians, Jews, Afro-Brazilians, and even Japanese, extends to the prostitution zone. In 'Balada do Mangue' we find 'polacas' and we see 'Blonds mulatas french women' ('Louras mulatas francesas'). In Bandeira's 'Não sei dançar' (I can't dance), from

Libertinagem, the poetic voice rejoices at how 'The Japanese also dances maxixe'. The poem performs the assimilationist powers of the dance with a syncretic phrase merging the African 'acugêlê' with 'banzai', a traditional East Asian exclamation meaning 'ten thousand years'. Twice, as in a refrain, the poem hails the scene as 'Tão Brasil!', *so Brazil*.

Music and dance indeed constitute spheres of Brazilian life that allow for such porosity. At their best, these encounters might even fulfil the promises of cultural diversity and of the syncretism so often celebrated as a national feature. More frequently neglected, however, prostitution also provided an arena of Afro-Jewish interactions, bringing together two of Rio de Janeiro's most marginalized social groups. That too we must recognize as '*so Brazil*'.

Notes

1 Tin Pan Alley was at first associated with the area around West 28th Street between Fifth and Sixth Avenues, becoming a metonymy for the city's music industry until radio and the phonograph supplanted sheet music. On the subject, see Jasen 2003, and for the Jewish involvement, Kanter 1982.

2 Two books and at least one dissertation have been dedicated to the subject: Samuel Malamud's *Recordando a Praça Onze* (Remembering the Praça Onze, 1988), Fania Fridman's *Paisagem estrangeira: memórias de um bairro judeu no Rio de Janeiro* (Foreign Landscape: Memories of a Jewish Neighbourhood in Rio de Janeiro, 2007), and Paula Ribeiro's PhD dissertation, 'Cultura, memória e vida urbana: judeus na Praça Onze, no Rio de Janeiro (1920–1980)' (Culture, Memory and Urban Life: Jews in the Praça Onze in Rio de Janeiro (1920–1980), 2008).

3 For a history of Jewish immigration to Brazil, see Lesser 1995.

4 Born in 1908, Malamud arrived in Brazil from Bessarabia in 1923. His extensively researched memoir, which he deems a 'depoimento', or testimony, was first published in Yiddish, and later expanded into an edition in Portuguese.

5 As the area loosely demarcated as Cidade Nova fragmented into the neighbourhoods of Catumbi, Estácio, Santo Cristo, and Rio Comprido, the term falls into disuse among those who lived there, perhaps partly in reaction to the negative connotations that it had acquired. Praça Onze seems to have been prefered by residents, especially after consolidation of the Mangue as a red-light district. Malamud specifies that for Jews it denoted not just the square but also the surrounding streets (1988: 17), which seems to have been generally the case.

6 For a total of 2,697. We can only speculate as to the extent to which Jews had dispersed by 1940. In 1950, their percentage of the population in the parish dropped to 5.5 per cent (Fridman 2007: 91).

7 See Ribeiro 2008: 245–56. During disputes, offensive terms came out, though the worst insult anyone interviewed by Ribeiro remembers was a Jewish woman being called a 'gringa' (172). 'Pau-de-arara', however, is most often derogatory. These villas were enclosed cul-de-sac clusters of one-storey houses, laid out rectilinearly. Valladares discusses how Backheuser's 1906 report mentions 'vilas' being built in Rio since 1890 by 'Sr. Arthur Sauer' of the Companhia de

Saneamento, at the time benefiting 5,102 individuals of the 61,060 intended (49).

8 The article appeared in *O Globo*, 5 December 2000. When I had the chance to speak with Pinduca and Celi in June 2008 and again in January 2009, I heard some of the same anecdotes retold by the journalist. My questions about the presence of blacks and baianos in the neighbourhood seemed to catch them by surprise. Alas, their own 'Vila do Éden' – officially called Vila Dr Alberto Sequeira – had a Tia Carmem. By the 1940s and 50s, when they came of age, however, the number of Afro-Brazilians had declined considerably. It is also noteworthy how in the interview for *O Globo* Pinduca seeks to illustrate the lack of prejudice by stating he married not a black woman but a 'mulata'.

9 Interview given to the MIS, 24 August 1966.

10 On New York City, see Katz 2005. For a narrative that takes more journalistic liberties, see Asbury 1928. Although research for this book involved the perusal of countless sources in the press and literature, a more complete understanding of these relations in Rio would demand research that falls outside of its scope, including court transcripts and police records.

11 The brewery was started in 1888 by Joseph Villiger, an engineer who, according to *O Globo* (2 May 2011), was Jewish. By 1907, under different ownership, it was already the country's largest brewery. A study of the company focusing on data from 1925 to 1935 concludes that although Afro-Brazilians did not appear to suffer discrimination Brazilians in general did. See Melo, Araújo, and Marques 2003.

12 This may also be, aside from all else, a matter of scale: according to their respective censuses, around 36 per cent of New York City's population was foreign-born in 1920, 46 per cent of Buenos Aires's in 1909, 35 per cent of São Paulo's in 1920, and slightly less than 21 per cent of Rio de Janeiro's in the same year. It is also worth adding that in Rio 72.1 per cent of foreigners were Portuguese, reducing tensions or a sense of kinship based on language differences. Italians comprised 9.2 per cent of the foreign-born population, followed by 7.6 per cent Spaniards (*Recenseamento do Brazil* 1922–30: lix).

13 The alufá Assumano lived at 191 (Guimarães 1933: 65). In an appendix, Fridman catalogues the addresses of several establishments and institutions related to Jewish immigrants (123–8).

14 Nélio Galsky writes about the fact in 'Judeus do Catete', *Boletim ASA* (*Associação Scholem Aleichem*) 83 (July–August 2000). Incidentally, the term gafieira appears to come from the French *gaffe*, in an allusion to the supposed faux pax or blunders committed by the working class that attended them.

15 Cony recounts the episode in a column published in the *Folha de São Paulo*, 7 July 2008.

16 See Gottlieb 2004. The Jewish presence in New York City was on another scale, more comparable to the impact of Afro-Brazilians in Rio, which has in turn also inspired a lengthy bibliography. Jews were 29 per cent of New York City's population in 1920 whereas blacks comprised only 2.71 per cent, according to that year's census.

17 All research of the Jewish press was conducted in the Samuel Malamud Collection at the Arquivo Geral da Cidade do Rio de Janeiro, in the 'jornais' folder. The *O Novo Mundo* was located in the Cidade Nova, on Senador Eusébio Street. In the archival folder containing Malamud's family photographs, there is a picture from

the 1920s portraying an Anita Malamud wearing carnival costumes.

18　Information on Jacob derives from his 1967 interview recorded at the MIS. The waltz project, orchestrated for Radamés Gnattali, did not go through because of opposition from RCA Victor executives.

19　On the trip to France, see Bastos 2004, and on the Batutas more generally, Hertzman 2008. For an excellent analysis of the influence of Brazilian songs in that specific composition, see 'The Bœuf Chronicles', Thompson 2008.

20　Other scholars have attempted a revision of the revolutionary role ascribed to that generation. See Camargos 2007 and Prado 1983.

21　The Monroe Palace was demolished in 1976, amidst great controversy.

22　See Nonato and Santos 2000 and Kessel 2001. The demolition was also tied to the exhibitions commemorating the centenary of Brazil's independence.

23　See Menezes 1992 and Caulfield 2000b: 69.

24　The external wall of one Lapa's buildings until recently had a painted panel depicting illustrious bohemians from the neighbourhood's past, with its iconic arches (from an eighteenth-century aqueduct) in the background. There we found João do Rio, Rosinha, Villa Lobos, Noel Rosa, Manuel Bandeira, Madame Satã, Portinari, and Di Cavalcanti.

25　Populations according to censuses for each city: Berlin, 4,024,286 (1925); Paris urban area, 4,850,000 (1921); New York City, 5,620,048 (1920); and London, 7,386,848 (1921). Other Latin American capitals: Mexico City, 1,029,000 (1930); Buenos Aires, 1,582,884 (1914) and 2,415,142 (1936). São Paulo's population catapulted from 579,033 in 1920 to 1,326,261 in 1940.

26　Freyre would go on to pen one of the classics of Brazilian sociology, *Casa-grande & senzala* (1933). Holanda also went on to write a seminal book, the aforementioned *Raízes do Brasil* (1936).

27　Patrício Teixeira (1893–1972), a guitar player, teacher, singer, and composer whose name did not remain as much in evidence as his counterparts', was born in the Praça Onze. Orphaned at an early age, he began working as a pedlar and later gained notoriety participating in major recordings (Lopes 2006: 130). He also recorded an interview at the MIS in 1966.

28　Favela began to be used as a generic expression during that decade (Abreu 1994: 35). The Favela Hill was also settled by veterans of the Canudos campaign to repress a settlement in the interior of Bahia, centred on the messianic leader Antônio Conselheiro. See Valladares 2005. The campaign itself became a symbol of the republic's relationship to the region and to its more destitute peoples, generating the now classic account by Euclides da Cunha, *Os Sertões* (1902).

29　These categories have obvious socio-racial implications. Valladares explores the transition from cortiços to favelas as the space of poverty and social threats (2005: 24).

30　The text was first published in the *Correio da Manhã* (18 March 1924).

31　On the subject, see Archer-Straw 2000. Tarsila illustrated Cendrars's *Feuilles de route* (1924), including a drawing of the painting 'A Negra' in the cover. She accompanies him during carnival in Rio. The following year, incidentally, she also illustrates Andrade's *Pau-Brasil*.

32　Sevcenko quotes the letter (1992: 283). Tarsila also recorded an interview at the MIS in 1969.

33　There is no comparable data for the 1920s, but a census from the late 1940s finds that 36 per cent of favela residents were of mixed race, 35 per cent black and 29 per cent white (Valladares 2005: 65). Although much more Afro-Brazilian than the rest of the city – 71 per cent of which was white, according to the 1940 census – favelas were evidently not racially homogeneous. In a painting of similar style, 'Carnaval em Madureira' (1924), Tarsila depicts carnival in the suburban neighbourhood, again portraying only blacks.

34 Marinetti's unpublished diary of the trip, recounting the visit to the Favela, appears in Rocha and Schnapp 1996. On Cendrars in Brazil, see Amaral 1970 and Fauchereau 2010.

35 See, for example, the *Brazam Guide* (1927).

36 *Criouléus* derives from 'crioulo', which in Brazil signifies a black person and can be used pejoratively.

37 Besides attention to Rio's cultural geography, the choice of neighbourhood might betray concerns of another order: the open 'o' of Nova (pronounced *nóva*) also provides a convenient assonant rhyme with Conservatório.

38 See Roland 2000 and Nascimento 2008. 'O mestre-sala dos mares', a samba from the 1970s, honours the rebellion's leader, João Cândido, known as the 'almirante negro' (the black admiral). The lyrics by Aldir Blanc and João Bosco echo the poem, singing of 'a battalion of mulatas' greeting the sailor in the port.

39 That same year, Mário de Andrade published *Ensaio sobre a música brasileira*, on his way to becoming a pioneering ethnomusicologist. *Macunaíma* had a total of seventeen chapters and an epilogue. The book was dedicated to Paulo Prado. I consulted E. A. Goodland's 1984 translation.

40 In an interview around four decades later, Mário de Andrade's friend and art critic Antônio Bento de Araújo Lima – mentioned as one of the 'macumbeiros' at Tia Ciata's house – says that the author of *Macunaíma* met Pixinguinha in October 1926, while he was already working on the 'rhapsody', when the Carioca musician was in São Paulo to present his spectacle *Urubu* with the Teatro Negro (Andrade 1988: 64 n.). Tia Ciata had passed away in 1924.

41 Zungu, translated earlier as house, connoted both poverty and a ruckus. In his taxonomy of the different types of prostitution in Rio, Ferraz de Macedo ranks the prostitutes of 'zungús' as the lowest kind (1873: 82). His book – one of the first to focus on the subject – cites sambas as one of the causes of clandestine prostitution (132).

42 On the history of 'racial democracy', see Guimarães 2002: 137–68. Apparently coined in the 1940s by Roger Bastide, a French sociologist and student of Candomblé, the expression entered the mainstream of racial discourses. It has since been critiqued for hindering efforts to confront the country's largely race-based inequalities. The 'three races' refer to the mixture of European, Indigenous, and African elements, all present in *Macunaíma*.

43 The capital of Pernambuco was sometimes also called an American Venice – including in the title of a 1924 documentary which Bandeira might have seen – but Brazilian Venice was the more usual epithet. Another suitable interpretation may be that 'americana' gives the verse an assonance that would be lost with 'brasileira'.

44 The painter was twenty years his senior. They lived together as a married couple from the mid-1930s until the 1950s. Several of her letters to the journalist – who was also an art critic – have been published. See Amaral 2003.

45 On the relationship between the two, see Gardel 1996.

46 At least in the Iberian context, cheganças involved simulation of battles against the Moors, incorporating singing, dance, and dramatic re-enactments. On the assimilation of Christian cultural forms in Central Africa before the 1600s, see Heywood and Thornton 2007.

47 Ranchos incorporated Bahian traditions tied to the Christmas cycle, a process in which Pernambuco native Hilário Jovino de Almeida played a major role. See Cunha 2001: 212–16.

48 'Evocation of Recife' is part of a collection of Bandeira's poems translated by Candace Slater (Bandeira 1989). Here, as elsewhere, I have consulted that edition but made significant alterations, often opting for more literal translations over poetic effect.

49 In 'Sambistas', Bandeira writes about a composition that Sinhô claimed as his own but that existed before his time. The poet wisely avoids pinning down the genesis of the song form: '[the] nocturnal world of samba, an impossible zone to locate with precision' (Bandeira 1993: 463).

50 See Caulfield 2000a: 47–8.

51 See the catalogue *Poéticas do Mangue* (2012).

52 See his woodcuts in Ribeiro 2005.

53 Rodman 1974: 204. Frank also describes the occasion (1943: 25–8).

54 There are regional exceptions: the second person, common in Portugal, is also used in parts of the north and south of the country.

CHAPTER FIVE

Writing the 'Cradle of Samba': Race, Radio, and the Price of Progress

Carnival is no more no less than [to take] the street.

Donga[1]

Streets are an obsolete notion.

Le Corbusier, *The Radiant City*

I

After so many modernist artists and writers turned their attention to the Cidade Nova during the 1920s, the neighbourhood was no longer a central space only for marginalized social and ethnic groups. Its role in Rio de Janeiro's lettered cartographies as a place inhabited by the poor, as we have seen, had been cemented. But in the 1930s the Praça Onze assumed a privileged role in narratives that began to define samba as a national genre, and Brazil as 'the country of carnival'.[2] This was accompanied by an interconnected development, with equally nationwide implications: racial mixture, previously feared and condemned, became increasingly valued by social scientists, musicians, journalists, and others. The case of the Cidade Nova, in this context, can elucidate a contradiction that has not been properly studied: just as the idea of a national identity founded upon mixture gained prominence and acceptance in the 1930s and early 1940s, a combination of technological, urbanistic, and political forces led to a more divided city.

But let us not get ahead of ourselves, since none of this happened overnight. Through careful analysis of sources like magazines and newspapers, Maria Clementina Pereira Cunha (2001) has traced the construction of an equivalence between carnival and nationhood, unveiling the process through which it became legitimized and widely accepted by the 1920s. Not all carnival celebrations were created equally, however. After the Pereira Passos reforms, Rio de Janeiro's carnival split roughly along socio-geographic lines: the private masked balls of European pretensions, attended by the elites and held at places like the Municipal Theatre; the *corsos*, decorated motor cars parading down Rio Branco Avenue; and, depending on who you asked, the barbarian and anarchic gatherings of the 'dangerous classes' *or* the authentic and spontaneous expressions of Brazil's 'African' populations, in the Praça Onze.

The carnival of the Praça Onze became the most popular among the lower classes of Rio de Janeiro not only because of its symbolic status in the 'Little Africa', but due to the square's proximity to increasingly populous favelas lacking suitable public spaces and to the Central Station that connected it to the suburbs. Despite the shift of major political institutions away from the Cidade Nova, the neighbourhood remained well served by public transportation networks, easily reachable from several corners of the city.[3] The Praça Onze, as Muniz Sodré argues, 'became a convergence point for the poor populations of Mangueira, Estácio and favela, favouring the territorial expansion of carnival blocos and cordões, as well as *rodas de samba*'.[4]

The Praça Onze's importance to the development of Rio's music transcends carnival. Besides samba gatherings and parties held in the houses of the Bahian matriarchs, a public cargo scale – located behind the municipal school facing the square, named Escola Benjamin Constant in 1897 – provided a rare outdoor space where sambistas could congregate year-round. The composers Carlos Cachaça (1902–99) and Cartola (1908–80), among the founders of the Mangueira Samba School and Recreational Society in 1928, look back on it with nostalgia in their famous 'Tempos Idos' (Bygone Days), from 1968: 'A school in the Praça Onze / eyewitness / and near it a scale / where the malandros went to dance' ('Uma escola na Praça Onze / testemunha ocular / e perto dela uma balança / onde os malandros iam sambar'). To arrive in the Campo de Santana from Mangueira took a short three-and-a-half-mile train ride. It was not incidentally known as the 'first stop' (estação primeira) – and we can imagine the residents of that favela traversed the area around the public scale often. It might be safe to presume that its visibility, coupled with the presence of workers from the nearby port waiting in line to use the scale, both enlivened the scene and inhibited police repression of those who went there to sing and dance.[5]

Although there is a vast body of literature on the subject of carnival, few authors resist a celebratory or nostalgic tone when addressing the Praça Onze of the initial decades of the century: it has become known as the 'cradle of samba'. The suggestion is that this bedrock of Brazilianness owes itself to the Cidade Nova's public square. The process through which the Praça Onze obtained this mythic or symbolic status, however, demands a closer look. Its place in the imaginary of the time was far more complex, and its role in the etiology of modern Brazilian identity far more ambivalent, than previously assumed.

One of the first detailed descriptions of carnival in the Praça Onze can be found in the climax of Graça Aranha's *A viagem maravilhosa* (The Wonderful Journey). Graça Aranha (1868–1931) hailed from a wealthy family in his native state of Maranhão, in the north-east. He became a judge at an early age, and in 1902 produced the novel *Canaã*, a great publishing success. Stationed in Paris as a diplomat during the heyday of the avant-garde, Aranha has often been credited as the driving force behind the Modern Art Week of São Paulo, which he opened with a lecture entitled 'Aesthetic Emotion in Modern Art'. A member of the Brazilian Academy of Letters since its foundation in 1897, at the early stages of the movement the older and prestigious Aranha lent a type of validity to the modernists. His support and involvement with that generation was not uncontroversial, and in 1924 he resigned from the Academy of Letters.

Aranha's much-anticipated second novel *A viagem maravilhosa* came out in 1929 and was not well received by critics. The only reprint seems to be from 1930, and the book has been largely forgotten since. Its final pages, however, offer some of the most suggestive contemporary representations of the Praça Onze carnival:

> Some days later Carnival explodes below. Wonderment of noise [...] Black melopoeia, mellifluous, bewitching, Candomblé. Everything is an instrument, flutes, guitars, reco-recos, saxophones, tambourines, cans, harmonicas and trumpets. Instruments without a name invented suddenly in the delirium of improvisation, of musical impetus. Everything is a chant. (379)

The prose breaks down syntax to give an impression of the delirious atmosphere: all senses are mobilized, and *everything* becomes subjected to an entrancing cacophony. From simultaneous instruments played in dissonance some type of synchronicity arises. But there is even more at play in this passage: 'Inside the sounds and the colours the smells move, the black smells, mulato smells, white smells, smells of all hues' (379). Such smells are not unlike those that Murilo Mendes finds in the maxixe-playing dance halls of his 'Noite Carioca'. Both are part of a persistent association in the literature of the period between musical experiences and the olfactory sense; and, not coincidentally, at the cusp of a moment where radio and the phonographic industry would render the experience of popular music as no longer inseparable from a bodily presence in certain kinds of often crowded environments. Here, the way in which these smells are synaesthetically assigned to racial terms also reveals Aranha's long-standing theoretical interest in incipient discourses of Brazil as 'a land of three races'.[6]

In a treatise of great influence after its publication in 1921, *A esthetica da vida* (The Aesthetic of Life), the author explores the Brazilian 'soul' as a combination of Portuguese realism and melancholy, the 'perpetual childishness' of Africans, and the 'metaphysics of terror' of Indians (Aranha 1925: 87–9). What he calls 'barbarian metaphysics', a hereditary result of the 'savage psychic elements of the primitive races which formed the nation', must be subdued for the Brazilian soul to obtain an 'essential unity to the cosmos' (96). In the lengthy essay, Aranha offers a programme for his countrymen to surpass the legacies of 'barbarian' ancestors and nature in their spiritual formation, among other things calling for a subjugation of animality.

In *A viagem maravilhosa* these tensions are dramatized without much subtlety in the carnival of the Praça Onze, the exponent of the black and 'barbarian' elements in Brazil's character. If the passage quoted earlier invokes a multiracial milieu, the narrative soon begins to dwell on what Aranha considered the African, feminine, and primitive aspects of the scene:

> Carnival. Everything effeminates. Glory of women. She, for her and by her. Universal inversion. Female-men. Male-women. Ancestral return to the lunar cults, to the nocturnal mysteries [...] The black woman triumphs, the mulata triumphs. Music, fanfare, processions, maxixe, samba.

In the Bakhtinian inversion of carnival, the text draws a clear correlation between irrationality, women, and blackness. As for the aesthetic merits of what he hears, if the poet Manuel Bandeira praised the lyric qualities of Sinhô's song writing and Villa-Lobos appreciated popular music, this narrator does not hold it in high regard: 'Bandstand music. Drum. Endless singing, confused, of black mouths, abysmal. Plangent melopoeia for wretched words'. More than an eccentric position, this is a voice that reflected the opinions of many – if not most – among the intellectual elites.

The creators of that 'barbaric rhythm' in Aranha's narrative are not individuals but a mass of blackness, portrayed metonymically through copious lists of African-originated artefacts, ethnic denominations, and foods (Aranha 1925: 381). At the height of the frenzy that the text conjures, a group of women from Bahia dances sensually. Portrayed and perceived as sexual objects, they entice men whose description becomes increasingly zoomorphic. While 'dancing, singing [and] shaking around their thick black lustfulness', they are 'sniffed' and 'followed by brazen, excitable gorillas of long lips, playing tambourines, jumping lasciviously'. Despite the overtly racialized descriptions, in an indication that this is not an exclusively

Afro-Brazilian scene, we hear from a Portuguese immigrant who succumbs
to his animality just like the rest of those 'excitable gorillas': 'If we had
Bahian women in Portugal, I wouldn't have left'.

After the raucous vignette, an authorial voice interjects and proceeds to
elevate the baianas to a religious sphere. In an abrupt change of tone, it is
as if Aranha were consecrating the primitive carnival of the Praça Onze as a
legitimate expression of the Brazilian soul – from the height of his position
as a writer. Now the baianas 'raise their round, flared skirts and dance', but
'the sensuality is religious'. The rhythm of ranchos is a 'sacred, grave and
profound drama'. Rather than debased and raunchy, 'Carnival spiritualizes
itself', and 'in its immense fountainhead it receives the currents of beliefs,
of cults, that transform themselves in festivities'. The author turns his
attention to the carnival manifestations that frequently went unmentioned
in the city's press, which preferred to cover masquerade balls in private
clubs, or adorned motor cars parading down Rio's central boulevard. Here,
the place that Little Africa assumes in this sacralized vision of cultural
authenticity is as immanent as the passage's conclusion is explicit: 'Into [the
Praça Onze] also flow the chants and melodies of all the people of Brazil'.

Not all in an increasingly fragmented lettered city concurred with
Aranha's interpretation of the Praça Onze carnival – carefully constructed
in accordance with ideological and nationalist precepts, but enchanted
nonetheless. A writer from the *Jornal do Brasil*, presents a more sceptical
view, representative of contemporary accounts in the press: 'The carnival
of the Praça Onze is private to the Cidade Nova. And it has, for that reason,
attractions and motifs that are exclusively theirs'.[7] That same day, the
newspaper transcribed an invitation to a pre-carnival ball at a gafieira in the
Praça Onze, where the Triunfadores Carnavalescos intended to raise funds
for Belisário Joaquim Rodrigues, who was jailed and lacked the means to
defend himself. The article claimed the man in question was a murderer,
and reproduced the invitation as evidence of police omission, allowing the
'dangerous classes' to act freely and without repression. It goes on to cite
another example of violence: according to the paper, at the same dance
hall, a certain Vicente Leôni (an Italian?) murdered his lover and committed
suicide with two gunshots to the head, all while the festivities supposedly
went on unperturbed. The article declares: 'The macabre maxixe continued
until sunrise'.

The Praça Onze might have served very different purposes in each of
these three narratives. All, however, chose to emphasize a type of 'otherness'
rather than mixtures. The insistence on the baianas, for example, serves to
distort their actual numbers: like Jewish immigrants, Bahians comprised
a small proportion of the city's total population, 1.49 per cent according

to the 1920 census. The term baiana may well have been used loosely (as it sometimes is today), and it is probable that their visibility also owes to their traditional dresses being used as a costume during carnival. Graça Aranha, however, presents an African 'other' as transformed into Brazilian via Bahia: 'África. Bahia. Brasil.', he writes. That source of authenticity, nonetheless, still appears as if removed from the rest of the 'civilized' city, somehow immune to its everyday and exotic to the implied readers.

II

In the less than three years between *A viagem maravilhosa* and the *Jornal do Brasil* article, quite a bit changed in the country's political and carnivalesque landscape. Aranha's novel sides with the '18 of the Copacabana Fort', the first in a series of revolts led by unsatisfied young lieutenants seeking various types of military and social reforms. Felipe, the character closest to incarnating the author, identifies himself as a communist and deems capitalism a form of oppression. The villain, Radagásio, 'order-loving' and ambitious but ultimately a parasitic arriviste, embodies the values and hypocrisies of the First Republic. Aranha's blunt attacks of the 'old order' in some ways anticipate the so-called Revolution of 1930, partly the consequence of dissatisfaction signalled in lieutenant revolts dating from the Copacabana Fort in 1922.[8] With president Washington Luís and the ruling coffee oligarchies further weakened by the stock market crash of the previous year, the *gaúcho* Getúlio Vargas (1882-1954) ascends to power in a military coup in 1930, breaking the grip of Minas Gerais and São Paulo on the presidency.

Barring an interval from 1945 to 1951, Vargas would not relinquish the office until his suicide. During his regime, the country underwent profound changes, including an accelerated industrialization of the economy, a centralization of the nation state, and the establishment of workers' rights – earning him the epithet of 'father of the poor'. A towering and polarizing figure, he presided as a dictator in his first term, and as an elected official after 1951. Brazil's longest serving president, Vargas became a fixture in popular culture during his time, and a subject of countless works of scholarship since.[9]

Meanwhile, in 1932, the newspaper *O Mundo Sportivo* introduced another change of lasting consequence – one that evidently does not draw comparable attention from political histories, but that had significant repercussions nonetheless. Under the helm of Mário Filho (1908-66), the newly established sports daily institutionalized an until then sporadic practice, treating carnival parades as competitive affairs.[10] Thus officially begins the era of the *escola de sambas*, literally samba schools, or associations that also function as clubs. Most researchers and sambistas consider the Deixa Falar in the Estácio neighbourhood the first of these organizations: its founders called themselves a 'school' in jest, since they considered themselves teachers, and because of a nearby Escola Normal. Ismael Silva, one of its leaders, spoke of being motivated to organize as a group out of the desire not to be beaten up by the police.[11] Regardless of technical differences between the Deixa Falar and existing ranchos, the contribution of these sambistas from Estácio had far more to do with innovations in musical form than with the organization of carnival parades (Sandroni 2001).

In the late 1920s, newspapers promoted a fad of contests related to carnival (Ferreira 2004: 274–5). Speaking about these events decades later, some Mangueira founders attempt to diminish the role of outsiders. They pinpoint the beginnings in a contest held in the Praça Onze, with the help of a 'turk' (meaning someone of Middle Eastern perhaps even Jewish descent) who let them expose trophies in his storefront.[12] The turning point, however, came after the fall of the First Republic. The carnival of 1931, the first after Vargas seized the presidency, was considered 'weak' by the press, marked by a dry law and the seeming exhaustion of previous forms of organizing the festivities (Ferreira 2004: 342) – counter-intuitive though it may sound to 'organize' carnival. Noticing the opportunity, the following year the *Mundo Sportivo* coordinated the parades of the escolas de samba. The event took place in the Praça Onze, and represented a watershed Rio carnival. Mangueira – the school Cartola and Carlos Cachaça helped create – emerged as the winner. They would win again in 1933, when newspapers estimated that 40,000 people accompanied the parades in the Praça Onze (345).

Besides the creativity of its members and the acuity of Mário Filho, the 'samba schools' benefited from the institutional support of Pedro Ernesto, appointed by Vargas as Rio de Janeiro's mayor in September 1931. In 1934, the event honoured the mayor and was held in the Campo de Santana. The following year the parades were made official and the escolas received financial support from the government (Costa 2007: 223). They were once again held at the Praça Onze, and remained there until the inauguration of the President Vargas Avenue in 1944. Carnival and samba had gone a long way since the backyards of the tias, and were now on the way to becoming a major industry directly involving tens of thousands of participants, capturing the eyes and ears of the nation every February or March. Previously looked down upon and even persecuted, these Afro-Brazilian expressions now unequivocally belonged in the public sphere, and were definitively incorporated into Brazil's image of itself and to the world. The song 'Tempos Idos' alludes to the impending transformations: 'It no longer belongs to the square / it's no longer samba from the terreiro / victorious it left for foreign lands' ('Já não pertence mais a Praça [Onze] / Já não é samba de terreiro / vitorioso ele partiu para o estrangeiro').

Not all samba admirers approved of the role ascribed to carnival and the prestige acquired by the genre – even among those who most probably gained from its rising prominence there was discomfort and criticism. Francisco Guimarães's *Na roda do samba* (1933), for example, expresses a prescient concern that samba's popularization among the cultural elites represented a threat to its authenticity and vigour. Its author, a journalist best known as Vagalume, witnessed the genre's early days in the 'old New City', 'where almost always balls took place in the living room and a mellow samba in the backyard' (Guimarães 1933 :43). Partaking in discourses of Rio as a divided city, he pushes the image even further. Only half jokingly, Vagalume suggests the image of not only two cities but of two separate countries entirely: writing about the poet, performer, and musician Eduardo das Neves (1874–1919), he declares that in the 'roda de samba, Eduardo always belonged to the Cidade Nova, because he considered himself a *foreigner* over there towards Botafogo' (97).[13]

Vagalume, who identified himself as a black man like Neves – the 'black artist that so greatly honoured the race to which I belong with pride' (81) – very clearly takes sides. He resents that 'samba was adopted in "chic" circles' (22), and that while 'in the past it was repudiated, mocked, ridiculed' today 'it is already well regarded by the men of letters, the poets, theatre writers, and even some of the immortals from the Academy of Letters!' (32). As if to distance it from the literary classes, he locates an origin in a past of purity, 'with no ambition of gold' (121), where sambas were created in mythic morros and became known only after they descended to Tia Ciata's house (117) and to the Praça Onze during carnival (218).

It is hard to ascertain whether Vagalume directed his criticism to anyone in particular. Donga speaks about occasions where Praça Onze musicians and distinguished writers got together to recite poetry and improvise sambas 'until dawn'.[14] Besides other examples we have seen, authors like Oswald de Andrade resorted to quoting popular songs in ambitious texts like his 'Manifesto Antropófago' (Cannibal Manifesto, 1928).[15] *Na roda do samba* at times strikes a protective tone that would characterize the approach of later intellectuals and journalists to popular culture: 'let the poets come, but they must respect the tradition' (178). Sambistas themselves, however, never seemed overly concerned with a threat from the lettered city, and in fact many lyrics suggest a two-way street.

While poets like Oswald de Andrade or Bandeira sought vitality in the vernacular, popular songwriters were quick to wear the mantle of

Poetry. Whether or not this type of reference can be understood as an expression of the porosity between popular and erudite in Brazilian music, the fact remains that sambistas not uncommonly sang themselves as poets: Noel Rosa in 'Palpite Infeliz' (Unhappy Remark), for example, draws no distinction between the two métiers: 'to make a poem over at Vila [Isabel] is child's play / even the trees dance to the sounds of samba' ('fazer poema lá na Vila é um brinquedo / Ao som do samba dança até um arvoredo'); in other famous verses, the Mangueira composer Nelson Cavaquinho and his partner Guilherme de Brito sing about the high regard in which the favela held poets like them: 'In Mangueira / when a poet dies / everybody cries. / I live at ease in Mangueira because / I know someone shall cry when I die' ('Em Mangueira / quando morre / um poeta / todos choram. / Vivo tranqüilo em Mangueira porque / Sei que alguém há de chorar quando eu morrer').

Vagalume's discontent with the state of samba, however, pointed to another incipient change of far greater consequence, brought about by the development of radio, the recording industry, and ensuing professionalization. In the late 1930s, radios became increasingly affordable to working-class families, and in 1945 an estimated 85 per cent of households in Rio de Janeiro and São Paulo owned one (McCann 2004: 23). The recording industry experienced a similar boom, with multinational corporations establishing local affiliates in the late 1920s, importing expensive technologies and able to invest in national distribution (25). Both industries were largely based in Rio de Janeiro and, unlike smaller Latin American countries, featured mostly national music. The radio, to an extent, became an arena of competing cultural projects within the Getúlio Vargas government. Yet, as Bryan McCann's *Hello, Hello Brazil* demonstrates, while the regime was able 'to carry out effective projects of cultural and civic persuasion', popular music 'proved relatively impervious to direct bureaucratic manipulation' (21).

As well as a stricter concept of authorship that hinged on copyright and a higher degree of professionalism among sambistas, the dissemination of songs through radio altered in fundamental ways the everyday experience of music. With the new medium, corporal presence, and along with it cultural geography, were much less integral: one no longer needed to be at a crowded house or in the sweat-filled dance halls of particular neighbourhoods in order to listen to samba. It could be done from home. It could be done in *more* homes, spread around the city and the country. And in that sense the musical forms gain in mobility, but the individual's experience is not conditioned by a physical relocation. Terms like samba and maxixe, for example, would no longer be indissoluble from the act of dance, increasingly referring only to musical genres and independent from bodily practices. Samba or maxixe no longer implied an 'event' that presupposed one's participation: rather, we are en route to what Guy Debord would call 'society of the spectacle'.[16]

Radio adds yet another stratum to processes of cultural transmission and circulation, another layer of cognitive mappings superimposed on those produced and projected by a lettered city. These must be understood as interrelated, and the dynamics are forever altered – radio, requiring equipment though not literacy, accelerates the speed at which cultural artefacts (a rhythm, a song, an idiom) travel in very immediate and evident ways. Products of cultural fermentation and assimilation that had taken shape over generations, involving transatlantic and inter-state diasporas, now moved across airwaves almost instantly, and could reach previously isolated backlands. If the city itself arguably enables an intensification of social encounters and cultural exchanges by grouping people of various backgrounds in concentrated spaces, an acceleration of these processes shaped by new technologies set off an unprecedented chain of reactions, with consequences that have preoccupied all kinds of commentators, from journalists like Vagalume to theorists like Marshall McLuhan.[17]

The new medium's political potential did not escape the attention of Brazilian government officials any less than elsewhere in the world: Lourival Fontes, the director of the Departamento de Propaganda e Difusão Cultural (Department of Propaganda and Cultural Diffusion) (DPDC), displays such awareness in a 1936 interview, exhorting his compatriots not to 'underestimate the work of propaganda and culture undertaken on the radio … it is enough to say that radio reaches where the school and the press do not, to the farthest points of the country, to the understanding of illiterates' (McCann 19). Radio deals a blow to the written word's near monopoly on the dissemination of 'official' Rio-centric or urban-centric information, produced from a centre that stood as a physical and familiar place in the mental maps of recipients. To a wider and partly rural audience, the music and news originated from the nation's capital, an almost off-mapped abstraction to listeners spread around the country. We may say that radio fractures the lettered city even further, to the point of rendering the metaphor outdated. If Manuel Antônio de Almeida wrote while having readers familiar with Rio de Janeiro in mind, radio spoke to a nation of continental proportions.

At the same time, considering how much samba's development owes to the milieu of the Cidade Nova, to a cognizant observer the peripheral neighbourhood again finds itself as a type of accidental centre: not only geographically, as in the nineteenth century, but as the place out of which a now at once national and cosmopolitan musical form radiates. In 1935, Arthur Ramos attempts to articulate the processes at hand:

But the 'malandro', the 'mulato bamba', the 'crioula', and the 'moreninha' are no longer content only with the Praça Onze. They took over the Avenue during Carnival; they invaded broadcasting; inspired popular composers; seized with excitement the city, all of Brazil [...] Continental syncretism completed the work. (Ramos 1935: 146)

Although – as we have seen – the Praça Onze's role in the formation of Rio's popular cultures owed a great deal to its interconnectedness relative to other parts of the city, Ramos, like Aranha, privileges the notion of a heterotopic space. To read Ramos retell it, these archetypal street characters, listed inside quotation marks, are all of a sudden no longer restricted within the Praça Onze's confines: to him, it as if they are woken up from an ancestral slumber and isolation to take over the capital and country, thanks to the annual carnival and new technologies.

Arthur Ramos (1903–49), an Alagoas-born physician who started out in forensic medicine, moved from Salvador da Bahia to Rio de Janeiro in 1934, where he would teach social psychology at the Universidade do Distrito Federal and head the Orthophrenology and Mental Hygiene section of the Instituto de Pesquisas Educacionais (Institute of Educational Research) (IPE). Among several other programmes the Instituto created, one by Anísio Teixeira explored radio and cinema as a means of spreading basic lessons about health and education to the interior, reaching 'illiterate and unfit individuals' before they moved to the cities (Dávila 2003: 36).

One of Brazil's most active and renowned intellectuals during the 1930s and 40s, Ramos was the first to attempt to write about the Praça Onze from the perspective of a social scientist. Quoted above, his *O folk-lore negro do Brasil: demopsychologia e psychanalise* (Black Folklore of Brazil: Demopsychology and Psychoanalysis) integrated a series of influential studies on similar subjects by the author, one of which was translated into English as *The Negro in Brazil* (1939) within just a few years of the original. His books have for the most part been out of print since they were first published. Ramos became associated with the rhetoric or ethos of 'racial democracy', like his contemporary Gilberto Freyre. In this work he sought 'a method of scientific exploration of the collective unconscious [of blacks]' (Ramos 1935: 12). Ramos proposes a confrontation of racial prejudices in the very preface, setting out to compensate for the lack of studies of blacks in Brazil and condemning the deliberate destruction of slavery records after abolition.[18]

Just as the culture shaped in the Cidade Nova and surrounding neighbourhoods like the Gamboa, Estácio, and Mangueira became increasingly affected by new technologies and by the entertainment industry, Ramos sought to explore its putative role as a repository of ancient and 'primitive' African practices: a place of totemic ceremonies, war and hunting dances, and sexual rites whose meanings had been lost, but that the author as an ethnologist claimed to recover. 'The Praça Onze, in Rio de Janeiro, has kept many African traditions', he writes (135). The need to clarify that the square is in Rio de Janeiro reinforces how Ramos was not addressing a local or even a contemporary public, but rather wrote self-consciously from within an academic tradition, to which he envisioned his work as a long-lasting contribution. It is a different mode, then, from those of novelists, musicians, travel writers, or journalists who we have been reading until now.

Like Vagalume, Ramos inverts the chronology and echoes the nascent truism that samba was born in the favelas, where it ostensibly remained hidden and untouched until the samba schools brought it down to the Cidade Nova: 'carnival unearthed samba from the hills', he writes, and 'the Praça Onze began to witness that which had until then been hidden in ignored recesses' (146). Whereas samba synthesizes a number of disparate musical traditions, Ramos reinforces the notion that its value derives from some type of purity found in the 'isolated' favelas. The institutionalization of parades, he suggests, undermines that 'purity', leading to a now worn-out assumption, still oft repeated, that 'samba began to be stylized in the escolas de samba' (147).

The Praça Onze's sudden fame and prominent role in the cartographies of cultural and intellectual elites is owed almost entirely to carnival. Ramos concludes his *O folk-lore negro do Brasil* by invoking the public square during the celebrations. The relevance of the passage to our study, as well as the difficulties of finding the book today, justify the lengthy quotations:

> Every year the Praça Onze de Junho, in Rio de Janeiro, receives an avalanche of this collective catharsis. There, carnival is only a pretext. [...] Carnival is a spectral vision of the 'culture' of a human group. The civilized explode their repressed instinctive life. But the primitive merely shows itself in his original spontaneity. It is the case with the Praça Onze, a conglomerate of an entire ancestral unconscious. There, the old images of the black continent, which were transplanted to Brazil, are periodically united.

These catharses might be collective and involve whites as much as blacks, but underlying Ramos's text we can identify a rigid racial dichotomy: on the one hand, 'primitive', 'spontaneity', 'ancestral', and 'old' are associated with descendants of the 'black continent'. Theirs is a culture in quotes. On the other hand, the instincts that need to be 'repressed' in daily life and the 'civilized' are grouped under an implicit, normative whiteness.

Unlike many other contemporary theorists of race, in Brazil and beyond, Arthur Ramos did not subscribe to the tenet that blacks were innately inferior. In a 1934 pamphlet meant to be distributed among parents of children in Rio's school system, he writes of how 'there are no superior or inferior races. But there are social groups that are culturally advanced or retarded' (Dávila 2003: 39). In that context, his descriptions leave clear which social practices are to be considered less advanced, and they conform to his theory of Afro-Brazilian culture as pre-logical. The influences of macumba and fetishism, he argues elsewhere, are an impediment against 'true scientific values' and should be combated through educational policy (40).

An interrelated but latent binary in Ramos's text proves to be even more revealing: the racial framework extends to how urban spaces are internalized. Ancestral African practices are encountered in the margins, favelas, or the Praça Onze during carnival. And, fittingly, by metonymy, 'avenues' will signify the modernized centre, as well as those more civilized upper-class neighbourhoods. This functions like a precursor to the post-Fordist use in Brazil of 'asphalt' to denote the non-favela city. It should not be deemed a coincidence, incidentally, that the vast majority of Vargas-era educational and political elites lived in the South Zone (78–9).

In Ramos's account, we read that 'the reveller from the avenues goes by that place and does not comprehend what he sees'. To him, the Praça Onze is the space where two poles meet and temporarily overlap, but the intrepid outsider who frequents the square once a year during carnival remains oblivious to all of its obscure codes. The author, then, positions himself as the informed interlocutor, hovering above, able to explain this exotic 'other' through the trained lenses of the scientist. 'But the ethnographer goes on registering', he writes. It is a subject that lies *lá*, over there, at the margins of lettered cartographies: amidst 'war and hunting ceremonies', where 'blacks exchange blows, carrying weapons, brandishing spears, dancing imitative pantomimes'. Carnival becomes a realm of 'totemic parades', of 'magical-religious fragments' found in 'macumba chants, in invocations, the preliminary rehearsals of "possession"' pervading the music and dance (Ramos 1935: 270).

As far-fetched as some of these associations might seem today, Ramos was positioning himself at the forefront of discourses not only in ethnography but also in psychoanalysis. His text frequently deploys concepts being developed in those disciplines to analyse the Praça Onze:

It is a phantasmagoria. Over an absolutely restricted period of time, we see the recapitulation of a whole collective life. Institutions that fragment, splinter, and are diluted. Their remainders are collected by the Praça Onze. A great grinder, a gigantic millstone, the Praça Onze elaborates the unconscious material and prepares it for entrance in 'civilization'. The Praça Onze is the censor of the black-African unconscious. The whole work that we find there is similar to the oneiric elaboration (*Traumarbeit*): condensations, symbolism, disguises, sublimations, derivations.

In Part VI of *The Interpretation of Dreams* (1900), Freud adopts the term 'Traumarbeit', translated as Dream Work, to describe the mechanisms involved in dreaming and its latent meanings. If dreams to him function as an interface between conscious and unconscious processes, the Praça Onze to Ramos functions as an interface between 'primitive' and 'civilized' Brazil – it is where the pre-logical African heritage filters into the modern world. The Praça becomes not only the 'censor' of 'the black-African unconscious' but the buffer between a lingering Brazil of the past and the desired country of the future.

As for the actual neighbourhood, with a culture and daily life evidently not limited to carnival, it becomes erased, in a sense, as its main square is transformed into a mythic place. Removed in time and space from the rest of the city, it is elevated (or reduced) to a symbol of the racial mixtures that characterize the country. That process is clear when Ramos pluralizes the Praça Onze, imagining similar squares throughout Brazil:

> The Praça Onze is the frontier between black culture and white-European culture, a frontier without precise boundaries, where institutions interpenetrate and cultures alternate. But the Praça Onze, for its part, is a symbol of all the Praças Onze disseminated by the focal points of black culture in Brazil. [...] [This] folkloric unconscious is a synthesis of an ancestral unconscious and of the inter-psychic unconscious. It is a structural content, a *Paideuma*.

The reference to Leo Frobenius's term 'Paideuma' – coined by the German ethnologist to describe a gestalt, the creation of meaning typical of certain social structures – suggests the Praça Onze carnival as the supreme and most significant expression of Brazil's black population. Yet Arthur Ramos's study culminates with the image of mixture in an urban environment, and it joins a wave of studies – particularly those of Gilberto Freyre – celebrating miscegenation as a valuable trait of Brazilian society.[19]

Seeking to privilege environment and culture over race, Ramos participated in new trends that sought to disprove the perceived inferiority of non-white Brazilians (Dávila 2003: 8). His vision of inter-penetrating cultures and fluid borders, however, must be detached from contemporary appreciation of plurality and hybridity, and should not be mistaken with the modernist search for authenticity or artistic inspiration in the 'primitive'. Rather, in the discourses and practices of social scientists and doctors at the time, racial mixtures were often conceived as a means of diluting the 'other', a solution to the problems of a country thirsty for modernity, but held back by large number of Afro-descendants – and, lest us forget, by the much smaller number of Jews, increasingly a target in the late 1930s.

Regardless of the array of divergent agendas and strategies among proponents of Brazil's miscegenation as a positive national feature, while these views entered the mainstream, carnival emerged as a showcase of socio-racial harmony, and the Praça Onze as its epicentre. By 1939 – in quite a departure from the *Jornal do Brasil* article seven years earlier – the weekly illustrated magazine *O Cruzeiro* claims the square's festivities as a 'choreographic parade of exotic types, a mixture of races and classes in the collective celebration of joy. Apotheosis of racial mixing [mestiçagem], carnival without prejudice'. Similarly celebratory statements, with striking lack of nuance, proliferate in the local press and among intellectuals. Not much later, the Portuguese poet, pedagogue, and publicist João de Barros (1881–1960) published a glossy volume on Brazil's resources, history, and tourist attractions where he praises 'the mixture, the heterogeneity of the people, of [social] layers, of nationalities' (1938: 203).

João de Barros, a friend of João do Rio and an enthusiast of Luso-Brazilian relations, had been elected to the Brazilian Academy of Letters in 1920. In his excursion to the Praça Onze, he highlights the 'marvellous spectacle of colour, animation and music' in the ranchos, and reiterates the notion of the square as heterotopic, a space unlike others but that nonetheless synthesizes the country. To the author it has a 'different' aspect. Amidst an environment of 'singular ecstasy' and 'unmatchable joy', he finds 'mixed up in the same maddening, infernal happiness, baianas in their picturesque dresses [...] Indians dressed in multi-coloured feathers, and washerwomen from Minho with their characteristic clothing' (204). These descriptions testify to carnival's plurality, and as in prior accounts there seems to be a dialectic between the Praça Onze as 'other' and 'familiar' operating here. In other words, writers experience the frenzy through particular filters and tend to recount it according to their own interests or the perceived interests of their readers, projecting desires and biases. While the scholar of 'black folklore' highlights what he identifies as remnants of African rituals, João de Barros notes the women with traditional wear of Minho, from his native Portugal.

Barros proves to be a useful source, and not only to corroborate the apparent super-human disposition of revellers who 'could not be defeated by fatigue or the need to sleep'. He notes the square's location near the Central Station, 'which unloads thousands of people coming from the suburbs' by train. Historians have discovered that a significant influx of suburban residents during carnival dates back to the end of the nineteenth century, based on passenger records (Soihet 2008: 66). Barros allows us to paint a more complete picture, one that helps to explain incongruences in the data: many people spent their nights in the square, and only returned to their homes after the four days of partying were over.

Beyond seeing their main public square flooded with people for four consecutive days (and perhaps partaking in the festivities), it is hard to determine how life changed for Cidade Nova denizens during the other eleven months of the year. With the heart of the neighbourhood solidified in lettered cartographies as the site of Brazil's most 'African' expression, it might be a cause of surprise that the percentage of self-identified blacks in the district containing the Praça Onze declined to numbers well below the city's average. According to the 1940 census, 11.3 per cent of Rio de Janeiro's total population declared itself as black, and 17.3 as pardo (mixed), compared to only 4 per cent and 9.8 per cent in the Santana district, respectively. Census statistics, then, contradict the expectations created by Little Africa's place in Rio's cultural geography. During the interwar period, suburbs and favelas appear to have concentrated population growth among the city's Afro-Brazilians.[20]

As Rio de Janeiro's population reached 1,759,277 in 1940, the uneven racial distribution of its population was accompanied by several gender imbalances. Although the city as whole was balanced (50.3 per cent of males), the Santana district had 12,342 men compared with only 7,948 women, which we can infer to be a result of greater numbers of male foreign immigrants. In another population shift, neighbourhoods like Copacabana now had disproportionate numbers of black women (6,719 versus 2,410 men), who presumably moved to the up-and-coming South Zone areas to serve as domestic servants in upper-class residences. It appears that the sons and daughters of immigrants who settled in the Cidade Nova were displacing Afro-Brazilians who had lived there earlier, although the neighbourhood continued to receive newly arrived Europeans. While approximately 38 per cent of the Santana district was inhabited by foreigners according to the 1906 and 1920 censuses, that number only declined to 36 per cent in 1940, even as the capital's foreign-born now totalled merely 12 per cent of the population (versus more than a quarter in 1906 and a fifth in 1920). Despite the fact that differences along social and ethnic lines were reflected in the city's spatial distribution, Rio de Janeiro gave several travellers the impression of a city without racial barriers. In a sense, the impression was justified, particularly in comparison with other major cities with near exclusive ethnic quarters: because of the several geographic accidents and settlement of hills, areas with disparate real estate values and living conditions remained in close proximity. Their residents in many cases shared the same public spaces. In a diary kept during his first trip to Brazil, in August 1936, Stefan Zweig (1881–1942) notes about the streets of Rio 'the same extraordinary miscegenation which will be confirmed to me as the most extraordinary thing of our times: the absolute absence of prejudice among the races – an observation I already make at a first glance' (1993: 170). Perhaps at a second glance the Austrian writer might have observed that this apparent lack of prejudice manifests itself chiefly among the lower classes or the socially marginalized, more racially mixed than the sometimes pardo but rarely black elites.

Zweig, one of the best-selling writers of the 1920s and 30s, would go on to author *Brazil: A Land of the Future* (1941). An enthusiastic tribute to the country's economic and human potential, published in several languages, the book repeatedly extols how all races 'live together in total harmony', contrasting this 'free and unrestrained intermixing' to tensions and divisions found elsewhere (Zweig 2000: 10). Amidst the impressions that led the author later to develop a utopian view of racial harmony in Brazil, it becomes clear through descriptions from his diary that the Mangue played a crucial and formative role:

> This Yoshiwara [red-light district in Tokyo] of Rio is unbelievable [...] women are displayed as in a storefront [...] a colourful mixture like I have never seen. Black women, dark as the night [...] look on dryly and indifferently like wooden statues; Frenchwomen with make-up, wearing skimpy blouses of garish colours or provocative shorts sing and scream, enticing clients; Jews from Eastern Europe promise the most exciting perversities; and, among them, the mulatas in all hues of milk-and-coffee; around five hundred women [...] as an illustration of all races and classes. (1993: 170)

The visit, narrated as fascinating, disturbing, and unforgettable in the diary, reappears in *A Land of the Future* in a passage that the author more or less buries under a section on 'things that will perhaps be gone tomorrow' (179). Hypothesizing that the Mangue 'will soon fall victim to civilizing ambition', he introduces it in the book as 'the one stretch of street that is not discussed' (179). Although off the map, as we have seen, the red-light district was no secret to the city's cultural elites, and it is somehow fitting that a foundational vision of Brazil's 'racial democracy' occurs based on an experience there: 'to us [Europeans]', he writes in the diary, 'the most impressive is the total mixture, the absence of preoccupations with any idea of race, so characteristic of this country. Blacks choose whites, whites go up to blacks, the street vibrates with intense activity' (170).

Zweig, himself of Jewish descent, explored the Mangue in the company of his editor Abrahão Koogan, a Ukranian-born Jew who arrived in Brazil in 1912. In a diary entry that he wrote en route to South America after departing from Lisbon, Zweig – who had attempted to maintain his anonymity among fellow passengers – remarks that only the Jewish immigrants travelling in third class interested him, amidst that 'monotonous atmosphere'. One of them recognized him as the 'greatest writer'. Once in the tropics, the author garnered considerable attention from authorities and the general public – and, likewise, there is quite a bit more that attracts his interest. When Zweig returns to the Cidade Nova after his visit to the red-light district, it is not to see the heart of the Jewish neighbourhood: 'At night, once again to the Mangue, where some musicians play Brazilian music' (177). For all we know he might have seen a show played by someone like Luiz Gonzaga (1912–89). The Pernambuco native and future 'King of Baião' (a rhythm from the north-east) began his artistic life in the capital by performing with his accordion in the red-light district.[21]

Once more, it is in the spheres of prostitution and popular music (and the two often went hand in hand) that Rio de Janeiro offered scenes permitting a visitor like Zweig to praise 'how the races mix among themselves with naturalness', in reference to people dancing at the 'clube Elite' (178). According to annotations in his diary, Brazil's best black musicians were asked to play due to his visit. The flautist and the *ganzá*, a percussive instrument, impressed Zweig. Among those 'macumba musicians' he intuitively senses how 'ancient motifs are impetuously mixed with new elements' (178). The Elite club in question was a famous gafieira of the 1930s, located in Frei Caneca Street by the Campo de Santana. Despite the reduced number of Afro-Brazilians inhabiting the neighbourhood, it is still in the Cidade Nova that we find many of Rio's spaces of multiracial sociability: the carnival of the Praça Onze, the red-light district, and the dance halls.

III

A notable pacifist during the First World War, along with others like French writer Romain Rolland, Stefan Zweig had left Austria in 1934, after Hitler's ascent to power. He lived in England and the United States before moving to Brazil in 1940, where he committed suicide less than two years later. The country Zweig hailed as the land of the future was by no means immune to the rising tide of Nazi fascism in Europe. On 30 September 1937, some four months before the scheduled presidential elections, sectors of the government denounced a communist plot given the name of 'Plano Cohen'. It would be used to justify the establishment of Getúlio Vargas's authoritarian Estado Novo (Silva 1980). The plot was forged, most probably by the fascist-influenced ultra-nationalist *integralistas*, congregated around the Ação Integralista Brasileira (AIB), a political party counting among its leaders Plínio Salgado (1895–1975), a writer who had been involved in the Modern Art Week of São Paulo.

The founding of the AIB in 1932 coincides with attention in the Brazilian press to the 'Jewish problem' (Martins 1992: 93–4). Rather than fear that they would hold the country back, attacks on Jewish immigrants focused on their supposed inability to join the mix. In his eugenicist *Raça e Assimilação* (Race and Assimilation), Oliveira Viana concluded that the 'Jewish group is infusible' (1932: 84). Viana would be elected as a member of the Brazilian Academy of Letters in 1937, and although his racial theories are challenged in later years they were by no means exceptional in the 1930s.[22] Henry Ford's *The International Jew* appeared in a Portuguese translation in 1933, and Anor Butler Maciel's suggestively titled *Nacionalismo: o problema judaico no mundo e no Brasil: o nacional socialismo* (Nationalism: The Jewish Problem in the World and in Brazil: National Socialism) was published in 1937. Jews were again seen as by definition incapable of assimilating, 'a race that excludes itself from national communion' (Maciel 1937: 14). Maciel proposes selective immigration laws to exclude their entrance in the country.

A biographical study of Zweig insinuates that he penned *Brazil, Land of the Future* under pressure from Vargas's regime, to recompense the Estado Novo, which was then enacting more stringent visa policies in relation to Jews, and expelling some under 'irregular status' (Dines 2004: 305). The systematic association of Rio de Janeiro's Jewish communities to communism – as well as the broader identification between immigrants and agitators – targeted the Cidade Nova, leading to Fania Fridman's use of the expression 'Red Praça Onze' (2007: 65). She documents several facets of the neighbourhood's political activities, including police action to thwart a protest against German persecution of Jews in 1933. In another episode, the suppression of a communist revolt, which had begun in the cities of Natal and Recife in November 1935, entailed a police incursion into a popular restaurant in the Praça Onze linked to the Brazkor (a Jewish organization analogous to the Red Cross, with a leftist orientation).[23]

Luis Martins, chronicler of Rio's bohemian nightlife, writes of a German orchestra playing sambas, and of a German bar with a Jewish waitress, full of 'people of colour', even after Hitler's grip on power (1964: 84–6). Although recreational spaces might betray a different impression, the persecution of Jews suspected of communist ties became relentless and often brutal. Amidst that environment, an exhibition of 260 Lasar Segall works in the National Museum of Fine Arts in Rio, organized by the Ministério da Educação (Ministry of Education) (MEC) in 1943, brought out familiar accusations against 'degenerate art', as well as the corresponding categories of 'Russian, Jew, and Communist' (Carneiro 2004: 63). The exhibit contained several of the works that would be reproduced in the *Mangue* album a few months later. While the repercussion in the press was by and large positive, an open letter to Gustavo Capanema, who headed the MEC, argued that 'it is not by dissolving characters in foolish scribbles or bringing the Mangue to the Fine Arts Museum that we shall work for our ideals'.[24] At the same time, the Nazi fascist-inspired integralistas claimed hundreds of thousands of members and owned several newspapers in the country (Fridman 2007: 67). In what must have been a highly loaded and symbolic gesture, they held a march in the Praça Onze on 25 July 1937 (71). The Jewish surname of the apocryphal Cohen Plan, then, should be understood as anything but arbitrary.

Capitalizing on the instability generated by the communist attempt at a coup two years earlier, Getúlio Vargas instituted his own coup after news of the so-called Cohen Plan was spread. On 10 November 1937, he declared a 'state of emergency', shutting down Congress, banning political parties, and declaring the Estado Novo. The measure of outlawing parties affected the integralists, who joined the opposition to Vargas, but the prohibition of racially specific political organizations also represented a setback for black movements (Hanchard 1994: 101–5). Although Afro-Brazilian political activities were far from an established and unified presence, the months preceding the Estado Novo had seen some promising signs of organization. In January 1937, for example, the Afro-Brazilian Congress of Bahia ended with the redaction of a text 'asking for the recognition of African sects in Brazil', until then 'persecuted as a form of witchcraft' (Martins 1976: 101). Attempts to mobilize beyond such measures were rendered increasingly difficult.[25]

Under the Estado Novo, Vargas gave himself dictatorial powers, and in 1939 ordered the creation of the Departamento de Imprensa e Propaganda (Department of Press and Propaganda) (DIP) to substitute a previous propaganda department and institute broad censorship of the press and arts (Williams 2001: 82–3). Political persecutions became more commonplace, although they were not unheard of before the coup: the benefactor of samba organizations Pedro Ernesto, for example, was imprisoned twice.[26] Probably the mayor whose administration most impacted Rio's social and cultural life after Pereira Passos, Ernesto figures much less prominently in the city's histories, even though he is a key figure to understand some of the tensions and changing relations between local government and national politics.

Nominated as the *interventor* or intervener of the Federal District in 1931 – as the office was known – Ernesto participated in the creation of the Partido Autonomista do Distrito Federal in 1933. After the party's major success in municipal elections, the Recife native was chosen by city councillors as the mayor of Rio de Janeiro in 1935, becoming the first elected administrator of Brazil's capital, albeit not by direct vote. Involved in the Aliança Nacional Libertadora (National Liberation Alliance) (ANL), an anti-fascist and anti-imperialist organization with affinities to leftist movements, he was jailed in April of 1936, accused of participating in the communist revolt to overthrow the government months earlier. Upon being released in 1937, Ernesto was acclaimed by the populace and became a vocal critic of the Vargas regime: that same year, he was once more imprisoned for three months, and left public life thereafter. In that interim Olímpio de Melo served as the city's mayor, but the day after instituting the authoritarian Estado Novo, Getúlio Vargas appointed as the Federal District's Intervener one of his new regime's close supporters, Henrique Dodsworth (1895–1975). He would remain in the position throughout the duration of the Estado Novo, until 1945.

Yet the Estado Novo entailed even deeper consequences to the future of Rio de Janeiro, and of the Cidade Nova in particular. To comprehend the process leading to the construction of President Vargas Avenue, we must backtrack about a decade or so. In late 1926, president Washington Luis appointed as Rio's Intervener his good friend Antônio Prado Junior, who hailed from a wealthy and traditional São Paulo family. An engineer by training like the city's two previous mayors, Prado Junior had no administrative experience beyond his involvement with a football club. Within months of taking office, he commissioned Alfred Agache to 'remodel, extend, and beautify' Brazil's capital. A positivist-influenced urbanist who co-founded the French Society of Urbanists in 1912, Agache jumped at the opportunity.[27] He belonged to a generation of French urbanists eager to put their theories into practice, and that saw cities of colonial Africa and Latin America as convenient testing grounds. The office he established in Rio produced an extensive report of the city's conditions, published in 1930, along with his proposed projects.

For all the comprehensive demographic studies, extensive analysis of water drainage, and careful statistical tables, the Agache plan treats the city to a great extent as a tabula rasa. Agache's vision conforms to preconceived ideals of what a city *should* be like. The plan was meant to take thirty to fifty years to be brought to completion. It proposed strict zoning laws and near absolute social segregation: aristocratic residential neighbourhoods and a university city in the South Zone; hotel, embassy, and business districts in the centre; a commercial zone to the north; and further out in the suburbs an industrial zone and residential areas for labourers. Although the plan showed some preoccupation with the social reasons behind the existence of favelas, including questions of land rights, it advanced the idea that they were inhabited by 'a sort of nomad population, averse to any and all rules of hygiene' (Agache 1930: 20). The obvious implication is that since they were inclined to be nomads forced relocation should not cause unease.

City planning at the time was still intricately tied to hygienism. Agache writes in the introduction to the plan that he wishes to be seen as a type of doctor, and adopts medical metaphors throughout. Nineteenth-century attitudes towards cortiços now applied to the favelas, which, like the Mangue, were often conceived as 'a city within a city'.[28] Agache's plan appears to be the first to address favelas directly, and marks a shift. It represents one of the earliest uses of the term in the plural, signifying a typology rather than the specific favela settlement of the Providência Hill. To the 'problem of favelas' – a 'leprosy', as the plan put it – Agache advocated 'total destruction' (190). Its residents would be transferred to labourer garden-villas where, in 'simple and economic housing, though hygienic and practical', they would undergo a 'first step of an education that shall prepare them for a more comfortable and more normal life'. Likewise, great portions of the Cidade Nova, including the Mangue and the Praça Onze, would be levelled under his plan, which envisioned a monumental avenue perpendicular to the Avenida Rio Branco.[29]

Like many other urban areas levelled during twentieth-century reforms, the neighbourhood displayed several of the elements sought by new urbanism today: mixed-used streetscapes, diversity of housing, a prominent public square, proximity to the centre, suitability for pedestrians, and integration to the rest of the city by a network of public transport. In the Agache plan the diverse neighbourhood, with an array of commercial, entertainment, and cultural options, became no more than an area of 'secondary commerce' (179), irrelevant to the 'businessmen' who, though less than 2 per cent of the city's population, were the central preoccupation of the proposals: 'There is nothing there [in the neighbourhood of the Mangue] that could be preserved' (179). It would be replaced with a large market, parking spots, and the Mangue Avenue (218).

News of the proposed changes circulated in the city even before the plan's publication, and was met with discontent among frequenters of the Praça Onze. Amidst increasingly polarizing debates about favelas – as we saw in the previous chapter – one of the most measured voices can be found in the views of a habitué of Tia Ciata's house. Upon hearing of plans to demolish the Providência, or Favela Hill, Sinhô wrote a samba both to announce and to protest against the measure, 'A favela vai abaixo' (The Favela's Coming Down):

> Minha cabocla, a Favela vai abaixo
> Quanta saudade tu terás deste torrão
> Da casinha pequenina de madeira
> Que nos enche de carinho o coração.

> [My *cabocla*, the Favela is coming down, / Oh, how you will miss this great lump of soil / And the wooden little house / That fills our hearts with tenderness[30]]

The song was recorded in 1928 by no less than 'the King of the Voice', Francisco Alves, accompanied by the prestigious orchestra of the Cassino Copacabana. Its success was such that Sinhô is sometimes credited as having intervened in debates among authorities, influencing the decision not to raze the hill. Addressing a cabocla – which cannot help but evoke Manuel Antônio de Almeida's nineteenth-century excursion to the Mangue – Sinhô's lyrics do not necessarily idealize the favela, but at the least they contest Agache's assessment that its residents are kinds of nomads. Rather, the song affirms their dignity, sense of belonging, and attachment to the place.[31] It ends by stating, 'I am going to live in the Cidade Nova / So that I can turn my heart towards the Morro da Favela' ('Vou morar na Cidade Nova / pra voltar meu coração para o morro da Favela'). Brodwyn Fischer sees the song as 'a radical manifesto, turning upside down the precepts justifying the visible poor's expulsion from Rio de Janeiro's central cityscape' (2008: 17).

A similar sense of ownership over the Cidade Nova's spaces could be found in reactions published in the Jewish press. A text from 1927, published in Yiddish, opens by stating that 'we have been afflicted by a great misfortune'. Without ever mentioning the Agache plan by name, the author explains that 'it is said that in the place of the Praça Onze, a market will be installed'. The article laments the loss of a public square where, under full-grown trees, 'lovers found refuge', a place which served as a 'resting spot for many night birds or for the numerous recently arrived immigrants, and even for some veterans with no resources or home'. Evoking the idea of a Jewish neighbourhood, the chronicler concludes that 'a blank page will appear in the history of our neighborhood. What a pity!'[32]

The unease over impending transformations appears to conflate Agache's designs for the Mangue with a reform carried out in the square months later, when beloved casuarina trees were cut down. But the sense of loss was not exclusive to Jewish weeklies – the city's mainstream press greeted the toppling of the square's trees with harsh criticism, calling it an 'unjustified

Figure 4   The Praça Onze being remodelled

crime'.[33] If the indiscriminate removal of casuarinas aroused indignation, the same cannot be said of pedestrian deaths in the neighbourhood. Some of Rio's magazines could hardly disguise their contempt for the Cidade Nova: a narrative recounting a ride through the city aboard a motor car focuses unsympathetically on its 'old aspects'. The Mangue, it remarks, 'always dark and dirty, will remain immune to the wonderful works of [...] remodelling, continuing to be useful only for photographs'. Another article, devoted to those places with the most disasters, deaths, and suicides in Rio, mentions how vehicles – in their 'immense fury' – traverse the Praça Onze on their way to the road along the 'sinister' canal. It cites statistics claiming that in the preceding year twenty-five people had died and 101 suffered injuries after being run over in the locale.[34]

Indeed, one of the guiding concerns behind the proposed reforms was the circulation of motor cars: central buildings, for example, had internal patios meant for parking. This model of urbanization inevitably recalls Le Corbusier's, which also prioritized cars. A rival of Agache, whose plans for Rio he disparaged as belonging to 'the classical school', Le Corbusier (1887–1965) visited Brazil's capital during the same period, in 1929. He also took an interest in the favela and devised plans from an aeroplane, sketching his own vision of raised highways cutting through much of the city.[35] The prospect of a city planned around the motor car excited the press and local elites. Rio's own mayor, Prado Junior, was an enthusiast of car racing, and they were increasingly an expression of power and modernity (Sevcenko 1992: 74).[36]

The very first edition of the upscale *O Cruzeiro*, billing itself as 'contemporary to skyscrapers' and 'the most modern of magazines', welcomed the Agache plan as 'in every aspect worthy of the hyper-civilized humanity of the twentieth century'.[37] Its inaugural editorial positioned the new publication as an heir of the Pereira Passos reforms, which through the straight line of Rio's Central Avenue had ushered colonial Brazil into the future. The article on 'Professor Agache' suggested that his vision would present the direction for Rio's next steps, containing the 'outlines of the magnificent capital of tomorrow'. Although the Favela Hill never was demolished, the French urbanist proved to be enormously influential among Brazilian city planners.[38] In Rio de Janeiro, as Brodwyn Fischer writes, 'Agache's plan served as a blueprint for some of the most important legislative and public works initiatives' of the mid-century (2008: 45), deepening some of the social inequities that already characterized the city.[39]

In the aftermath of the 1930 revolution that brought Getúlio Vargas to power, the monumental projects were largely set aside. The new regime distrusted and sought distance from anything related to the First Republic, and Pedro Ernesto was critical of the plan (Abreu 1988: 86). It was a matter of time, however, before the plan's ideas resurfaced. Urbanists of that first generation, after all, could be accused of anything but humility, and inserted themselves at the centre of aesthetic, political, and policy debates, assuming the function of a 'social elite' in line with earlier republican authorities similarly influenced by Comte's positivism.

Agache considered urbanism to be 'a Science and an Art, and above all a social philosophy' (1930: 1). This triple status, which urbanists demanded and acquired, also points to a growing distance between the poets of modernity and modern technocrats, coincident with the shrinking place of the former in what we have been deeming the lettered city. Although it becomes exceedingly difficult to speak of centralized production of knowledge in the twentieth century, urbanism's claim to both art and science in a sense sought a monopoly of the creative and technical forces shaping what it meant to live in a city. When we read Manuel Bandeira's poetry expressing interest in the 'language of the people', or referring to the Mangue as *aqui* (here) and not *lá* (over there), it may be interpreted as the lettered city's embrace of 'spoken language' and the marginal. It could also, however, signal the poet's increasingly marginalized voice and displacement from the centre: expulsed from the *polis* at last, or at least outspoken by urbanists.

IV

After the establishment of the Estado Novo, under Henrique Dodsworth's administration, technocratic city planners had their way: the intention of building a monumental avenue across the Cidade Nova was revisited. Official justifications were to a great extent of a functional order: to facilitate traffic out of the financial centre. But a pervasive ideological component behind its rapid construction became apparent in discourses of the tightly controlled press and of the authorities, as well as in the avenue's names and the symbolic dates chosen for inaugural ceremonies. The completed Avenida Presidente Vargas boasted an impressive width of 300 feet and a length of two and a half miles, leading from the central Candelária Church to the Praça da Bandeira. Initially to be called Avenida 10 de Novembro in honour of the anniversary of the Estado Novo (Lima 1990: 128), the dictator's title ended up prevailing. Construction and demolitions began on 19 April 1941, with a grand inauguration on 7 September 1944, timed to coincide with the Independence Day military parades.

The project was conceived in 1938, six years after the completion of Mussolini's Via dell'Impero in Rome and contemporary with Hitler's equally ambitious plans for a north–south axis cutting across Berlin. Like the President Vargas, both were monumental avenues designed in a straight line, and were envisioned as fitting grounds for theatrical military processions.[40] Despite the Estado Novo's ideological affinities to the Axis powers, Brazil aligned with the Allies, including the United States, officially entering the Second World War on 22 August 1942. Though the project of the Vargas Avenue suffered an obvious influence from its Italian and German counterparts, the nationalist climate promoted by the Estado Novo was exacerbated during the war and most probably had an impact on how its precedents were to be located – not in foreign countries but in the earlier Avenida Central.

The scale of the intervention certainly recalls the Pereira Passos reforms, and the press eagerly established a connection between the two. An editorial of the *Diário Carioca* from the week before the inauguration entitled 'From the Avenida Central to the Presidente Vargas' associates resistance to the prior reforms to 'conservative elements' – 'reactionary traditionalists' who believed that Ouvidor Street 'would resist indefinitely to the competition' (1 September 1944). No specific criticism of the 'new and majestic avenue' is acknowledged, and potential critics are pre-emptively dismissed. Another editorial of the same newspaper, two days later, reasons that 'not always are these efforts of the government duly understood', and that 'there are even those that proffer severe criticism, not always thought out and fair'. If

Figure 5   The Avenida Presidente Vargas, view of the Candelária Church

Passos – and by implication Dodsworth – 'were to have stopped in view of the accusations and the campaign waged against him, Rio would perhaps still be full of dead ends and sordid streets, incompatible with its condition as the capital of a great Nation'. The text concludes by praising the new avenue as heir and update of the first: 'In this manner Rio takes on new clothing, gathering majestic aspects and seeing its progress gain a decisive and fast-paced rhythm'.

With the facades built under the First Republic – variations on the French eclecticism of the École des Beaux-Arts – considered irredeemably old-fashioned, the city's new public buildings had to keep pace with advances in other areas. In the 1930s, as it happens, a new generation of Brazilian architects were at the forefront of architectural modernity, exuding confidence and determined not to lag behind the newest trends. The design team for the fourteen-storey building that was to host the Ministério da Educação e Saúde (Ministry of Education and Health) (later, the Ministério da Educação e da Cultura (Ministry of Education and Culture) (MEC)), an organ created during the Vargas regime, included Lúcio Costa, Affonso Eduardo Reidy, and Oscar Niemeyer. All would go on to become some of the country's most influential architects. The building, completed in 1942 but only inaugurated in 1945, was located on the site of the levelled Castelo Hill. It was among the first to incorporate bold elements of the International Style – reinforced concrete, pilotis, and a shading system known as brise-soleil. The use of Cândido Portinari's modernist *azulejos*, traditional painted ceramic tile-work, made reference to Portuguese heritage. Although the extent of Le Corbusier's direct role in the celebrated final design has been the object of controversy, his influence remains undeniable.[41]

The monumental designs for two other buildings, facing the new avenue, have received considerably less attention from architectural historians. The imposing Army Headquarters (now known as the Duque de Caxias Palace) and the new Central Station were inaugurated not long before the President Vargas (Fig. 5). Like the MEC, both were commissioned by the state, were widely covered by the press, and sought to project the image of a modern nation. The two neighbouring skyscrapers, however, share certain architectural elements that immediately set them apart from the more original MEC, which stood on the other side of downtown Rio, towards the bay. Their designs embodied a competing version of what modernity meant, and remain crucial to understanding the internal tensions that pervaded Brazil's political and social life during the Estado Novo (1937–45).[42]

Unlike constructions related to the Passos reforms, the President Vargas projects did not take their cues exclusively from architecture based in France. In his project for the Army Headquarters, Cristiano Stockler das Neves, a graduate of the University of Pennsylvania, sought to ally the Beaux-Arts classical spirit with practical aims developed by North Americans. Urban historian Evelyn Werneck Lima, our most important source for this set of interventions, suggests the influence of Hugh Ferriss's *The Metropolis of Tomorrow* (1929), which conceives of numerous tower edifices resembling ziggurats for the business district of Manhattan. The Army Headquarters, designed and built before Brazil joined the Allies, has elements bearing great similarity to projects by Albert Speer and Wilhelm Kreis in Third Reich Germany, reminders of the Estado Novo's ideological ties to the Axis Powers. The imposing symmetric spatial arrangement of its facade – vast ten-storey wings on both sides of a twenty-three-storey tower building – were meant to evoke a general marching in front of his divisions (Lima 1990: 66). The layout and position of the building in relation to the avenue took into account its use as a stage for military parades; a function highlighted by weeklies with nationwide distribution in their Independence Day spreads, which eagerly covered the very first parades after Brazil's official entrance into the war. Magazines like the *Revista da Semana* and *O Malho* dedicated several pages to photographs of marching soldiers, with the building's massive facade and tower frequently in the background.

The other major undertaking concomitant to the Vargas Avenue, a new Central Station, had also already been proposed by Agache. José Marianno Filho, an important architect at the time, criticized how the approved project kept the new building on the site of the old railway station, rather than moving it to the Praça da Bandeira, as the French urbanist had suggested in his – as Filho emphasizes – very costly commissioned plans.[43] Right beside the Army Headquarters, the new main railway station certainly seems to reference its neighbour through the iconic tower, scale, and use of similar materials.[44] Begun in March 1936, the building's design was altered during the Estado Novo dramatically to increase its proportions and monumentalism, resulting in an art deco tower of twenty-nine floors, inaugurated on 29 March 1943. Adorned on its four faces with enormous clocks spanning six of the top floors, the new building was Rio de Janeiro's tallest skyscraper, and Brazil's second after the Edifício Martinelli in São Paulo. Its horizontal ribbon windows, evoking industrial buildings, were among Le Corbusier's 'five points' of modern architecture. Media coverage of the inauguration, timed to coincide with the station's eighty-fifth anniversary, highlighted the clock as one of the four largest in the world.[45]

Every aspect related to the new avenue had strong symbolic value. In her work on the subject, Lima analyses how specific attributes of the architecture and planning aimed to project power and enable social control (1990). Official rhetoric – particularly in regard to the avenue – attempted to insert the interventions within discourses of the DIP. The goal was to substitute the culture of bohemianism and celebrations of malandros with the exaltation of discipline, highlighting the importance of a work ethic.[46] This echoes in the language of politicians and in the press. The *Revista da Semana*, for example, praises the new Central Station as a 'brilliant demonstration of labour and of progress' (10 April 1943). In a speech to commemorate the opening of the first portion of the Avenue in 1941, Dodsworth stresses 'the value [...] of the national worker' (Lima 1990: 30).

On that same occasion, Dodsworth drew attention to the purportedly practical aspects of the new avenue, in an implicit attempt to discourage associations with the aesthetic preoccupations of the belle époque's Avenida Central. The justifications offered by the Intervener, however, conform to the objectives of the Passos reforms: 'we are not dealing with a spectacle for the city's beautification, but with the fulfilment of a programme that attempts to solve economic problems of traffic and sanitation'.[47] The term 'sanitation', ubiquitous in nineteenth-century city planning, gains new contours in the context of urban policies enacted in Europe during the 1940s. Here, it evokes not only the demolition of cortiços, but also the language adopted by the Vichy regime to legitimize destruction of buildings inhabited primarily by Jews in the Marais quarter of Paris. Both of the prior plans for a major avenue connecting Rio's Centro to the North Zone – Sampaio's in 1922 and Agache's in 1930 – spared the Praça Onze, and the exact location of the Estado Novo's thoroughfare raises troubling questions.

The main drive to demolish over 500 buildings in Rio de Janeiro, several of which constituted the so-called Jewish neighbourhood, nonetheless seems to have been mostly related to economic pressures. The role that real estate speculation played could not be more evident. Several blocks had their houses levelled with the objective of financing construction through the sale of empty lots at higher values than those paid as reparation to previous owners. In a 1940 speech to the Associação Brasileira de Imprensa (Brazilian Press Association) (ABI), the engineer Edison Passos announces that 'the avenue will increase in value' (Lima 1990: 34). Newspaper advertisements four years later indeed capitalize on the land's appreciation. One, in the *Diário Carioca*, makes the pitch: 'Prefeito Frontin Edifice in construction on the greatest artery in the world, the President Vargas Avenue [...] the most valuable area in Brazil' (6 September 1944).

Over and above narrower interests, the reform's execution, tearing through vibrant and diverse neighbourhoods, was to a great extent motivated by ideological purposes. According to the narratives pushed in the press, the avenue stood as the Estado Novo's great gesture to affirm its place in the country's future, and the country's place on the world stage. It would herald the nation's commitment to modernity and progress. The much-touted gains, excluding temporary improvements in road traffic, were of a mostly symbolic order. The unacknowledged costs, for the many who saw their homes and neighbourhoods vanish, were of course of a tangible as well as symbolic nature.

The impetus to build the avenue was animated by an almost obsessive desire to compete with other metropolises, particularly the Argentine capital. The *Diário Carioca* praises Dodsworth, 'who thought, rightly, that Rio needed to possess something as grandiose as Buenos Aires, so proud of its Avenida de Maio, like Paris with its wonderful Champs Élysées' (1 September 1944). Two days later, the same newspaper welcomes 'one of the greatest improvements undertaken in Rio de Janeiro [...] in accordance with the programme outlined by the head of the nation'. 'The avenue', it goes on, 'endows this capital with a public thoroughfare in the style of the most famous in the world's great metropolises', concluding that 'there is no one who does not feel pleasure in traversing it, admiring the speed and perfection with which its opening was achieved'. A page later, a large picture accompanies the triumphant headline, in bold letters: 'Second among the World's Largest Avenues'.

The Sunday edition of *A Manhã* joined the chorus with particular panache. At a time when the world war dominated front pages, the newspaper directed by modernist writer Cassiano Ricardo would dedicate its prime spot to a picture of the new avenue, with the caption: 'one of the most important in the universe [...] it gives to the city an appearance worthy of its grandiose nature' (3 September 1944). In order to illustrate its dimensions, the daily printed a diagram comparing the new avenue's width with those of other 'great modern arteries' in Berlin, Buenos Aires, Paris, and Santiago. An identical comparative feature conspicuously appears in other newspapers during the week of the inauguration. Beyond the reproduction of diagrams most probably distributed by the DIP, the newspapers' mixture of state-fed lines and unbridled enthusiasm betrays a certain disconnect from empirical reality or even rudimentary logic, especially where they merely echo urbanist orthodoxies of the day. The same *A Manhã* approves the destruction of 'a considerable part of the old city, dark and meagre', expressing gratitude that the city can at last bid farewell to the 'old traditional make-up of colonial Brazil [...] where low and dark houses impede the flow of air'. The solution to air circulation, presumably, would be the construction of tall buildings.

Such descriptions of the razed quarters, in addition, contradict those of less partial voices. Just a few years earlier, the Portuguese architect Raul Lino (1879–1974), in a book about his travels in Brazil, depicts the Cidade Nova as defying the expectations produced by a neighbourhood of the lower classes: 'Dark dead end streets, alleyways, dumps? By no means. It is a network of wide streets, grid-like and regular [...] It is a neighbourhood flooded with sunlight. One could therefore not use here the adjectives with which we commonly endow such places' (1937: 69). Information from census records indeed shows that the district possessed far more infrastructure than the city's average. All roads were paved, 87.5 per cent had access to transport, the literacy rate was 84.1 per cent, and only 8 per cent of buildings were non-brick. Among its households, 100 per cent had sewerage, water, and electricity.[48]

But there was no braking to the march of progress and modernity. Few technological advances embodied those ideals more than the motor car, and it was in its service that the avenue came into existence. The car too, ultimately, was also part and parcel of the ideologies of progress. A comment in the *Correio da Manhã*, accompanying the aforementioned diagrams that compared the width of various avenues, reveals the imperative reasoning: it explains that the President Vargas Avenue could not be considered the world's widest owing to a central garden which reduced its 'useful space' (3 September 1944). The 'useful', then, pertains to vehicles.[49]

In the very last scene of *A viagem maravilhosa*, a sombre Radagasio arrives at the Praça Onze in a motor car, trying to reach the train station in order to escape carnival. We can imagine such a scene in this book's cover photograph. The revellers force the vehicle to stop. As a result, the novel ends with the narrator describing the wealthy protagonist swallowed by the crowd of baianas, and by the 'barbarian rhythm' of the multitudes (Aranha 1929: 382). Decades later, during carnival people would still temporarily reclaim the streets of Rio. Yet less than twenty years after Aranha's novel, the cars would be too many and too powerful, and in their name the Praça Onze itself was run over, in order to make way for the monumental President Vargas Avenue. The neighbourhood that owed its development to a road providing access from the royal residences to the administrative centre would meet its fate with a highway superimposed onto the former Landfill Road: but we have now entered the age of automobiles. Their demands and their velocity will far surpass anything imaginable in the long-gone 'tempo do rei', the time of the king.

Notes

1 Quoted from an interview recorded at the MIS, 2 April 1969.

2 *O País do Carnaval*, an almost ubiquitous expression today, was the title of the first novel by the Bahian author Jorge Amado (1912-2001), published in 1931.

3 The Senate and the seat of the republican government – the Itamaraty Palace from 1889 to 1898 – both moved south. The executive power went to the Catete, where it remained while Rio was capital. The Cidade Nova remained a crossroads of transportation lines. *Maxambomba* vehicles used the Praça Onze as a hub (Santos 1934: 239). The square was twenty minutes away from the Praça XV via streetcars that left every four minutes during the day (417).

4 Sodré quoted at Moura 2004: 107. This study explores how the institution of the 'roda de samba' – the practice of samba around a circle, frequently in a corner bar or backyard – helped to shape the genre, constituting a vital social space in Brazilian culture.

5 See Hertzman 2008, which reconsiders narratives of samba's repression and brings light to what he calls the 'punishment paradigm', often overstating the extent to which popular music was in fact persecuted. Accounts of sambistas being harassed by the police, at any rate, permeate oral histories of samba. See, for instance, Soihet 2008: 176-8.

6 See Haberly's *Three Sad Races* (1983), a study of racial and national identity in authors like Machado de Assis and Mário de Andrade. The title quotes from a

sonnet by Olavo Bilac. Racial mixture and national consciousness were crucial themes to Brazilian intellectuals. See, for example, Prado 1931. For an analysis that contextualizes these discussions and their antecedents – not inclusive of Aranha – see Vainfas 1999.

7 My systematic though not exhaustive research of newspapers and magazines produced relatively few references to the Cidade Nova, compared to the profuse coverage of carnival in other parts of the city. I arrived at this article, from 9 February 1932, through a reference in Tinhorão 1997: 152. The text, despite stressing a difference between the Praça Onze's carnival and the rest of the city, was in fact partly celebratory. For further mentions of Praça Onze's carnival in the press, see Soihet 2008: 59–77.

8 On the movement that became known as *tenentismo*, see Borges 1992; for a study focused on its relationship to urban middle classes, see Forjaz 1977.

9 There is an extensive bibliography on Vargas; the best starting place might be Fausto 2006. In English, see Levine 1998.

10 Although there are earlier records of competitions between grandes sociedades and ranchos (Ferreira 2004: 269–71), the first disputes between samba groups were reputedly organized in 1929 in the Engenho de Dentro by Zé Espinguela, one of the founders of the Mangueira Samba School.

11 Their desire was to replicate the well-behaved and respected ranchos while introducing a sound that allowed one to sing, dance and parade at the same time: hence the *bum bum paticumbum prugurundum* of Ismael Silva's onomatopeic expression, used during an interview at the MIS (16 July 1969), to denote the new rhythm. See Carvalho 1980.

12 The story is told in an interview of the Velha Guarda at the MIS (27 January 1968).

13 A multi-talented artist, Eduardo das Neves worked as a clown, wrote verses, sang, played the guitar, and was a pioneer of the phonographic industry – popular for his versatility, political satires, and humour. On Neves, see Vasconcelos 1977: 282–3; Abreu 2005: 277–9; Tinhorão 2006: 103–11; Hertzman 2008: 187–97.

14 In his interview at the MIS, Donga reminisces about these events in the Praça Cruz Vermelha, attended by figures like Catulo da Paixão Cearense, Afonso Arinos, Olegário Mariano, and Hermes Fontes.

15 In a metaphor that pervades Brazil's cultural history, the manifesto proposes anthropophagy as a response to European cultural domination: Brazilians must 'devour' the foreign, metabolizing it into something new. One passage of the text alludes to the maxixe 'Cristo nasceu na Bahia' by Sebastião Cirino and Duque (1927). The manifesto was published in the first issue of the *Revista de Antropofagia* (1928).

16 To Debord, 'the spectacle is not a collection of images; it is a social relation between people that is mediated by images' (1992: 4). Here we are faced with a similar process, where relations are mediated by sounds instead. On the cultural industry and transformations in samba, see Fenerick 2005.

17 McLuhan (1967) was among the first to explore how new media changed the ways in which people perceive the world. The effects of radio as a mode of cultural transmission might also be related to Lefebvre's (1970) suggestion of a breakdown between the traditional opposition between city and village, where rural areas – served by supermarkets and with economies interconnected to industrial centres – become part of what he deems *le tissu urbain*, or urban tissue.

18 In 1890, the then minister of finance Rui Barbosa had ordered that records of slavery be burned, as they constituted a reminder of that 'blemish' in the country's history. Debates surrounding the episode also consider the action as a response against demands for compensation by slave owners, who had incurred losses with abolition. See Lacombe 1988.

19 There is an extensive bibliography on Freyre and the shifts that his thoughts on miscegenation crystallized and catalyzed. For a study that connects new-found racial discourses with samba's elevation to symbol of national identity, see Vianna 1999. For a discussion that situates Brazil in a Latin American context valuing miscegenation – what the author calls 'cultural browning' – see Andrews 2004.

20 The 1940 census was the first to collect racial data after 1890. According to the census, 28.9 per cent of the city was non-white. Compared to Santana's 14.1 per cent of non-whites, 30.6 per cent of Gamboa's residents were in the same category. In some suburban districts like Pavuna, Madureira, and Anchieta, Afro-descendants comprised at least 40 per cent of the population. See Fischer for a table with comparative data on all of Rio (2008: 31). The first census conducted in favelas, published in 1949, estimates that their population of 138,837 – 71 per cent of which was non-white – accounted for 7 per cent of the city's total (Valladares 2005: 64–5).

21 Gonzaga arrived in the capital after his service in the military, and was taken by a man he met in the streets to play in the Mangue. While there he 'made money from all over the world' playing for foreign sailors, according to his interview at the MIS, recorded 6 September 1968.

22 Artur Nehl Neiva, in a piece published in the *Revista de imigração e colonização*, critiques racial theories and Aryanism. Citing Viana's book, he argues against the notion of Jews as a racial group: 'there are white and black, tall and short Jews' (Neiva 1944: 407). This periodical was consulted in the Samuel Malamud collection of the Arquivo Geral da Cidade.

23 Fifty-four Jews were imprisoned for interrogation, and some were deported. See Fridman 2007: 65–74. The revolt, deemed pejoratively as the 'Intentona Comunista' (Communist Conspiracy), arose from within the military ranks (Pinheiro 1992).

24 The letter by Augusto de Lima Jr was published in Recife's *Jornal do Comércio*, 28 May 1943, and is reproduced at Carneiro 2004: 63. In my own research at the archives of the Museu Lasar Segall in São Paulo, I found that reactions like this were not the norm. An article by Nicanor Miranda in the *Estado de São Paulo*, 8 June 1944, for example, expresses pride at how Brazilians celebrate two paintings by Segall that had been considered 'degenerate' in Nazi Berlin. The archives contain several folders with newspaper clippings related to Segall and his work, apparently collected by the artist himself.

25 Hanchard discusses the limitations posed by the close relationships between Afro-Brazilian political strategies and 'expressive cultural practice[s]' during the 1930s (1994: 99–141)

26 Under the administration of Ernesto, who was a doctor, public services like schools and hospitals were significantly extended. See Sarmento 2001.

27 The term *urbanisme* is sometimes attributed to him. See Stuckenbruck 1996.

28 Benjamin Costallat (1990: 37) uses the phrase to refer to favelas in the 1920s.

Bandeira describes the Mangue in Segall's album with the same phrase, reinforcing the notion of both spaces as similarly 'othered', or heterotopic.

29 Though the most influential, Agache's plan was not the first to envision such an avenue: an Avenida da Independência had been proposed during Carlos Sampaio's administration (1920-2), and there were precedents dating back to Montigny.

30 I have used Fischer's translation, with minor adjustments. See her detailed analysis of the song, which serves as a starting point to her discussion of Agache and the reception of his plans (2008: 15-18).

31 Sinhô's song also condemns the 'ingratitude of humanity', imposing 'desabrigo' (destitution or homelessness) to the people of the favela: joining a long line of sambas that would protest against policies of forced removal in later decades.

32 Published anonymously in the weekly *Dos Iídiche Vochenblat*. A typed translation, in Portuguese, was found among Malamud's papers, so he might well be the writer.

33 Quoted from the *Fon-Fon*, 31 March 1928. The 7 April edition of the same publication refers to protests in 'almost every newspaper', but defends cutting the trees with an ironic tone, as it would spare them from the 'martyrdom' and 'suffering' of living in the Praça Onze.

34 The article appears in *O Malho*, 28 February 1928. The previous text was quoted from the *Fon-Fon*, 12 January 1929.

35 See Le Corbusier's *The Radiant City*, where he reproduces an image from Agache's plan next to his own, without identifying the rival by name (1967: 223).

36 For a study of cars in Brazilian history, see Wolfe 2010.

37 *O Cruzeiro* debuted on 10 November 1928. The main article on Agache was written by Dr J. A. Mattos Pimenta, an active member of the Rotary Club and among the first to campaign for the elimination of the *favelas* (Valladares 2005: 41-5).

38 Agache would later work on plans for Recife, Porto Alegre, and, more famously, Curitiba.

39 To Fischer, 'its zoning and construction standards were the basis for the 1937 building code, the most important Carioca urban legislation of its era' (2008: 38). She shows how the code was both segregationist and burdensome, although it was often easier for the wealthy to get around some of its regulations (44-9).

40 On Berlin, see Helmer 1985. On Rome, see Painter 2005. Focusing on the Brazilian case, Lima explores how urban spaces were used as a 'theater of power' (1990: 102-12).

41 There is a lengthy bibliography on the MEC's place in architectural history. See, for example, Fraser 2000 and Deckker 2001.

42 An argument could be made that the Avenue's buildings and the MEC responded to antagonistic currents within Vargas's regime: one, led by the DIP, more aggressively nationalist and with totalitarian leanings; the other 'softer' and more willing to compromise, centred around education minister Gustavo Capanema, who the MEC building would later be named after. The portrayals of the three buildings in the local press favoured the version of progress and modernity represented by the Army Headquarters and the Central do Brasil, although the MEC became canonized among international architects even before its inauguration. See Carvalho 2010 and Deckker 2001. On the Estado Novo, see Williams 2001.

43 Lima (1990: 88) quotes from Mariano Filho's *Debates sobre estética e urbanismo* (1943).

44 There is a relevant, if obvious, difference in their functions – one serves as a public space, the other forbids entry to the non-authorized.

45 Architects Adalberto Szilard and Geza Heller were primarily responsible for the final design, a modification on Roberto de Carvalho's original project (Lima 1990: 84).

46 The effort included legal measures like a decree from 1939 forbidding celebrations of *malandragem* (Matos 1982).

47 Dodsworth never backed down from the reform, authoring an unapologetic book over a decade later (Dodsworth 1955), defending its legal and technical underpinnings.

48 The numbers given are for the Santana district, cited from data collected by Fischer (2008: 31) from 1933 and 1940. The city's respective averages were: 33.7 per cent (roads paved), 10.8 per cent (access to transport), 81 per cent (literacy rate), 26 per cent (non-brick), 31.7 per cent (with sewerage), 57.5 per cent (with water), and 43.9 per cent (with electricity).

49 Acclaim for the new avenue was juxtaposed by a type of ridiculing of public transportation as 'picturesque', outdated, and reserved for the poor. During the week of the avenue's inauguration, coverage of the opening of a new line of express bondes to the suburbs of Engenho Novo, Muda, and Tijuca, relegates the event to the uneducated, trouble-making masses: 'There were people who did not want to get off the bonde at the proper stopping point', the *Correio da Manhã* complains, 2 September 1944. The article shares the page with another entitled: 'In Brazil there is no Place for Racism'.

CHAPTER SIX

'It's (Mostly) All True': The Death of a Neighbourhood and the Life of Myths

I

What if the plans to build three vast highways crossing Manhattan in New York City in the 1960s had gone through?[1] While we may only speculate about the consequences to New York, in a sense something equivalent happened in Rio de Janeiro two decades earlier. The President Vargas Avenue tore through the heart of a Jewish neighbourhood, the former Little Africa, a Syrian stronghold, and eliminated the Praça Onze, one of the few public spaces enjoyed by residents of nearby favelas, as well as by the many Europeans, naturalized citizens, and native Brazilians who lived in its vicinity.[2]

Rio de Janeiro's loss of the 1940s is a familiar tale of top-down modern urbanism and of the dawn of the automobile age. New York City itself had several neighbourhoods in the Bronx and elsewhere destroyed during the 1950s and 60s for new highways. Around the same time, an interstate was built right through New Orleans's Tremé, and Johannesburg lost one of its few non-segregated areas with the clearing of Sophiatown during Apartheid.[3] Today, in cities like Beijing and New Delhi, countless continue to be uprooted from their neighbourhoods in the name of progress. Despite its geographic centrality and vital role in the cultural life of a national capital, the Cidade Nova met its demise relatively early in what turned out to be a global phenomenon. The President Vargas Avenue, on the one hand, followed those interventions of the late nineteenth and early twentieth centuries inspired by the Baron Haussmann's Parisian boulevards and seen throughout the world's major cities – including, of course, belle époque Rio. On the other hand, it was also in line, as we have suggested, with Nazi fascist influences, signalling a moment of urbanism attuned to totalitarian aesthetics and aims, as well as city planning in function of the car.

While European urban areas rebuilt in accordance to new precepts were often those that had been ravaged during the Second World War (Diefendorf

1989), in American cities great portions of the urban fabric were torn down not by bombs but by bulldozers, in order to make way for 'modern arteries' and buildings. It must be recognized that to a great extent the functioning of our contemporary metropolitan centres rely on some of these interventions. The President Vargas Avenue, for example, acts as an important traffic connection between Rio's centre and its North Zone and suburbs. But the persistent state of desolation and abandonment of much of the Cidade Nova and adjacent areas, long after its construction, hardly serves as a postcard for early to mid-century urban reforms.

Brazil in the 1940s did not have someone like a Camillo Sitte some fifty years earlier or a Jane Jacobs twenty years later, to critique then orthodox city planning or to galvanize dissent and help put a stop to an increasingly ambitious and authoritarian modern urbanism.[4] And any such critical stance would most likely accomplish little during the repressive and controlling Estado Novo. Yet, in spite of censorship, the President Vargas Avenue faced some protest, as popular musicians and poets found ways of voicing discontent. When construction began, demolitions targeted the middle of the avenue, the section between the Praça Onze and the Campo de Santana. Lúcia Silva, in her dissertation (2006), argues that the idea was to subdue the area of greater symbolic value, where there would most likely be more resistance.[5] As she notes, the inauguration of that first segment – a ceremonial cutting down of trees in 1942 – was inconspicuously held on a Saturday night, as if politicians had been seeking not to call attention to the project at that stage (2006: 216). The only opposition acknowledged in the press concerned colonial churches in the avenue's path.

Amidst the apparent near-unanimous support for the project, a samba from 1942 registers dissatisfaction with the disappearance of the square. The song 'Praça Onze', by Herivelto Martins (1912–92) and Grande Otelo (1915–93), became an enormous hit during that year's carnival.[6] Years later, the actor Grande Otelo spoke of reading about the end of the square in an article claiming that a bust of Getúlio Vargas would be put in its place.[7] He wrote lyrics on the subject, lamenting the square's demise but welcoming the homage to the dictator.[8] Otelo showed it to a number of sambistas who were not interested. After much insistence, the composer and performer Herivelto Martins – with whom he worked at the Urca Casino – kept the theme but changed the lyrics:

> They are ending the Praça Onze
> There will no longer be samba schools, no
> The frame drums cry
> All hills cry

Favela, Salgueiro
Mangueira, First Station,
Put away thy tambourines, put them away
Because the samba school won't parade
Farewell my Praça Onze, farewell
We know that you will disappear
You take with you our remembrance
But you shall remain eternally in our hearts
And some day a new square we shall have
And your past we shall sing.

[Vão acabar com a Praça Onze / Não vai haver mais escola de
samba, não vai / Choram os tamborins / Chora o morro inteiro
/ Favela, Salgueiro / Mangueira, Estação Primeira / Guardai
os vossos pandeiros, guardai / Porque a escola de samba não
sai. / Adeus minha Praça Onze, adeus / Já sabemos que vais
desaparecer / Leva contigo a nossa recordação / Mas ficarás
eternamente em nosso coração / E algum dia nova Praça nós
teremos / E o teu passado cantaremos]

The song protests in an elegiac and apparently resigned tone, yet in the
end preserves a degree of hope, revealing the yearning for a more just
future. It leaves clear that those who 'cry', those who lose with the avenue's
construction, are the music's practitioners and devotees, as well as the
inhabitants of the favelas, the hills of some of the descendants and heirs
of Little Africa.

The so-called 'cradle of samba', as the square became known in the
city's cultural cartography, was scraped from Rio de Janeiro's landscape
by the same government responsible for using the musical form as an
instrument of national unification.[9] While popular music penetrated 'high
society', overcoming stigma and increasingly accepted by cultural elites, the
environment that in many ways enabled its formation was largely destroyed,
and those social groups rooted there were once again in Rio's history forced
to move further out of the city's centre, dislocated to distant suburbs and
precarious favelas.

Like the many displaced by the forces of modernization, samba also had
to find ways of adapting to new conditions. Herivelto Martins and Grande
Otelo, for example, who circulated in the capital's 'nobler' spots, performing
in casinos, sensed that to be appreciated by the elites, to become a carnival
success without attracting the attention of censors, their song had to diverge
from the tone of lament in the lyrics. As a union leader, Herivelto had been
schooled in the arts of compromise. The recording of the Trio de Ouro,

of which he participates, creates a sound with the upbeat style typical of samba schools, privileging the *tamborim* (a small frame drum), the *surdo* (a large bass drum), and for the first time adopting the whistle as a rhythmic element.[10]

The song helps to disprove the truism of samba's co-optation by the Estado Novo, demonstrating not only the complexities of cultural production in the 1940s, but also suggesting that sambistas of the Vargas era deserve some of the credit usually given to middle-class composers of the late 1960s, who managed to skirt censorship and offer veiled criticism of authoritarian regimes. Their repertoire displays a range of tactics to subvert expectations of the market and of the state's cultural apparatus. Analogous examples of creative resistance to the regime's restrictions abound throughout Brazil's cultural life, including the local Jewish press. The first issue of the *Imprensa Israelita* to follow the prohibition of publishing in foreign languages, for example, commemorates the Estado Novo's anniversary in good Portuguese, but opens from right to left, as its version in Yiddish did.[11] Without breaking the law, the Jewish newspaper registers opposition to it.

Another samba responding to the Avenue's construction appears to conform to the Estado Novo's ideology but proves to be more subtle and layered. The song, by Little Africa frequenter Gastão Vianna (?–1959) and accomplished flautist Benedito Lacerda (1903–58), evidences the (partial) success of the DIP's intentions of subjugating cultural expressions to the ideal of a united and productive nation: 'The Praça Onze disappeared / But samba can be made anywhere / Here comes the Getúlio Vargas Avenue / Which will be pride of this beautiful capital' ('Desapareceu a Praça Onze / Mas o samba se faz em qualquer local / Vem surgindo a Avenida Getúlio Vargas / Que será o orgulho desta linda capital').[12] At the level of the written word the government's propagandist objectives seem fulfilled, but the percussive rhythm and back vocals (the *pastoras*) evoke the Praça Onze's former terreiros. Contrary to the Trio de Ouro's version of 'Praça Onze', the dissonance in 'Vem Surgindo a Avenida' (Here Comes the Avenue) is between the sanitized lyrics and the rhythm of Afro-Brazilian religious ceremonies. The flagrant contradiction between sound and sense complements the song, as if it were pointing to the contradictions within the very programme of a government that at once legitimized popular music and wiped out one of its most meaningful places.

II

It took an outsider of uncommon sensibility to capture the significance of samba in Brazilian society, and the profound consequences of the Praça

Onze's disappearance. Orson Welles (1915–85) arrived in Rio de Janeiro in February 1942, the year following his first feature film, *Citizen Kane*. Appointed as a Special Ambassador during the war, he travelled to Latin America at the behest of Nelson Rockefeller, then a major stockholder and member of RKO Pictures' board of directors. The effort was part of the Good Neighbor Policy, seeking to counteract the influence of Axis powers in Latin America and to forward the interests of the United States. The Hollywood studio would foot the bill for Welles's film, with the Office of Inter-American Affairs guaranteeing against potential financial losses.

After *Citizen Kane*, while directing *The Magnificent Ambersons*, Welles had been contemplating a variety of projects, including a history of jazz. He supervised shooting in Mexico of an animal christening ceremony, and an episode entitled 'My Friend Bonito' would have later integrated the larger *It's All True*, the unfinished film's title. The Wisconsin native came to Rio de Janeiro amidst carnival celebrations, and it is difficult to overstate the impact that the experience had on him. For months to come, Welles would nurture his fascination with samba and with Brazil's popular culture, out of which evolved one of the episodes of *It's All True*, focusing on carnival. Even after his departure from South America, the director kept attempting to make a fictional film called '*Samba*', about interspersed love stories involving an Irish and American woman, the Brazilian man that she ends up with, and the American who loses her, played by Welles. It was to be set in 'the world's loveliest city', during 'the strange, the fabulous, the violent, the inexpressibly beautiful carnival of Rio'. The project, for which he developed an argument, screen treatment, and production outline, did not seem to have convinced Hollywood executives.[13]

While in Rio, Welles shot footage of carnival in black-and-white and Technicolor – over 30,000 feet of the latter, according to reports in the Brazilian press, where he was quoted as saying that 'the carioca carnival is the only institution in the whole world completely devoid of commercial spirit'.[14] In a radio broadcast, Welles later described the experience as akin to 'trying to capture a hurricane'. The venture involved a twenty-seven-member crew, from both RKO and Welles's Mercury company, and filming extended into June 1942. It also mobilized local authorities, at least initially: records from around the time of carnival show that Police Chief and Nazi admirer Filinto Müller offered his support, and several newspapers published photos of Welles and RKO vice-president Phil Reisman meeting with Getúlio Vargas and DIP director Lourival Fontes, among others.[15]

Preparations for the film entailed extensive research on Brazil, as had been the case with other Latin American countries. Several hundred pages were written on major literary and historical figures, events, and cultural or socio-economic issues, including a range of topics like the Amazon, positivism, race relations, mining, and the church.[16] As Welles spent time in the country, it became increasingly clear that his true interests lay elsewhere: the milieu of the Praça Onze seemed to attract him the most. The filmmaker did not measure efforts to understand the social context of samba and the history of carnival. Besides the research staff that had already been assembled to produce the general reports, local experts were commissioned to write specifically about popular music and culture. Among them we find radio personalities, musicians, writers, and journalists such as Almirante and Haroldo Barbosa.

This unprecedented undertaking left us a substantive body of literature which has largely not been explored, with texts like 'Samba Goes to Town', by Alex Viany, 'The Truth about the Samba', 'Formation of the Carnival Spirit', 'How Different Races and Peoples Contributed to Carnival', and 'The Whys of Rio's Carnival', by Rui Costa, and yet another series on carnival by Giussepe Ghiaroni.[17] In a twenty-something-page memo to Welles entitled 'The Genealogy of Samba and other Aspects of an Unquiet Life', screenwriter Robert Meltzer synthesizes different opinions and theories about the musical phenomenon's development. After interviewing practising authorities, 'folklorists', musicians, and 'old friends and drunken companions' – including Little Africa mainstay Patrício Teixeira – Meltzer, an amateur jazz musician, wrote a well-informed and perceptive piece, touching on themes like the choro's connection to the Brazilian 'polka' and the controversy generated by Gonzaga's maxixe in the presidential palace. He ends up, in his own words, with 'a residue' of what 'might be called The Truth about Samba'. Passages from these pioneering but largely forgotten studies and testimonies gave great importance to the Praça Onze, while lacking the condescension of Arthur Ramos's and Graça Aranha's previous writings on the subject.

Orson Welles also enlisted the help of the two composers behind 'Farewell Praça Onze'. He hired Herivelto Martins as the assistant director, choreographer, and composer. Grande Otelo, the star performer, was cast as a malandro and the 'spirit of Carnival'. Welles's close relationship with the two would develop into a strong friendship, and both Brazilians later described their many nights together during the North American's stay in Rio.[18] Otelo would have also been a character in the feature 'Samba'. Even when already back in the United States, Welles tried to sell him to Hollywood executives in the screen treatment as a 'black blend of Mickey Rooney and Chaplin', an artist 'with as much talent as anybody I've ever met'. Neither of the projects came to fruition, however, and It's All True was aborted after changes in RKO's direction, despite all the time and resources that had been invested, and notwithstanding Welles's pleas to be allowed to complete it. Most of the reels were purportedly dumped into the Pacific Ocean, although in a message to his 'good friends in Brazil' the director claims to have purchased the film in its entirety from RKO.[19] He wanted to incorporate existing footage of the Praça Onze, for example, into the '*Samba*' project.

It becomes clear, then, as film scholar Robert Stam has demonstrated, that Welles's experience in Brazil represented far more than an 'adventure' in the tropics. Likewise, as Stam also shows, it becomes apparent that the direction taken by *It's All True*, and the filmmaker's attraction to Afro-Brazilian expressions, bothered both local officials – not particularly interested in promoting an image of blackness abroad – and North American executives, aware that a great parcel of their domestic public would not welcome a movie with black protagonists.[20] Reception in Brazil of the *Citizen Kane* director's trip was initially very positive. Occasionally, outlets expressed some bewilderment at the foreigner's peculiar attraction to the popular classes, implying that interest in the Praça Onze could be no more than perfunctory. In an edition of the *Dom Casmurro* magazine from February, for instance, we read: 'this giant is now in Rio. What aspect of Carnival will his bizarre taste register in Technicolor? Will he watch the farewell of the Praça Onze? [...] Or will he find the Praça Onze too excited and dangerous, exchanging the acrid taste of the cachaça for the subtle aroma of the posh champagne from dazzling casinos!'

Afro-Brazilian culture had already become part of the repertoire through which the country represented itself to the world, but *It's All True* appears to have crossed a line.[21] By April, the tide had turned. Press coverage began to complain about the filming of favelas, and Welles's advisers were held responsible for how – as an article's headline proclaimed – 'Carioca Carnival is Going to be Very Dark on the Screen'. The newspaper laments that 'Welles's dignitaries have been hiring black "artists" from the hills', and concludes:

> Without doubt the informers of Mister Orson Welles are committing a grave injustice to the people and to our customs, without knowledge of the DIP, where several writers and journalists [...] with the best sense about Brazilian things, could better conduct these details and avoid the collection of cinema sequences in which only black people figure, as though Rio were another Harlem district.

The North Americans were obviously sensitive to these charges, since they had such articles translated.[22]

The discomfort with race extended to a dismissal of any notion of samba as a representative or worthwhile phenomenon. In what became a battle over national identity, Vinicius de Moraes calls Welles 'a great Brazilian', one who was 'beginning to know Brazil, or at least an important side of the soul of Brazil, better than many sociologists, than many novelists'. Another commentator, on the other side of the aisle, articulated anxiety over how the film distorted 'our aspect of a civilized nation', blaming Welles's counsellors for letting him film – 'to his delight' – 'no good half-breeds' and 'dances of negroes'. As a third writer put it, summarizing the attitudes towards samba of many among the ruling elites: 'if it were only Culture'.[23]

One of the great virtues of *It's All True* had been its 'self-conscious effort at targeting a Latin American as well as US audience' (Benamou 2007: 46). This turned into one of the reasons it became unviable, paradoxically. A central episode in the film, after all, focused on an urban Brazil that constituted an embarrassment to a significant portion of the educated audience, and remained somewhat of a mystery to those sympathetic to it. Aside from those who denigrated samba, the Praça Onze and its surroundings were opaque even to researchers who welcomed its place in the national imaginary. That much transpires from the unpublished texts written at Welles's request, though they are nonetheless valuable sources for information about the neighbourhood, and on how it was perceived by lettered observers who doubled up as participants. Ghiaroni (1919–2008), a poet and journalist of humble background, saw the Praça Onze as 'Carnival's liver, if not Carnival's heart', and thought that 'our popular music, being a simple thing, is made by simple people'. He stresses that the square was dominated by blacks, and writes that during the festivities people slept on doorsteps because streetcars did not run at late hours. To Ghiaroni, in São Paulo's dance halls the races were separated 'by personal and moral laws', whereas in Rio the 'customers are a mixed-up throng of whites, blacks, and half breeds'.[24]

Alex Viany (1918–92), who would serve as *O Cruzeiro*'s Hollywood correspondent from 1945 until 1948, paints a similar picture of the square, evoking Lima Barreto's suggestion of a class bond that trumps racial identification. He also comes closer to being celebratory of the Praça's function within the city:

> Praça Onze is like the African Embassy in Rio during Carnival. Its feasts are the biggest social events for the Carioca negro. Those feasts are like gigantic Harlem jam-and-swing sessions elevated to the highest degree. They are really unique in the whole world. And they can't be imitated. [...] The white workers also go to Praça Onze during Carnival. There, among their negro brothers they are happier and more free than in the middle-class Carnival hangouts, Avenida Rio Branco, or than in beautiful but snobbish Copacabana.

Viany echoes some of Ghiaroni's claims about mixtures between races, but adds a different perspective to the by-now familiar representations of Little Africa. Unlike other authors, Viany realized that the square does not only act as a centripetal force for black Brazilians during carnival. It also played a centrifugal role, functioning as a 'centre of irradiation' that 'can be taken as a democratic symbol'. The Praça Onze, which Viany constantly links to the favelas, is therefore anything but a ghetto. To the author, it shapes the city's everyday, exerting an influence even on language: 'Slang is born there and takes only a few days to take the city', he writes, adding that 'there you'll find the most genuine freedom in thinking and speaking'.[25]

Countering the vision of a space that only comes alive during carnival, Viany speculates – not without a dose of paternalism – about the neighbourhood's social life, and the political agency of its residents: 'The psychology of Praça Onze is, naturally or complexly, one of force. The workers, negroes or whites, are used to fighting for their rights, even if they haven't sufficient knowledge to distinguish right from wrong. But they had to fight to live, to get jobs, to eat – and they go on fighting'. According to him, reactions to the President Vargas Avenue's construction were resigned, and people also expected that their hills would be demolished. They believe in progress, Viany writes, and went along with the urban interventions out of a wary expectation that 'they must have better houses in better conditions by then'. The obelisk of Vargas, to have been erected in the former square, would act as a reminder to the government of its promises. The obelisk, as we know, was not built, and many of the promises were not kept.

III

Although we will never know how It's All True would have turned out, it is possible to get a sense of how Welles envisioned 'The Story of Samba'. The uncompleted project generated two documentaries by the director Rogério Sganzerla (1946–2004), Nem tudo é verdade (1986) and Tudo é Brasil (1997), as well as It's All True: Based on an Unfinished Film by Orson Welles (1993), under the direction of Richard Wilson, Myron Meisel, and Bill Krohn. Based on the recovered footage and interviews conducted for these movies, along with Stam's aforementioned work, Catherine Benamou's It's All True: Orson Welles's Pan-American Odyssey (2007), and archival findings, we can attempt to reconstruct some of the director's insights and intentions.

The section on carnival was to be accompanied by another episode shot in Brazil on the 'jangadeiros', a group of rafters who travelled for over sixty days at sea from the north-eastern state of Ceará to the national capital in order to voice their grievances to the president.[26] The urban piece, in a similar vein, sought to do more than illustrate the 'simple' and festive nature of its subjects. Welles frequently took care to dispel the notion that 'Brazilians think seriously of nothing but dancing and singing and indulging in other aspects of Carnaval'.[27] At the same time, his project recognized the complexities and plurality within the music, and was to have included an 'anatomy of samba', presenting some of its instrumentation and variants (Benamou 2007: 106-7). What jumps out here, however, is the contrast between the Praça Onze's one-dimensional place in lettered cartographies – as the locus of popular carnival – and the richer texture that it gained in Welles's view. And although the film toed the government line when speaking about the Vargas Avenue's construction, it broke the official silence regarding the losses implicated by the constantly heralded march of progress.[28]

As both Stam and Benamou have also shown, Welles's film was inserted in certain cinematic traditions while proposing a highly original approach to the relationships between sound and image, as well as between fiction and documentary. In the manner of Walter Ruttman's *Berlin: Symphony of a Great City* (1927) and other city symphony films, *It's All True* conveyed visual impressions in a semi-documentary style, with external travelling shots coupled with an at times anthropocentric gaze, in the Flaherty vein. If works of the symphony genre create continuity between the images and even suggest a type of narrative through use of musical scores, Welles's movie seemed to have music as an even more integral component of its formal structure: in his own words, 'music had to do more than complement the picture – it must dictate what was to be seen' (Stam 1997: 231). Grande Otelo explains that the Urca Casino ceded its artists, and that several songs, including carnival hits from 1942, were either recorded live, in synch at Cinédia Studios, or for playback in Odeon studio sessions.

Samba on the screen was not particularly new or revolutionary: in the 1930s and 40s Brazil's popular music would be the main ingredient of popular and lucrative features known as *chanchadas*. They absorbed elements from the revue, showcased acts by radio stars, and were clearly influenced by Hollywood musicals. *Alô Alô Carnaval* (1936), a major success, had in its cast names like Almirante, Noel Rosa, and Carmen Miranda. It also included the Bando da Lua, one of the first samba groups to harmonize their vocals according to the style in vogue in the United States. They would accompany Carmen Miranda to Hollywood and participate in several of her films. Produced by the local Cinédia in partnership with Waldow Film, *Alô Alô Carnaval*, like other chanchadas, meant to entertain above all else: among humorous dialogues, action scenes, and musical numbers, they venture into parodies or critiques of things such as the Brazilian predilection of foreign culture, but never threaten nationalist sensibilities.

The Rio de Janeiro segment of Welles's *It's All True* received the collaboration of Cinédia Studios and artists associated to it. Chanchadas, like the radio, were not closed off to black artists: Grande Otelo's presence, after all, was pervasive. Yet, black musicians in general made less money than their white counterparts, and public praise of their work often covered for racism (McCann 2004: 16). Something similar occurred in the film industry: blacks were relegated to caricatured roles, and their numbers were disproportionately small. The frequently on-screen Bando da Lua, for instance, only had white members. Welles's footage, then, anticipating neo-realists and the Cinema Novo, in part simply by virtue of shooting outdoor scenes like Ruttman or Dziga Vertov, had black men and women featuring prominently on the screen. His roster of musicians and bands included Little Africa luminaries like Pixinguinha and songs like 'Lamento Negro' (Black Lament), besides other Afro-Brazilian artists, among them Ataulfo Alves, Horacina Corrêa, and Carmen Costa. At first, Welles had difficulties hiring black extras, since almost only whites would respond to newspaper ads for people of 'good appearance'.[29]

A contemporary counterpoint might be illustrative. On 24 August 1942, just two days after Brazil joined the Allies in the war effort, Walt Disney premiered in Rio de Janeiro its sixth animated feature, *Saludos Amigos*. Commissioned by the US State Department as part of the Good Neighbor policy, it was also a partnership with RKO. In the film that introduced the character of Joe Carioca, known in Brazil as Zé Carioca, we again see samba centre stage. Besides using some of its best animators, Disney enlisted several of Brazil's most important musicians, like Aloysio de Oliveira, who sang Ari Barroso's 'Aquarela do Brasil'. *Saludos Amigos* received Academy Award nominations for Best Sound, Original Music Score, and Best Song. While skirting race, the anthropomorphized parrot Zé Carioca embodies several traits of the malandro, and the feature combines animated sequences with Technicolor images of carnival. Unlike in *It's All True*, however, this time we are in a virtually all-white carnival, in a virtually all-white city.[30]

Welles, taking a stab at his country's cinematic establishment, wrote that Rio's carnival 'defies studio representation', 'hopelessly beyond the scope of any Hollywood spectacle' (Stam 1997: 121). In one of the versions of the *It's All True* script, it is defined as 'Fourth of July multiplied by a million'. Nonetheless, besides external footage shot during carnival, he did attempt to recreate the Praça Onze in the Cinédia Studios, in Technicolor. According to Herivelto Martins, Welles closely followed the advice of his locally assembled team of sambistas, striving not for a stylized version but for maximum realism (Norberto and Vieira 1992: 103–4), which included techniques like the use of decoy cameras. Attempts to replicate the square's carnival included as many as 229 Brazilian extras. On a day when one of these scenes was being filmed, Waldo Frank visited Welles, in the company of Oswald de Andrade. The New York-based writer described the 'fabulous' setting and the 'fabulous' price that the 'dark men and women' had been paid to be there. But, when the singing begins, he writes, 'in a moment, the time, the place, the money, are forgotten'. Extras and director are 'possessed'. Frank seems to share in the enchantment: 'I could listen to Brazilian folk music forever. It is unfathomably beautiful and unfathomably profound' (Frank 1943: 42).

Orson Welles seemed to comprehend or have an intuition about what the Praça Onze's disappearance meant for the city's cultural life and future. In an interview years later, Grande Otelo recalls the following episode: 'And then there was a very beautiful scene [...] as if we were in the Praça Onze, and a boy [...] came walking through a long avenue, he looked towards a lamp post and it had a sign: Praça Onze'. Nostalgically, he concludes: 'When the boy looked, the sign fell, meaning that it was the end of the Praça Onze'.[31] With some minor differences, the scene is described in Richard Wilson's shooting log, adding that it would be intercut with Otelo saying farewell to the square, as the song 'Farewell, Praça Onze' plays like an echo. After a fade out, the film would show Welles on the roof of a soon to be demolished building overlooking the Praça, with a representative of the government announcing new housing projects: 'model homes' both for those displaced by the President Vargas Avenue's construction and for favela residents. Welles did shoot footage in nearby hills, and we can only speculate about whether his final editing would have highlighted incongruences in the official line.[32]

In another episode loaded with meanings that are not likely to have escaped those involved in the film, the song 'Batuque no morro' was performed simultaneously in two symbolic spaces that stood for socio-racial polarities: the white Linda Batista in the Urca Casino and the black Grande Otelo in the Praça Onze, both singing about a cultural expression from the favelas. The musical scene's contrapuntal montage bridged the city's divide: while we do not know how the footage and editing would have contrasted the prestigious casino of the upper classes with the humble public square, the dual performance brought together the Cidade Nova and the South Zone locales in the studio. A juxtaposing of places separated by geography and class that only filmmaking, and perhaps music, could allow for. As if to take even further the cinematic integration of the city's extremities, it was carried out in the North Zone, where the Cinédia Studios were located.

The montage could be characterized as celebratory of miscegenation and as a proponent of the myth of Brazil as a land of racial harmony, were the movie not cognizant of the tragic consequences of the Praça's destruction, particularly to largely non-white favela residents. In treatments from later months, Welles wrote about the scene that 'the contrast is one not only of voices, but of directions'. Noting carnival's trend 'indoors to the Baile and the Casino', he explains that 'the Carnival of traditions is a celebration of the streets alone'.[33] Welles seemed conscious of what those spaces conjured, and their depiction as side-by-side disregards the usual foreigner's itinerary, cinematic conventions, and perhaps even subverts the hierarchies by which urbanists and politicians privileged the South Zone of Urca's casino over areas like the Cidade Nova. The scene in a sense breaks down or approximates the *here* and *there* of Manuel Antônio de Almeida's nineteenth-century narrative.

This was already an imaginary Praça Onze, recreated through the memories of its frequenters, all aware of how their actual square – at the time under construction – would soon vanish. *It's All True* was most likely the first to transpose samba to the screens in order to articulate a collective anxiety, a political awareness, or at least for more than entertainment.[34] Some two decades later, a more experimental and politicized theatre and the Cinema Novo would follow suit, turning popular music into a centrepiece of their aesthetics. Yet, in the 1940s, Welles appears to capture something that escaped the press, politicians, and urbanists rallying behind the construction of the President Vargas Avenue. While the movie seemed to tap into or find inspiration in cultural porosity, the demolitions entailed by the new reform would play a decisive role in the further spatial segregation of Rio de Janeiro along socio-economic lines. It is as if Welles perceived the imminent changes, situating the imperilled cityscape in a recent past and in an imaginary plane, recalling the literary procedures of Machado de Assis a few decades earlier.

Some of these urban transformations were familiar to Welles from close parallels in recent US history, and had been in his mind prior to his arrival in Brazil. In Welles's Pan-American imaginary, as Stam suggests, Grande Otelo and Pixinguinha replaced Duke Ellington and Louis Armstrong, who were to be central to his never made 'Story of Jazz' (Stam 1997: 123–4). If samba and jazz could function in a continuum, so did Brazil's aggressive pursuit of progress, embodied in the construction of the Avenue and modelled after a North American push for the motor car. This had provided a central subtext to *The Magnificent Ambersons*, a movie on which RKO executives tagged a happy ending, since Welles had to surrender editorial control after travelling to Rio. To cite one of the film's critics, the picture's concern 'was the childhood of America itself: the genteel time before the arrival of the automobile'. Amidst Rio's aggressive urban reforms, it is as if Welles saw Brazil embarking on a similar path.

Itself palimpsestic, 'erased' by studio executives and later partly recovered by moviemakers, scholars, and the personal remembrances of those involved, *It's All True* integrates and sheds light on the multilayered fabric of the Cidade Nova and of Rio de Janeiro. Unfinished, it would never be able to circulate, and in that way insert the Praça Onze in cognitive mappings of moviegoers from Brazil and abroad; and, perhaps, we can speculate, impact those decision-makers who thought so little of the neighbourhood.

IV

The Cidade Nova's disfigurement was motivated not only by short-term real estate speculation and pressures to improve the circulation of cars, but by ideological reasons, disregarding both humane and long-term practical concerns.[35] In one of the dialogues written for *It's All True*, Orson Welles speaks of how the Praça Onze would leave 'saudades', which he defines as a 'heartache – something like that – sentimental memory, lonesomeness – a longing remembrance of something past, or of someone gone away'. More than ten years after the avenue's inauguration, Henrique Dodsworth's book about its achievement does not recognize any of the price that was paid. He opens defiantly: 'The necessity of a violent surge of progress has not yet abolished, in Brazil, the spirit of resistance against realizations that exceed common standards' (1955: 5). There is only one mention of the public square, in passing.

Today, any sense of the Cidade Nova as an actual place seems to have vanished. When the neighbourhood's name is mentioned to long-time residents of the Morro da Providência, the former Favela Hill, it produces puzzled looks. Mentions of the Praça Onze, however, often awaken fond memories of childhood carnivals and affordable cinemas.[36] Amidst brand new glass towers, the Sambódromo, dilapidated structures, a polluted canal and vacant lots used to store junk cars, one would be hard-pressed to imagine the area's past. Given this current state, it is worth asking whether some of the writers and artists of the previous chapters would not have had a more accurate sense of the far-reaching consequences of the avenue's construction than the technocrats and ideologues behind it.

Rather than wrap a critique of modern urbanism on the limits of objectivity and the perils of scientific empiricism, perhaps we ought to ascribe its most dramatic failures precisely to a disregard for the tangible, everyday contingencies and possibilities of life in an urban environment. The metaphors privileged in discourses of the press and city planners in the 1940s took up a longstanding tradition of speaking of the city as a human body (from the Renaissance to the Chicago School): one newspaper in Rio de Janeiro argued that 'with the evolution of mentalities, under the influx of renewal principles, the heart of the city should also evolve'. Another maintained that 'in a short while the concrete highway will contain all the palpitation and life of the metropolis'.[37] References to modern, wide streets as arteries abound, including in the writings of Alfred Agache. Yet in this case the organic images conceal the most dehumanizing processes: in the arteries flowed not people but machines, motor cars, military units, translated into control of capital and power concentrated in the hands of a minority.[38]

By the mid-1940s one can no longer claim the innocence of early twentieth-century fascination with technology. We must historicize, not make excuses. According to an edition of *A Manhã* from the week preceding its inauguration, the new avenue responded to the 'necessity of giving the centre of our wonderful city an aspect worthy of its growing economic importance, with the vertiginous elevation of its culture, with the sudden prestige obtained by the country as a nation comparable to the greatest and most powerful of the civilized world' (3 September 1944). When those words were printed, *civilized world* of course referred to a continent amidst the carnage of the Second World War.

In a radio broadcast Orson Welles speaks about his trip to Rio de Janeiro as 'the end of civilization as we know it', following the comment with his characteristic boisterous laughter.[39] This half-joke, which might at first seem a repeat of the familiar trope of the backwards tropics, gains new meaning once we again consider how the so-called civilized world found itself engulfed in a brutal war. It is a tragic irony which Welles himself explores: in a scene from *Citizen Kane*, explaining his disbelief that war was imminent, the protagonist tells a reporter that European leaders are too intelligent to embark on a project that would mean 'the end of civilization as we know it'. After two devastating wars, that would not be such an undesirable thing, if one allowed 'civilization' to preserve its geopolitical connotations, reified in the Brazilian press. 'To arrest the meaning of words once and for all, that is what Terror wants', declares Jean-François Lyotard in *Rudiments Païens* (Certeau 1984: 165). In the most modest of ways, perhaps Welles's playful comment helps to halt what Terror wants.

Even on the eve of the Estado Novo, not all were swept up by the forces of civilization and progress. Some asserted their allegiances to the concrete level of the neighbourhood, transcending the abstracting values of modernity. Noel Rosa, against the grain of urban development, where Copacabana beach assumed precisely the status of symbol of modernity,[40] writes a song where the first-person reasons: 'I was born in Estácio / And cannot change my blood type / You bet that a palm tree from the Mangue

/ Cannot live in the sands of Copacabana' ('Nasci no Estácio / Não posso mudar minha massa de sangue, / Você pode crer que palmeira do Mangue / Não vive na areia de Copacabana'). The 'X do Problema' of its title, the 'crux of the matter', concerns leaving the Estácio neighbourhood. The invitation to become a movie star poses a problem to Noel Rosa's lyric voice, a woman who directs a samba school. The song's persona, given the choice, opts for the unglamorous neighbourhood and the Mangue's palm trees over a palace and banquet, as a form of recognition of local affiliations and certain values ('Sou independente, conforme se vê'; 'I'm independent as you can see'). Amidst the maelstrom of modernity and nationalism, Noel Rosa celebrates the particularities of the familiar, without any hint of intransigence towards the new. Copacabana was just not for him.

In an increasingly utilitarian, so-called pragmatic world order dictated by short-term bottom lines, our more creative artists, poets, musicians, or filmmakers might continue to be dismissed as irrelevant to everyday life, out-of-touch dreamers when contrasted to the seriousness of 'real world' statistical tables. Yet where the metaphors of urbanists and the state-controlled press were frequently misleading and inadequate, a popular composer's verses emerge as far more attuned to the complexities and contradictions of living in a rapidly changing city. Orson Welles was prescient, and so were Herivelto Martins and Grande Otelo. The Praça Onze ended, buried under a highway like so many other public spaces and affectionate references of our cities: run over by the march of time. The songwriters were mistaken, however, to think that there would be no more samba schools or carnival parades. They were too entrenched in Rio de Janeiro's cultural cartography and 'consciousness'. Whether or not certain purists agree, samba has strengthened since, itself a form of palimpsest, retaining elements of the past while acquiring new forms.

A number of songs from the mid-1940s, taking up the theme of the Praça Onze's end, in fact proclaim its resilience. Besides the more famous version, maintaining that the square will remain 'eternally in our hearts', several other forgotten sambas suggest a similar fate, rendering the Praça Onze as a seemingly intractable state of mind: 'it did not die and it will not die [...] those born in the Praça Onze cannot forget' ('não morreu nem morrerá [...] quem nasceu na Praça Onze é difícil esquecer') sings one. Another claims that 'those who cried wasted their time', 'to us it will never end / [...] / the square continues to exist' ('perdeu seu tempo quem chorou a sua morte', 'pra nós nunca há de acabar / [...] / a praça continua a existir'). And a third, despite the loss – 'Who saw you then, who sees you now Praça Onze / cut up into wide streets / doesn't tire from seeing with nostalgia / the President Vargas Avenue' ('Quem te viu, quem te vê Praça Onze / retalhada em ruas bem

largas / não se cansa de olhar com saudades / a avenida Presidente Vargas')
– reaffirms in the refrain: 'Praça Onze / Praça Onze / I keep in my heart your
bronze plaque' ('Guardo no peito a tua placa de bronze').[41]

All of these songs, like the Praça Onze that Orson Welles included in his
vision for *It's All True*, connect remembrance with singing ('and your past
we shall sing'). Music, and by extension poetry, dance, and other artistic
forms, become not only a mechanism to uncover submerged layers but also
an instrument to resist 'erasures'. An assurance that current and future
struggles (whatever they may hold) will maintain a link to an invisible past,
to cherished and shared memories, so long as one sings. At least that seems
to be these sambas' suggestion.

Notes

1 The Lower Manhattan Expressway, an eight-lane elevated highway, was set in
motion by Robert Moses, the 'master builder' who famously asserted that 'cities
are for traffic'. Like plans for the Mid-Manhattan Expressway and the Cross-
Harlem Expressway, it did not come to fruition. On Moses, see Caro 1974.

2 The area between the Candelária Church and the Campo de Santana concentrated
Syrian merchants who often lived on the second floor of their establishments. See
Ribeiro 2000.

3 On New York, see Berman 1982: 287–348. On Sophiatown, see Goodhew 2004.

4 See Sitte's *The Art of Building Cities*, first published in German (1889), a vigorous
defence of the city square against what the Austrian architect saw as the sterility
of modern planning. On Sitte, see Schorske 1981: 62–72. Also see Jacobs's
watershed critique of contemporary Moses-style urban renewal, *The Death and
Life of Great American Cities* (1961).

5 The stretch was also less valued, entailing cheaper reparation costs than the area
closer to the Candelária Church (Lima 1990: 80). Beginning demolitions there
might also have given the project a sense of inevitability.

6 The song won a prestigious competition sponsored by the Fluminense Football
Club, along with another now classic song, 'Ai que saudades da Amélia', by
Ataulfo Alves and Mário Lago.

7 According to newspapers that I consulted, the monument was an obelisk rather
than a bust. A commission of workers supposedly sponsored the obelisk to
honour Vargas. The plans were cancelled at the president's request – per *A Manhã*
(3 September 1944) – since the materials required could be better employed in
'immediate necessities' related to the war effort. The potential to slow down
traffic was also mentioned in the article.

8 The original lyrics, as recounted by Grande Otelo in Rogério Sganzerla's
documentary *Nem Tudo é Verdade* (It's Not All True, 1986) read: 'My people, this
year the school won't parade / let me explain / we no longer have the Praça Onze
/ for our emotions. / There, where the women showed us their moves / a great
man in bronze / will be by everyone remembered'.

9 On samba and national identity, see McCann 2004: 41–95; with a greater focus

on race, see also Davis 2009: 31–4. On nationalism and samba under the Vargas era, see Tupy 1985.

10 The Trio de Ouro was composed of Herivelto, Nilo Chagas, and Dalva de Oliveira, all active in radio. They recorded the song at Columbia with Castro Barbosa and the Regional de Benedito Lacerda.

11 *Imprensa Israelita*, 7 November 1941. On censorship and samba, particularly of the malandro, see McCann 2004: 65–7.

12 The song was recorded in 1942 by Cyro Monteiro and Nelson Gonçalves at RCA Victor. This and all subsequent recordings were accessed in the archives of the MIS.

13 The material amounts to over eighty pages of text. Different versions of the screen treatment, including drafts, can be found among the Orson Welles materials at Indiana University's Lilly Library (box 16, folders 24, 25, 26).

14 Quoted from the *Diário de São Paulo* and the *Diário de Notícias*, 20 February 1942. Newspaper clippings of virtually any mention of the director in the national press were kept, and often translated into English. They can now be found at the Lilly Library. For more details of the filming, see Benamou 2007: 47–8.

15 Filinto Müller (1900–73) visited the Gestapo's Heinrich Himmler in 1937, and his tenure as Police Chief (1933–42) was marked by arrests and persecution of political dissidents. The *Meio Dia* published a note where Welles thanks him for the police's 'generous and wonderful cooperation' with filming activities (28 February 1942). Several photographs show Welles with important officials, including Müller (see box 35, folder 4, Welles materials, Lilly Library).

16 Among the subjects we find Santos Dumont, Oswaldo Cruz, Casimiro de Abreu, Diogo Feijó, Tomás Gonzaga, José do Patrocínio, Barão de Mauá, Chico Rei, and Xica da Silva, as well as a mix of topics including sugar, coffee and rubber cultures, gaúchos, diamonds, Bahia, Fortaleza, Cuiabá, Belém, São Paulo, the Jangadeiros, Bandeirantes, and Macumba.

17 Other collaborators included Edmar Morel, Ayres de Andrade Junior, Luiz Edmundo, Aydano Couto Ferraz, Ernani Fornari, and Clóvis de Gusmão. Almirante signed texts about songs by 'cangaceiros' and tied to funerals, congadas, bumba-meu-boi, and 'the famous challenges of the North' (box 18, Welles materials, Lilly Library).

18 Herivelto recounts Welles's desire to join him on a humble vacation house in the Ilha do Governador, as well as the long nights the three spent together in bars and in his Catumbi home. He also recalls early mornings at the studio, where a prompt Welles would reproach the Brazilians' tardiness (Norberto and Vieira 1992: 101–4).

19 The undated document appears to be a telegram (box 23, folder 14, Welles materials, Lilly Library).

20 See 'Pan-American Interlude: Orson Welles in Brazil, 1942' (Stam 1997: 107–32). Stam highlights Welles's 'nonracist approach' and the 'audacity' of the project, stressing the director's relationship to Afro-Brazilian culture and black Brazilians as well as the 'racial subtext to some of the opposition' to the film, a 'subtext recapitulated [...] in the discourse of many of Welles's critics' (109).

21 A 1942 issue of the magazine *Travel in Brazil* published by the DIP shows a black man and a woman dancing on the cover with *frevo* umbrellas. Elsewhere, it includes black Brazilians and two *baianas*, as well as a piece by Mário de Andrade.

22 See 'The Favelas in the Film of Orson Welles', in the *Diário da Noite*, 22 April 1942; the quoted text came from the *Meio Dia*, 28 April 1942 (box 18, folder 11, Welles materials, Lilly Library).

23 Vinicius is quoted from *A Manhã*, 30 April 1942; the second text comes from *Cine Rádio Jornal*, 20 May 1942, signed by Gatinha Angorá, while the last quote is Enéas Viany's, from a text found among the Welles manuscripts (box 18, folder 11, Welles materials, Lilly Library).

24 See box 18, folder 14, Welles materials, Lilly Library. 'Half-breed' is the North American translation.

25 See box 19, folder 7, Welles materials, Lilly Library.

26 On the 'jangadeiros' episode, see Benamou 2007 and Stam 1997: 107–32.

27 Quoted from the transcript of a radio broadcast (18 April 1942) (see box 9, folder 37, Welles materials, Lilly Library).

28 The film's treatment contains a visit to Vargas, who says the director has his 'sympathies'. In a dialogue with a government authority, which was to include images of the avenue's model, the reform is presented as a solution to the city's problems. The same scene, however, would also have Otelo speaking about the loss of the square (box 16, folder 22, Welles materials, Lilly Library).

29 He attempted to hire around 100 black extras out of a total of 400, but only eight or ten of the 1,000 who showed up at the RKO offices were not white, according to an article in the *Diário de Notícias*, 29 March 1942. The ads specified 'boa aparência' as a requisite, which can function as racial code in Brazil (see box 18, folder 9, Welles materials, Lilly Library).

30 As a document of US diplomacy, much remains to be said about *Saludos Amigos*. When compared to misconceptions and stereotypes about Latin America in contemporary Hollywood, Disney's film defies certain expectations: although a parrot, Zé Carioca speaks eloquent Portuguese (rather than Spanish), and it is Donald Duck – the monolingual North American – who strikes the viewer as the buffoon, unable to understand his host. For more detailed and different takes, see Stam 1997: 119–20 and Benamou 2007: 42–5. On US–Brazil relations during the war, see Tota 2009.

31 Grande Otelo is quoted from about forty minutes into Sganzerla's *Nem tudo é verdade* (1986).

32 See fact sheets for the filmed sequences in Benamou (2007: 310–15).

33 Treatment dated from 2 July 1943 (box 16, folder 22, Welles materials, Lilly Library).

34 Nelson Rodrigues's *Vestido de Noiva* caused somewhat of an uproar by incorporating a samba song into a play staged in Rio's Municipal Theatre in 1943.

35 Plans to build skyscrapers, for example, were rendered impractical owing to the high maintenance costs of structures built above a former marsh: costly water-pumps were needed to avoid flooding in the basement levels.

36 I am grateful for Dona Odette, Dona Chiquinha, and Dona Leda for their kindness and willingness to speak with me, when I visited the Providência in June 2011.

37 The citations are from *A Manhã*, 3 September 1944 and the *Diário Carioca*, 2 September 1944. For a history attuned to this genre of imagery, see Sennett 1994.

38 A vast literature analyses the intersections between urban form and power. See Lima's reading of President Vargas Avenue along Foucauldian lines (1990: 87–9).

39 Quoted from Welles 1998: 192. A recording is heard in Sganzerla's *Tudo é Brasil* (1997).

40 See my 'Mapping the Urbanized Beaches of Rio de Janeiro' (Carvalho 2007) and O'Donnell 2013.

41 Quoted songs, respectively: Teófilo Miranda's 'Praça Onze' (Euterpe Ltda.); 'A Praça Onze não morreu', recorded by Marly Monteiro and Luiz Mergulhão at Star; and 'Praça Onze', of which no information remains beyond the title and the recording itself. They were all found in the MIS archives. For a more comprehensive study of the square in popular song, including more recent examples, see Thompson 2009.

Conclusion: The Future Revisited: Where Has the Past Gone and Where Will it Go?

Brasil
Tua cara ainda é o Rio de Janeiro
3 × 4 da foto e o teu corpo inteiro
Precisa se regenerar.
[Brazil / Your face is still Rio de Janeiro / The 3 × 4 photo and your whole body / Must regenerate]

Aldir Blanc, Moacyr Luz, and Paulo César Pinheiro, 'Saudades da Guanabara'
(1995)

I

The future envisioned with the construction of the President Vargas Avenue did not arrive, at least not according to plans. Built during the Second World War, espousing a style that could be associated to the losing side, the avenue can be ascribed to what Beatriz Jaguaribe calls modernist ruins, the 'fracturing of a previous ethos that was never fulfilled and has already become dated' (2001: 343). Many of the skyscrapers imagined for the area were never built. Rather than usher a new era of progress, the reforms left Rio with a thoroughfare that would be considered by a prominent architect as 'the ugliest in the world'.[1] It would also leave Rio a more divided city.

The port area neighbourhoods, along with Brazil's primordial favela, the Providência, became increasingly cut off from the rest of the city and entered a period of accelerated decadence. After the loss of so many buildings, residents, and references like the Praça Onze, the Cidade Nova never recovered its protagonism in Rio de Janeiro. This reduced importance cannot be detached from the growth of a city that reached a population of over 2.3 million in 1950, a number that would more than double by 1980 and exceed 6.3 million in 2010. No single urban space, or configuration of places, could claim to have as much centrality in the socio-cultural fabric of such a megalopolis.

At any rate, Rio's centre of gravity – or at least its most visible spaces –

kept shifting towards the South Zone and the beachfront. The 1937 building code established the city's central areas as a commercial zone, paving the way for a process that reduced their diversity and vitality. Levelling of the Santo Antônio Hill during the 1950s freed up new spaces for construction in the Centro, rendering the area around the President Vargas Avenue less crucial for development.[2] The traditional port neighbourhoods fared worse: in 1936, the Santos Dumont airport had been inaugurated in the entrance of Guanabara Bay, taking Rio's most noble gateway elsewhere. Once Brazil's major port, Rio's facilities also continued to lose their relative importance, surpassed by the port of Santos in the state of São Paulo. Beginning in the 1950s, a series of new elevated highways privileged the South Zone and adversely affected the neighbourhoods that had once been part of the 'greater Cidade Nova'.[3] One of these freeways, mentioned in the introduction, ran perpendicular to the President Vargas Avenue, close to the former Praça Onze. It sought to improve the flow of traffic from the centre to the burgeoning South Zone, through the Santa Barbara tunnel inaugurated in the early 1960s.

Upon going through the Santa Barbara tunnel today, we might be reminded of Georg Simmel's 'Bridge and Door'. On one side we encounter the affluent Laranjeiras neighbourhood. On the other, the Catumbi is markedly poorer, has fewer trees, and feels like a different city altogether. Neighbouring the Cidade Nova, this area suffered with the construction of the elevated highway, and also stands as a shadow of its former self. Prior to the tunnel, the two neighbourhoods had fairly similar architecture and socio-economic make-ups. The urban intervention brought them closer, but it also pulled them apart. Like Simmel's bridges and doors, which we have discussed as an analytical touchstone behind the concept of porosity, the tunnel separates as much as it connects. Something comparable could be said of the President Vargas Avenue.

All of these new transportation networks facilitated access from the suburbs and the South Zone to the centre, but they also led to a more sprawling and uneven city. At the same time, legislation against residential uses in the former New and Old Towns was consolidated in the mid-1970s.[4] As Rio became less compact, and as urban infrastructure continued to prioritize the upper classes as well as car owners, spatial segregation grew. In the process, the Cidade Nova became a mere passageway for most of Rio's inhabitants. For those lingering residents, it was a devalued place. While certainly not absent from the city's past, the neighbourhood remained absent from how this past was told, narrated, commemorated. Despite its important role in cultural and urban histories, the Cidade Nova has been mostly relegated to footnotes.

In the meantime, the South Zone's place in the itinerary of tourists and the repertoire of postcards had long been assured. The streetcar going up to the Sugar Loaf Mountain opened in 1912, followed by the statue of Christ the Redeemer on top of the Corcovado Mountain, inaugurated in 1931. In the 1950s, the emergence of Bossa Nova music and beach-going culture irrevocably altered Rio de Janeiro's image. Copacabana and Ipanema were now powerful symbols in Brazil's cultural cartographies. Likewise, some of the city's most visible favelas were also located in wealthier regions. Marcel Camus's *Black Orpheus* (1959), based on a play by Vinicius de Moraes, would catapult the Babilônia Favela in Copacabana to the world's screens.[5] When Michael Jackson and Spike Lee shot a music video in Rio for the song 'They Don't Care About Us' (1996), they opted for the Santa Marta Favela, in Botafogo. Orson Welles seemed to be the last illustrious visitor to take a keen interest in the Providência.[6]

The Cidade Nova, however, never ceased to have a special place in Rio's carnival. After the disappearance of the Praça Onze, samba schools paraded in the Rio Branco Avenue for three years. In 1946, the first carnival after the war, they were held in the President Vargas Avenue. Each samba school chooses a yearly theme around which they develop a song, floats, and costumes. After 1948, by law, these had to be 'national'. In 1966, the Portela samba school won with *Memoirs of a Militia Sergeant* as its topic; in 1970, Salgueiro honoured the Praça Onze.[7] Throughout the 1950s and 60s, the competitive parades generated growing interest from the press, tourists, and the state, amplifying its presence outside of Rio.[8] In the early 1970s, Rede Globo began to broadcast them nationally. The parades gained prominence in advertising, and would become a centrepiece of two major television stations' programming.[9] By the second half of the 1970s, temporary stands built along the President Vargas Avenue already hosted over 100,000 participant spectators (Farias 2006: 225). Again, the future did not conform to plans: this was quite a different spectacle from the military parades that had been imagined for the site.

Responding to pressures from the entertainment industry, samba schools, and other sectors of the population, the state government built the Sambódromo in time for the 1984 carnival. The massive structure ran parallel to the elevated highway that led to the Santa Barbara tunnel. During the year, the parade ground was used as a regular road, and some of its spaces, like the viewing boxes, accommodated a public school. The combination of building material (reinforced concrete), functionalism, and a curvilinear decorative arch reveals the indelible touch of Oscar Niemeyer, who had attained celebrity status as the architect of Brasília. One block away from the President Vargas Avenue, the location made logistical sense: the major samba schools, from the North Zone or the suburbs, were used to the place, metro service improved access, and that stretch of the Cidade Nova had already been receiving other important constructions.[10] By the relative proximity to the former Praça Onze, the Sambódromo could also invoke the symbolic weight of its memory.

Critics often remark that the Sambódromo 'domesticates' the parades, turning the transgressive experience of carnival into a product that the cultural industry can assimilate. Indeed, television has become an inseparable part of the spectacle. In 1986, when around 50,000 people paraded, over 1,000 television professionals already covered the events (Farias 2006: 252). Today, the parades have reached another scale, involving hundreds of thousands of people and several hundred million dollars.[11] Although the majority of participants hail from Rio's lower classes, much of the coverage revolves around famous artists and television celebrities. It is not our intention here to enter into debates about a loss of 'authenticity', or the development of carnival into a massive industry. It is worth exploring, however, how the Sambódromo may offer insight into some of the urban transformations undergone by Rio as a whole.

In *Laws of Chance: Brazil's Clandestine Lottery and the Making of Public Life* (2011), Amy Chazkel analyses the role of regulating public spaces and criminalizing certain practices in the construction of a new relationship between urban denizens and the state. Referencing discussions around the 'tragedy of the commons', Chazkel introduces the concept of 'urban enclosure' to explain the process of privatization, regulation, and monetization of public life, especially during the early years of the First Republic. Her book accounts for a measure of porosity that this 'enclosure' gained in Rio, where despite the 'expropriation of resources and rights', those 'left outside the metaphorical (or actual) fence were not merely swept aside' (Chazkel 2011: 11). Enclosure becomes understood as 'part of a cycle of informalization'. Although illicit, the lotteries that she writes about have remained a fact of Rio's daily life.

Leaving aside the direct connections between these lotteries and Rio's carnival parades – jogo do bicho has often financed samba schools – the concept of enclosure can be useful to help us understand the Sambódromo's role in Brazil's most popular festivities, and in the city's urban development. In this case, mass media become crucial arbitrators. They appropriate forms and profits, determining the length of parades, as well as both creating and reflecting the public's expectations.[12] As the extraordinarily inventive and exuberant event turns the space into a sort of temporary 'open-air studio', the metaphorical (or actual) fences are not unfamiliar to a capitalist order: even though a 'popular sector' has relatively low prices, the stands are only accessible to those who pay an entrance fee, and few can afford the costumes through which one gains the right to parade. But those who wish to participate can find informal ways of avoiding the prohibitive prices.[13]

The Sambódromo, then, though part of a process harkening back to the 1880s, does not quite represent the much less metaphorical 'enclosures' experimented with in Latin American cities since the 1980s. The paradigm in the title of Teresa Caldeira's *City of Walls: Crime, Segregation, and Citizenship in São Paulo* (2000) applies to several metropolises. Rio is no exception. Beginning in the 1980s, many of the city's residential buildings had gates added to their exteriors, intruding onto the sidewalks. A real estate boom stretched the city towards the West Zone neighbourhood of Barra da Tijuca, where a model consisting of shopping malls and private, enclosed condominiums has prevailed. More car-dependent, more walled, this is not the same Rio as the one in which French anthropologist Lévi-Strauss arrived in 1935:

> As I strolled [...] I noticed something special about the narrow, shady streets which cut across the main avenue: the transition between the buildings and the roadway was less obvious than in Europe. [...] In fact, the street was not just a thoroughfare; it was a place where people lived. (Lévi-Strauss 1992: 85)

The city's thoroughfares today are less so a place where people live, where 'Western civilization's' 'contrast between house and street' has been abolished (85).[14] In that sense, Rio is like every other modern metropolis that at some point answered to Le Corbusier's call for the 'death of the street' during the mid-1920s.

But even the President Vargas Avenue, a turning point in the city's urban history, did not resist the subverting practices of pedestrians. A popular street market, the Camelódromo, lies adjacent to the multi-lane thoroughfare. When a well-known Caetano Veloso song from the 1960s suggests that we take a stroll down the President Vargas Avenue, there is a measure of irony in the lyrics. At the time, those 'broad streets' served as a parade ground for military bands and the Mangueira samba school alike. Yet, even today, anyone strolling down the Avenue would not lack company, at least not in certain stretches.[15] In front of Central Station, elaborate performers – from clowns to salespeople hawking cleaning products – compete over pedestrians' attentions. The Avenue has continuously been a site of carnival blocos and major political protests. As Sérgio Bloch's recent film about the avenue shows, the President Vargas's chaotic environment has enthusiasts as well as critics.

Everyday tactics seem to have always flourished in Brazil's urban life. Even in Brasília, the quintessentially utopian modernist city, planned spaces quickly acquired unintended uses. In an often-cited example, storefronts that had been designed to open towards the grassy areas of residential complexes, quickly reverted to the traditional set-up: their 'backs', facing the streets, were adapted to serve as the storefront. The anthropologist Hermano Vianna, who grew up in Brasília, hints at the unexpected uses that punks made of the planned city.[16] In Rio itself, there was a time when no one could imagine that an underpass in the neighbourhood of Madureira would host a weekly 'Black Music' party; or that, on New Year's Eve, millions would gather in the Copacabana beachfront, most wearing white. Rather than just a failure of top-down planning, these improvisations can signal a success of bottom-up appropriation. Subversions or manipulations of planned spaces are by no means exclusive to Rio, or Brazil. We are, after all, following the trail of Michel de Certeau's *The Practice of Everyday Life*, and comparable examples abound in contemporary studies about urban cultures.[17]

There are other ways, however, in which Rio's cultural dynamics could indeed be considered out of the ordinary: many among the poorest and wealthiest live in extremely close proximity, sharing public spaces, slang, football chants, and musical tastes. These areas of contact, however, coexist with stark disparities in access to services, goods, and a myriad of rights and opportunities. As the city's development from the 1940s onward accentuated divisions, Rio never ceased having a tradition of 'transcultural mediators', to quote a category used by Hermano Vianna. In this very book, we have seen Manuel Antônio de Almeida, João do Rio, Chiquinha Gonzaga, Noel Rosa, Orson Welles, and several others build bridges across social, racial, political, or spatial lines. There have been many others since: from the visual artist Hélio Oiticica, who lived in the Mangueira favela, to Zeca Pagodinho, a musician whose popularity knows few boundaries.

Rio de Janeiro's delicate dynamic between its extremes – *morro* and *asfalto*, 'hill' and 'asphalt', favela and non-favela – became unsustainable when urban violence exploded in the 1990s. As the armed drug traffic began to control territories inside many of Rio's favelas, 'enclosure' acquired new meanings in the city's daily life. While some in the upper classes could always choose to move into walled compounds, others in favelas cannot avoid being subjected to wars between rival drug traffic factions, often involving corrupt police forces. When armed conflicts break out, residents sometimes find themselves unable to return to their homes. During that decade, in an environment where it had become common to speak of a Brazilian apartheid, urban interventions like the Favela-Bairro programme were devised to smooth out transitions from the 'hills' to the 'asphalt'.[18]

After the Candelária Church and Vigário Geral massacres in 1993, Rio seemed to have hit rock bottom. In that context, Zuenir Ventura's *Cidade partida* was bold not just for exposing the city's divisions, or the inner workings of drug traffickers. Rather, it was perhaps even more daring because of how it insisted on being hopeful. The book ends with a dialogue between Zuenir and a drug dealer, hinting at how those who in fact organize and profit from the drug trade do not live in favelas. There were positive signs, however, after one year and a half of research, visits to Vigário Geral, and active participation in civil society's response to the tragic massacres. By the time that Zuenir Ventura completed the book, three ambitious projects conceived during its gestation appeared to be firmly under way: the aforementioned Viva Rio NGO; the Casa da Paz (House of Peace, an art centre, and umbrella organization in the location where the Vigário Geral massacre took place); and the Fábrica da Esperança (Factory of Hope, an NGO providing a host of services in the Acari favela). Before the end of the decade, only the movement based in the South Zone, the Viva Rio, continued to thrive. The creator of the Casa da Paz, a sociologist from Vigário Geral called Caio Ferraz, fled to the United States after receiving death threats from the perpetrators of the massacre. The Fábrica da Paz, which had won several prizes, would eventually close after the police allegedly found great quantities of cocaine stored there, and its founder-director became involved in an unrelated political scandal. At the turn of the century, Brazil had emerged from a long period of military dictatorship (1964–85), with the right to elect a president by direct vote restored. In 1992, Congress impeached the first elected president, Fernando Collor de Mello, who was implicated in a corruption scandal. A new democratic constitution (1988), an economic plan that brought rampant inflation under control (the Plano Real, 1994), a strengthened civil society and free press all seemed to point towards better days for the country. Brazil's former capital and most visible city, meanwhile, remained steeped in crisis.

So where does the Cidade Nova fit into this scenario? If the neighbourhood had been a crucial crossroads, a starting point through which to reflect about the cultural history of the national capital, it was no such thing after the 1940s. According to census data, the reduced area now demarcated as the Cidade Nova had 8,077 residents in 1980, and only 5,466 in 2010; a small fraction of the nineteenth- and early twentieth-century populations. If the neighbourhood had been a space where various experiences of Rio could overlap, a point of contact between its different sides, it now shielded and disconnected City Hall from the rest of the city. The 1970s building housing the municipal government is set back from the President Vargas Avenue in typical modernist fashion. Except that whereas other buildings from the modernist canon are set back from a vibrant street, Rio's City Hall has stood instead like a towering, isolated island in a new Cidade Nova where few people venture.

As the Cidade Nova receded into oblivion, the favelas became increasingly less marginal and more visible, in ways that threatened the city's established order. Not long after Zuenir Ventura's *Cidade partida* came out, a samba by Wilson das Neves and Paulo Cesar Pinheiro gives voice to anxieties from the 'asphalt'. 'The day when the hills come down [people from favelas descend] and it's not carnival', the song goes, 'no one will be left to see the last parade'. In the best samba tradition of mixing protest and humour, Wilson das Neves's mellow voice describes an ominous 'civil war' scenario, where each section of a samba school would be a gang; costumes would be weapons; gunshots the soundtrack. The theme: 'a cidade partida', the divided city.

The notion of Rio de Janeiro as a 'cidade partida' became deeply ingrained, and while porosity never stopped coexisting with inequities and division, the city's tradition of circulation, exchanges, and common ground seemed to be in peril. A journalist known as Tim Lopes, who worked for the Globo television network, was one of countless Cariocas who revelled in the always renewed and continued presence of music in Rio's daily life. Unlike countless other Cariocas, he worked for a powerful media organization, and his story was widely publicized, causing great commotion. Lopes had been writing a book about samba and the Mangueira samba school. He received an award, in 1994, for a piece on Funk Carioca, one of the innovative musical genres that originated in marginal areas, and then swept the entire city. In 2002, Lopes went to the favela Vila Cruzeiro, intending covertly to record images from a funk party, where there had been reports of sexual exploitation of minors and drug dealing. He was discovered. Drug lords tortured him, and chopped his body into pieces with a Katana, a Japanese sword.[19]

II

Conversations about Rio de Janeiro's decline nearly became a national sport during the years of more acute crisis. Speculation often located the turning point in 1960, when the city lost its status as a national capital to the newly inaugurated Brasília. After this transition, the municipality acquired state status under the name of Guanabara. In 1975, the city was incorporated into the state of Rio de Janeiro as its capital. Others blamed Rio's decadence on this fusion.[20] Even if Brazil's face was still Rio de Janeiro, as the samba 'Saudades da Guanabara' (Nostalgia/Longing for Guanabara) stated in the mid-1990s, this could no longer be taken for granted.

The Vargas era had been marked by efforts to render regional or local histories as 'Brazilian', and to promote a language of brasilidade, or 'Brazilianness', that incorporated a modern vision for the country. Initiatives endorsed or created by the federal government – involving art, architecture, museums, historical landmarks, and overseas expositions – reached far beyond the federal capital. In the immediate wake of the Estado Novo, there was a sense in which 'hegemonic claims to brasilidade remained elusive' (Williams 2001: xviii). In subsequent decades, Rio de Janeiro seemed to lose space in Brazil's political, economic, and cultural landscape. São Paulo became the country's industrial powerhouse and largest city. Brasília became the capital. Samba, Vinicius de Moraes would sing, 'was born over there, in Bahia'.

There have always been competing symbols of nationhood in Brazil, but even throughout all of these changes it is still difficult to dispute Rio de Janeiro as the city that most readily identifies the country abroad, and the place with which most Brazilians identify national symbols. Beatriz Jaguaribe deems the city a 'synecdoche for a Brazilian ethos' (2001: 332). The inverse could also apply. Brazil is vast, diverse, and heterogeneous. There can be little in common between people inhabiting the same city, let alone between those living in the Amazon basin, in the backlands of the Northeast, or in German-speaking towns in the South. Cultural discourses and practices, nonetheless, have cultivated common denominators that to some extent translate a 'Rio de Janeiro ethos' into particular narratives about the nation.

When discussing Brazil, the triad of football, soap operas, and samba are clichés, but they are powerful and meaningful ones. Rio's major football clubs are national. Each Brazilian capital has its popular local clubs, but one finds a great number of devoted fans of Rio's Vasco da Gama in the Amazonian city of Manaus, in Brasília, or in the interior of Paraná.[21] Soap operas, watched by housemaids and their employers alike, are disproportionately filmed and set in Rio de Janeiro. And samba has continued to be an 'agent of national unification' (Vianna 1999: 107). Although each region or city celebrates carnival differently, there are Sambódromo-like structures and samba schools in São Paulo, Florianópolis, Macapá, and other places throughout the country. We cannot underestimate the influence on these phenomena of Rio-based Globo, Latin America's largest media conglomerate. Certain symbols, at any rate, radiated so successfully from Rio de Janeiro that they became national, and not just Carioca.

The centrality of Rio to national narratives would be reaffirmed even after the city lost its status of federal capital. In 1960, the new Guanabara state chose as its official anthem a carnival song from the 1930s, 'Cidade Maravilhosa' (Marvellous City), which declared Rio to be the 'coração do meu Brasil' ('the heart of my Brasil'). Similar declarations are difficult to imagine elsewhere. At the end of the introduction of *Cidade partida*, Minas Gerais-born Zuenir Ventura writes that Vigário Geral, where the massacre had occurred, is a 'metonymy of Rio, just like Rio is the part that can be taken as the whole of what's known as Brazil' (Ventura 1994: 14). Later, he suggests that a certain Carioca pretence could be a double-edged sword. The city's congressmen tended to speak for the nation, neglecting local interests. This ambition would manifest itself through the names of newspapers. In other places, they refer to their location: the *Folha de São Paulo, Estado de Minas, Diário de Pernambuco*. In Rio, they refer to the country as a whole, or even beyond: *Jornal do Brasil* and *O Globo* (140).

So what does all of this have to do with the Cidade Nova? In one sense, not all that much. The neighbourhood, as we have seen, played a major role in the development of cultural forms that became widely hailed as national, like choro, samba, and carnival. These manifestations, however, have kept evolving in various directions, and maintain very few direct ties to the Campo de Santana, the Praça Onze, or the Mangue. In another sense, however, the urban spaces studied here matter quite a bit. The Cidade Nova's history can be understood as paradigmatic of the types of mixtures that have served as sources of vitality for Rio de Janeiro's, and indeed Brazil's cultural formation. Processes whereby marginalized cultural practices became central to lettered cartographies, or where certain lettered circles embrace orality, also occurred elsewhere. If these relationships have been shaped by comparable forms of porosity in other contexts, the Cidade Nova's history sheds light on particular dimensions of this quality.

Samba, samba schools, and to a lesser extent figures like Tia Ciata moved from the margin to the centre, resulting in a configuration which would have been impossible to predict in the nineteenth century: even white elites often explain and perform their collective identities as Brazilians through a cultural repertoire historically tied to urban poverty, marginality, and non-whites. Samba became a 'shared musical idiom', as Hermano Vianna argues, 'rather than being the property of a single ethnic group or social class' (1999: 86). We should be careful not to overstate the Cidade Nova's role here. The making of samba was itself more complex, as other works on the subject highlight. And, besides samba, analogous processes occurred with other cultural practices like forró, capoeira, feijoada, funk carioca.[22]

The Cidade Nova, again, matters both for how it was paradigmatic and for how it was exceptional. Within Rio's urban history, heterogeneous poor populations were never exclusive to the neighbourhood, although its particular diversity finds few parallels anywhere. It was not unusual for marginal spaces during the nineteenth century to be represented as threatening, inferior, backwards. But the Cidade Nova's combination of lower-class inhabitants, central location, and rather decent infrastructure during the same period stands apart. The gradual inversions that its spaces produced and reflected, as we have seen, tell us a great deal about broader transformations in how culture gets disseminated, and in what gets to be considered culture. From a place that was marginal in lettered cartographies, but central to particular cultural geographies, the Cidade Nova became central to particular lettered cartographies, but was largely obliterated from actual cultural geography. After the construction of the President Vargas Avenue, the latter prevailed: the neighbourhood was mostly forgotten, and, barring exceptions, remained absent from personal experiences and historical narratives.

Even its past, in other words, can be considered porous. The neighbourhood's very material histories became absorbed in discourses that might have had little to do with everyday life there – Brazil as a mixed country; progress as a sixteen-lane avenue – but that nonetheless impact the future, for good or for bad. All of this continues to serve as a reminder that there are winners and losers in urban modernity. Much of the writing about cities over the past several decades has taken up the challenge of identifying who benefits and who suffers under modernization. Rio de Janeiro is no exception in that regard. Contemporary studies by and large recognize the historic debt towards descendants of slaves, for example. 'Racial democracy', exposed as a myth and holding increasingly less valence in intellectual and public policy circles, tends to be exhausted as an ethos.

Fewer appear to conclude that where one sees cultural inclusion, social exclusion or racial discrimination must not be an issue. Few, at the same time, affirm the inexistence in Rio de Janeiro's past of ethnic ghettoes in the European or North American mould. That this follows from historical, geographic, and socio-political contingencies – rather than from a Carioca predisposition for tolerance and mixing – has been made abundantly clear. But that certain identitary gaps might not be unbridgeable has to be considered as well, lest we throw the baby out with the bathwater.

Rio de Janeiro changed in significant ways during the period covered by this book, and that continued to be the case during the period of its research, gestation, writing, and rewriting. As steep and daunting challenges remain, the accumulation of certain conquests, local and national, appear to be accelerating. These might be as uneven as they are undeniable, but a democratic state of rights seems to be more entrenched. As of this writing, one of the official City Hall slogans for new urban initiatives evokes Zuenir Ventura's descriptor: Cidade Integrada, or Integrated City. In preparation for the 2014 World Cup, the 2016 Olympics, and in response to Rio's housing shortage, several billion dollars are currently being invested in the infrastructure and development of the port zone and parts of the Cidade Nova. In very material ways, the city as palimpsest becomes evident:

recent excavations unearthed the Valongo Quay, an arrival point for African slaves.[23] Although the long-term consequences of these interventions cannot be predicted, it is clear that the areas that this book focuses on will once again become central to Rio de Janeiro's future.

So what to make of this Porous City, after the Marvelous City, the Divided City, and now the Integrated City? To some extent, porosity seeks to be disruptive, by accounting for Rio's mixtures, openness, and fluidity as well as its inequities and asymmetries. The concept, at the same time, participates in a long and vibrant tradition of national interpretation that stresses the coexistence of antagonistic forces: from Sérgio Buarque de Holanda's ambivalent 'cordiality', to Antonio Candido's 'dialectic of roguery', and José Miguel Wisnik's 'poison-cure'. The Cidade Nova's local history had enormous consequence to Rio de Janeiro as a whole. Its past, regardless of where it has gone or of where it may go, continues to speak to Brazilian cultural histories and to various ways of being in the world, an urban world.

If this author may then end with a more personal note: I first came across the neighbourhood of the Cidade Nova through a musical experience. When I heard 'Bum-Bum Paticumbum Prugurundum' as a young child in Rio de Janeiro, the contagious song seemed rather cryptic. A samba from the traditional Escola de Samba Império Serrano, it had been written for the 1982 carnival (the first for which I was alive). Beto sem Braço and Aluísio Machado's lyrics offer a devastating critique of the massive proportions gained by the parades, increasingly run like businesses. The title refers to Ismael Silva's onomatopoeic explanation of samba's rhythm. None of that I understood as a child, but the refrain produced a mystery: 'Oh Praça Onze / thou art immortal / your arms cradled samba / your apotheosis is triumphant' ('Ó Praça Onze / tu és imortal / teus braços embalaram o samba / a tua apoteose é triunfal').

What and where could this place be? Its several layers of complexities (Afro-Jewish–Brazilian and so on) came into view since, through a combination of chance encounters, musical or literary experiences, and hard-nosed research. Inscribed in the very etymology of palimpsests one finds the Greek *pálin* ('again'). The Cidade Nova and its Praça Onze are perhaps not *immortal* as the song claims – and it is unlikely to be enough – but may their pasts surface yet again as a reminder of where we have been, and of what we are capable.

Notes

1 The opinion is emitted by no less than Lúcio Costa, who authored Brasília's master plan. It is quoted from a document entitled 'Constatação', identified as V.C.03-03272 in the digitized archives of the Casa de Lúcio Costa.

2 The Irish clergyman Robert Walsh reports on how Imperial authorities already contemplated levelling the Santo Antônio Hill (1831: 459). Several of Rio's postmodern buildings, including the Municipal Cathedral, are located in its former area. The levelling also enabled construction of the waterfront Flamengo Park, landscaped by Roberto Burle Marx.

3 Including Perimetral Avenue, now being demolished as part of the port area's revitalization. The one-and-three-quarter-mile-long Rebouças tunnel (1967) connects the south and north zones, via an elevated highway in the latter's case. The same occurs with the Santa Barbara tunnel, where only the south zone side does not have an extensive elevated highway. By 'greater Cidade Nova' one should infer the Catumbi, Estácio, and Santo Cristo neighbourhoods. One of the few major public investments privileging the north zone was Maracanã stadium, built for the 1950 World Cup.

4 See, especially, Decreto 322, 1976. For a history of twentieth-century Rio focused on regulatory law, the most authoritative study to date of the connections between urbanization and poor peoples' citizenship rights is Fischer 2008.

5 The French filmmaker portrays the favela as an exotic and mythical locale. Set during carnival, *Black Orpheus* became one of the most successful films in Portuguese, winning the Best Foreign Language Film Academy Award (1960). For a critical reading, see Stam 1997: 157–78.

6 That has begun to change in recent years, and the Providência now promises to enter touristic itineraries. In 2008, before current 'pacification' efforts had begun, the French photographer JR took his Women Are Heroes Project there, pasting images of residents – often close-ups of eyes – in building facades.

7 As today, themes varied widely, often including Afro-Brazilian symbols, Rio's history, national folklore, regional traditions, and literature. There was increased pressure to privilege nationalist sentiment after 1964, under the military dictatorship (Farias 2006: 244).

8 From 1957 to 1962, first division schools paraded in the Rio Branco, while the second division stayed in the President Vargas. Around this time, tourist agencies began promoting the event (Farias 2006: 173). Stands were added in 1962, and the following year parades returned to Vargas Avenue. Judges included prominent names like Roberto Burle Marx, Edson Carneiro, Iberê Camargo, and Lúcio Rangel.

9 TV Globo began broadcasting them in 1971. By 1980, over half of Brazil's households had a television set (Farias 2006: 242). By then, parades were timed. Later in that decade, TV Manchete – founded by the aforementioned Adolfo Bloch – also began to broadcast the parades.

10 These included the Globo newspaper headquarters in the mid-1950s, and later, in the 1970s and early 1980s, the metro station, City Archives (AGCRJ), Calouste Gulbenkian Arts Center, a post office headquarters, and City Hall. Most are marked by the influence of brutalism in Brazil's architectural modernity.

11 According to official estimates of the Riotur for 2012, around 850,000 tourists visited Rio during carnival, and the event represents an injection of 628 million dollars into the city's economy. It is not clear how this was calculated, but the figures were widely disseminated in the press and on the agency's website.

12 An edition of *Veja* magazine, for example, shows that banners in the stands calling for direct elections were excluded from television broadcasts (14 March 1984).

13 Those willing and able to pay for costumes that cost from hundreds to thousands

of dollars – frequently tourists or upper-class Cariocas – indirectly subsidize the many members of a given samba school community that parade for nothing or for more affordable prices.

14 Of Lévi-Strauss, it must also be noted that he famously compared the Guanabara Bay to a 'toothless mouth'. He is often cited as an example of a traveller unimpressed with the city's natural beauties, but one might find a measure of 'enchantment' in the metaphor.

15 The song 'Enquanto seu lobo não vem' (Before Mr Wolf Gets Here), from *Tropicália: ou Panis et Circensis* (1968), goes: 'A Estação Primeira da Mangueira passa em ruas largas / (Os clarins da banda militar …) / Passa por debaixo da Avenida Presidente Vargas' (The First Station of Mangueira goes by broad streets / (the clarions of a military band) / goes by under the President Vargas Avenue).

16 See column in *Folha de São Paulo*, 15 February 2004.

17 Certeau differentiates between 'strategy' and 'tactics', where the latter 'must constantly manipulate events in order to turn them into opportunities' (1984: 480). For recent studies that prioritize this dimension of urban life, see Nutall and Mbembe 2008 and De Boeck and Plissart 2004.

18 On the Favela-Bairro programme, see Rosa Duarte and Magalhães 2009. On the drug traffic, see Zaluar 2004.

19 On Tim Lopes, see Sant'Anna 2002 and Souza 2002.

20 See Freitag 2009. Niterói had been the state capital until the fusion.

21 The Brazilian Football Federation (Confederação Brasileira de Futebol) (CBF), is housed in Rio. All public opinion studies indicate that Rio's teams are comparatively more popular in other regions of the country than those from other states (such as a poll undertaken by Datafolha in 2010, for example).

22 On the north-eastern musical and dance genre, see Draper 2010; on capoeira, see Oliveira and Leal 2009; on the 'national' bean stew dish, see Fry 2005; and on Rio's funk, see Vianna 1988. On samba, see also Lisa Shaw's social history (1999) and Marc Hertzman's history of race and music in Brazil (2013).

23 It is being preserved as a site of archeological importance. Robert Walsh described the miserable conditions in the late 1820s, when this was one of the busiest slave markets in the world: 'The poor creatures are exposed for sale like any other commodity' (1832: 179). The programme to revitalize the area is called Porto Maravilha (Marvelous Port), echoing the moniker of 'cidade maravilhosa'.

Acknowledgements

S everal people helped me during the process of researching, writing, and publishing this book. At Harvard, where this project was first nurtured, Nicolau Sevcenko inspired me to think broadly and take risks. Joaquim-Francisco Coelho taught me to listen and learn in so many ways. Tom Conley's insights proved to be far-reaching and decisive. I am grateful to the Romance Languages and Literatures Department for the intellectual mentorship, friendships, and support. Initial research benefited from grants by the David Rockefeller Center for Latin American Studies, the Nancy Clark Smith Funds, and a Jorge Paulo Lemann Fellowship.

At Princeton, I found a stimulating environment in which to develop the book. The Department of Spanish and Portuguese Languages and Cultures has been a wonderful academic home. I would like to thank Angel Loureiro, Gabriela Nouzeilles, Marina Brownleee, Ron Surtz, and Rubén Gallo. Rachel Price and Germán Labrador Méndez, fellow Assistant Professors, have been the best colleagues, readers, and friends anyone could imagine. Pedro Meira Monteiro saw this book come into being over the past few years. It owes a great deal to his readings of earlier versions, and to our conversations. Flora Thomson-DeVeaux, while living in Rio as an undergraduate student, helped me with research and read the manuscript with her usual acumen. Grants from the University Committee on Research in the Humanities and Social Sciences and from the Program in Latin American Studies, as well as a sabbatical year, allowed me to conduct further research in Brazil and complete the book.

During the past few years, I have benefited enormously from Lilia Schwarcz's incisive comments and advice. Kenneth Maxwell has taught me to think more like a historian, and helped to improve the manuscript. The following colleagues also read the manuscript or parts of it, and I am deeply thankful for their input and encouragement: Arcadio Díaz Quiñones, Barbara Weinstein, Beatriz Jaguaribe, Codruta Morari, Gabriel Duarte, Hermano Vianna, Jeremy Adelman, João Biehl, José Miguel Wisnik, Marc

Hertzman, Marta Peixoto, Max Weiss, Serge Gruzinski, and Stuart Schwartz. José Marcelo Zacchi has been a crucial interlocutor. Bryan McCann, initially an anonymous reader, provided generous feedback and support. Another anonymous reader shared expertise, and made valuable suggestions.

I would also like to acknowledge the following for their support, suggestions, or kind assistance: Alida Metcalf, Amy Chazkel, Andréa Melloni, Antonio Feros, Beta Martins Ferreira Castro, Bob Stam, Carol Sá Carvalho, Celi and Maurício (Pinduca) Benkes, Clémence Jouet-Pastré, Cristina Zappa, Dain Borges, Ed Telles, Elio Gaspari, Ellen Chances, Esther Schor, Fábio Durão, Farès El-Dahdah, Fred Coelho, Graziella Moraes da Silva, Gyan Prakash, James Green, João Moreira Salles, Jorge Schwartz, June Erlick, Julia O'Donnell, Leonardo Pereira, Lilian Martins Ferreira, Luisa-Elena Delgado, Mariana Cavalcanti, Mariano Siskind, Mario Gandelsonas, Nelson Vieira, Nick Nesbitt, Nicola Cooney, Noah Eaker, Paulinho Fonseca, Piers Armstrong, Rachel Valença, Rob Karl, Rodolfo Franconi, Ronaldo Lemos, Sérgio Bloch, Tera Hunter, Tom Levin, Vanessa Grossman, Vivian Caccuri, and Zuenir Ventura.

Most of all, thank you to my wife, Michael Elizabeth Rozas, who has been a wonderful partner throughout the many adventures, discoveries, and setbacks behind this project.

For their integrity, professionalism, and efficiency, I would like to thank Anthony Cond and the team at Liverpool University Press. I am also grateful to George Stoll for making the maps, Kate Murphy for the index, and Sue Barnes and Lucy Frontani at Carnegie Publishing.

A book can be an attempt to honour people no longer among us, while trying to reach unknown readers. It can also be a way to accrue debt with those in our lives. To the many not mentioned above, who were part of this in more oblique ways, muito obrigado.

Works Cited

Newspapers and Magazines

A Columna
A Manhã
A Noite
Boletim ASA (Associação Scholem Aleichem)
Cine Rádio Jornal
Correio da Manhã
Diário Carioca
Diário da Noite
Diário de Notícias
Diário de São Paulo
Dom Casmurro
Dos Iídiche Vochenblat
Estado de São Paulo
Folha de São Paulo
Fon-Fon
Gazeta de Notícias
Gazeta do Rio de Janeiro
Imprensa Israelita
Jornal do Brasil
Jornal do Comércio (Recife)
Jornal do commércio
Jornal dos Sports
Kósmos
Meio Dia
O Cruzeiro
O Globo
O Malho
O Mundo Sportivo
O Novo Mundo
Revista da Semana
Revista de Imigração e Colonização
Travel in Brazil
Veja

Principal Archives and Special Collections

Academia Brasileira de Letras, Rio de Janeiro
Arquivo Geral da Cidade do Rio de Janeiro
Arquivo Histórico do Itamaraty, Rio de Janeiro
Arquivo Nacional, Rio de Janeiro
Biblioteca Nacional, Rio de Janeiro
Centro de Pesquisa e Documentação, Fundação Getúlio Vargas, Rio de Janeiro
Cinemateca do Museu de Arte Moderna, Rio de Janeiro
Houghton Library, Special Collections, Harvard University
Instituto Moreira Salles, Rio de Janeiro
Library of Congress, Washington, DC
Lilly Library, Indiana University, Orson Welles materials
Museu da Imagem e do Som, Rio de Janeiro
Museu Lasar Segall, São Paulo

Works Cited

Abreu, Martha de. 1989. *Meninas perdidas: os populares e o cotidiano do amor no Rio de Janeiro da belle époque*. Rio de Janeiro: Paz e Terra.

—— 1999. *O império do Divino: festas religiosas e cultura popular no Rio de Janeiro, 1830–1900*. Rio de Janeiro: Editora Nova Fronteira.

—— 2005. '*Mulatas, crioulos, and morenas*: Racial Hierarchy, Gender Relations, and National Identity in Postabolition Popular Song: Southeastern Brazil, 1890–1920'. In Pamela Scully and Diana Paton, eds. *Gender and Slave Emancipation in the Atlantic World*. Durham, NC: Duke University Press.

Abreu, Maurício de. 1988. *Evolução urbana do Rio de Janeiro*. 2nd edn. Rio de Janeiro: Jorge Zahar Editor.

—— 1994. 'Reconstruindo uma história esquecida: origem e expansão inicial do Rio de Janeiro'. *Espaço & Debate* 37.

Agache, Donat Alfred. 1930. *Cidade do Rio de Janeiro, extensão, remodelac o, embellezamento*. Paris: Foyer brésilien.

Akerman, James R. ed. 2006. *Cartographies of Travel and Navigation*. University of Chicago Press.

Alencar, Edigar de. 1981. *Nosso Sinhô do Samba*. Rio de Janeiro: Edição Funarte.

Allain, Émile. 1886. *Rio-de-Janeiro, quelques données sur la capitale et sur l'administration du Brésil*. Paris: L. Frinzine et cie.

Almeida, Manuel Antônio de. 1941. *Memórias de um sargento de milícias*. Introduction by Mário de Andrade. São Paulo: Livraria Martins.

—— 1999. *Memoirs of a Militia Sergeant: A Novel*. Trans. Ronald W. Sousa. New York: Oxford University Press.

Almeida, Renato. 1942. *História da música brasileira*. Rio de Janeiro: F. Briguiet.

Almirante. 1977. *No tempo de Noel Rosa*. Rio de Janeiro: Francisco Alves.

Amado. 1944. Jorge. *O País do Carnaval*. São Paulo: Livraria Martins Editora.

Amaral, Aracy A. 1970. *Blaise Cendrars no Brasil e os modernistas*. São Paulo: Martins.

—— 1998. *Artes plásticas na Semana de 22*. São Paulo: Editora 34.

Amaral, Tarsila do. 2003. *Aí vai meu coração: as cartas de Tarsila do Amaral e Anna Maria Martins para Luís Martins*. Ana Luisa Martins, ed. São Paulo: Editora Planeta do Brasil.

Andrade, Mário de. 1962. *Ensaio sobre a música brasileira*. São Paulo: Martins.

—— 1944 [1928]. *Macunaíma*. São Paulo, Livraria Martins editora.

—— 1988 [1928]. *Macunaíma: o herói sem nenhum caráter*. Telê Porto Ancona Lopez, ed. Brasil: CNPq.

Andrade, Oswald de. 1990 [1925]. *Pau-Brasil*. São Paulo: Editora Globo.

—— 1991. *O santeiro do mangue e outros poemas*. São Paulo: Editora Globo.

Andreatta, Verena. 2006. *Cidades quadradas, paraísos circulares: os planos urbanísticos do Rio de Janeiro no século XIX*. Rio de Janeiro: Mauad X.

Andrews, George Reid. 2004. *Afro-Latin America, 1800–2000*. New York: Oxford University Press.

Antelo, Raul. 1989. *João do Rio: o dândi e a especulação*. Rio de Janeiro: Timbre/Taurus.

Aranha, Graça. 1925. *A esthetica da vida*. Rio de Janeiro: Garnier.

—— 1929. *A viagem maravilhosa*. Rio de Janeiro: Garnier.

Araújo, José de Sousa Azevedo Pizarro e. 1820–2. *Memórias históricas do Rio de Janeiro e das províncias anexas a jurisdição do Vice-Rei do Estado do Brasil, dedicadas a el-rei Nosso Senhor D. João VI*. Rio de Janeiro: Imp. Regia.

Archer-Straw, Petrine. 2000. *Negrophilia: Avant-garde Paris and Black Culture in the 1920s*. New York: Thames & Hudson.

Asbury, Herbert. 1928. *The Gangs of New York: An Informal History of the Underworld*. New York: Knopf.

Assis, Machado de. 1962. *Obra completa*. Afrânio Coutinho, ed. 3 vols. Rio de Janeiro: J. Aguilar.

—— 1996. *A semana: crônicas*. John Gledson, ed. São Paulo: Editora Hucitec.

—— 2000. *Esau and Jacob: A Novel*. Trans. Elizabeth Lowe. New York: Oxford University Press.

—— 2001. *Machado de Assis: crônicas de bond*. Ana Luiza Andrade, ed. Chapecó: Argos Editora Universitária.

—— 2007. *Machado de Assis afro-descendente: escritos de caramujo*. Eduardo de Assis Duarte, ed. Rio de Janeiro: Pallas.

—— 2008. *A Chapter of Hats: Selected Stories*. Trans. John Gledson. London: Bloomsbury.

Azevedo, Aluísio. 1889. *Fritzmac: revista fluminense de 1888, em prosa e verso, em 1 prólogo, 3 atos e 17 quadros*. Rio de Janeiro: Luiz Braga Junior.

—— 1926. *A Brazilian Tenement*. Trans. Harry W. Brown. New York: R. M. McBride and Company.

—— 1980. *O cortiço*. Belo Horizonte: Editora Itatiaia.

—— 2000. *The Slum: A Novel*. Trans. David H. Rosenthal. Oxford University Press.

Azevedo, Manuel Duarte Moreira de. 1877. *O Rio de Janeiro; sua historia, monumentos, homens notáveis, usos e curiosidades*. Rio de Janeiro: Garnier.

Bachelard, Gaston. 1969. *The Poetics of Space*. New York: Beacon Press.

Backheuser, Everardo. 1906. *Habitações populares: relatório apresentado ao Exm. Sr. Dr. J. J. Seabra, Ministro da Justiça e Negócios Interiores*. Rio de Janeiro: Imprensa Nacional.

Baker, John Martin. 1838. *A View of the Commerce between the United States and Rio de Janeiro, Brazil*. Washington, DC: printed at the office of the *Democratic Review*.

Bakhtin, Mikhail. 1981. *The Dialogic Imagination*. Austin: University of Texas Press.

Bandeira, Manuel. 1989. *This Earth, That Sky: Poems*. Trans. Candace Slater. Berkeley, Calif.: University of California Press.

—— 1993. *Poesia completa e prosa*. Rio de Janeiro: Editora Nova Aguilar.

Barbosa, Francisco de Assis. 1964. *A Vida de Lima Barreto*. Rio de Janeiro: Civilização brasileira.

Bardi, Lina Bo. 1999. *Lina Bo Bardi*. Marcelo Carvalho Ferraz, ed. São Paulo: Instituto Lina Bo e P. M. Bardi.

Barreto, João Paulo de Mello. 1939. *História da polícia do Rio de Janeiro; aspectos da cidade e da vida carioca*. Rio de Janeiro: A Noite.

Barreto, Lima. 1978. *The Patriot*. Trans. Robert Scott-Buccleuch. London: Rex Collings.

—— 1988. *Diário do hospício; O cemitério dos vivos*. Rio de Janeiro: Departamento Geral de Documentação e Informação Cultural.

—— 1989. *Numa e a ninfa*. Rio de Janeiro: Livraria Garnier.

—— 1997. *Triste fim de Policarpo Quaresma: edição crítica*. Paris: Coleção Archives/ UNESCO.

Barros, João de. 1938. *Brasil, por João de Barros, José Osório de Oliveira [e] Gastão de Bettencourt*. Lisbon: Edições Europa.

Bastos, Rafael José de Menezes. 2004. *Les Batutas in Paris, 1922: An Anthropology of (In)discreet Brightness*. Florianópolis: Universidade Federal de Santa Catarina, Programa de Pós-Graduação em Antropologia Social.

Beccari, Vera d'Horta. 1984. *Lasar Segall e o Modernismo Paulista*. São Paulo: Editora brasiliense.

Benamou, Catherine L. 2007. *It's All True: Orson Welles's Pan-American Odyssey*. Berkeley, Calif.: University of California Press.

Benchimol, Jaime. 1990. *Pereira Passos: um Haussmann tropical: a renovação urbana da cidade do Rio de Janeiro no início do século XX*. Rio de Janeiro: Biblioteca Carioca.

—— 1999. *Dos micróbios aos mosquitos: febre amarela e a revolução pasteuriana no Brasil*. Rio de Janeiro: Editora Fiocruz.

Benjamin, Walter. 1989. *Reflections: Essays, Aphorisms, Autobiographical Writings*. Peter Demetz, ed. New York: Schocken Books.

—— 2005. *Selected Writings*, vol. 2. Marcus Bullock and Michael W. Jennings, eds. Cambridge, Mass.: Belknap Press.

—— 2007. *Illuminations: Essays and Reflections*. Trans. Harry Zohn; Hannah Arendt, ed. New York: Schocken Books.

Berger, Paulo. 1980. *Bibliografia do Rio de Janeiro de viajantes e autores estrangeiros, 1531–1900*. Rio de Janeiro: SEEC-RJ.

—— 1983. *O Rio de Janeiro de ontem no cartão postal*. Rio de Janeiro: Rio de Janeiro Arte.

Berman, Marshall. 1982. *All That is Solid Melts into Air: The Experience of Modernity*. New York: Viking Penguin.

Bibliotheca brasiliense. 1907. Rio de Janeiro: Typographia do 'Jornal do commercio'.

Blanchot, Maurice. 1982. *The Space of Literature*. Trans. Ann Smock. Lincoln: University of Nebraska Press.

Borges, Vavy Pacheco. 1992. *Tenentismo e revolução brasileira*. São Paulo: Editora brasiliense.

Brazam Guide to Rio de Janeiro, São Paulo and the Principal Points of Brazil, compiled by Cora L. Brown. 1927. Rio de Janeiro: Brazilian American.

Broca, Brito. 1960. *A vida literária no Brasil, 1900*. Rio de Janeiro, José Olympio.

Bueno, Alexei. 2002. *Gamboa: desterro e resistência*. Rio de Janeiro: Relume Dumará.

Bunbury, Charles James Fox. 1981. *Viagem de um naturalista inglês ao Rio de Janeiro e Minas Gerais*. Belo Horizonte: Editora Itatiaia.

Cabral, Sérgio. 1996. *As escolas de samba do Rio de Janeiro*. Rio de Janeiro: Lumiar Editora.

Caldeira, Jorge. 1995. *Mauá: empresário do Império*. São Paulo: Companhia das Letras.

—— 2007. *A construção do samba*. São Paulo: Mameluco.

Caldeira, Teresa. 2000. *City of Walls: Crime, Segregation, and Citizenship in São Paulo*. Berkeley, Calif.: University of California Press.

Camargos, Marcia. 2007. *13 a 18 de fevereiro de 1922: a Semana de 22: revolução estética?* São Paulo: Lazuli Editora; Companhia Editora Nacional.

Canclini, Néstor García. 1995. *Hybrid Cultures: Strategies for Entering and Leaving Modernity*. Trans. Christopher L. Chiappari and Silvia L. López. Minneapolis, Minn.: University of Minnesota Press.

Candido, Antonio. 1993. 'Dialética da malandragem'. *O discurso e a cidade*. São Paulo: Duas cidades.

—— 1995. *On Literature and Society*. Trans. Howard S. Becker. Princeton, NJ: Princeton University Press.

Carneiro, Maria Luiza Tucci. 2004. *Judeus e judaísmo na obra de Lasar Segall*. Cotia, SP: Ateliê Editorial.

Caro, Robert A. 1974. *The Power Broker: Robert Moses and the Fall of New York*. New York: Knopf.

Carvalho, Bruno. 2007. 'Mapping the Urbanized Beaches of Rio de Janeiro: Modernization, Modernity, and Everyday Life'. *Journal of Latin American Cultural Studies* 16.3.

—— 2010. 'A Tale of Three Buildings: Brazil's Estado Novo'. *ReVista: Harvard Review of Latin America*. Special issue on architecture (spring/summer).

—— 2011. 'Palimpsests Remapped: Everyday Life in Retrospect'. *Spaces and Flows: An International Jounal of Urban and ExtraUrban Studies*. 1.1.

Carvalho, José Murilo de. 1980. *A construção da ordem: a elite política imperial*. Rio de Janeiro: Editora Campus.

—— 1987. *Os Bestializados: o Rio de Janeiro e a República que não foi*. São Paulo: Companhia das Letras.

—— 1990. *Formação das almas e a República que não foi*. São Paulo: Companhia das Letras.

—— 2007. *D. Pedro II*. São Paulo: Companhia das Letras.

Carvalho, Lia de Aquino. 1980. 'Contribuição ao estudo das habitações populares: Rio de Janeiro (1886–1906)'. MA thesis. Universidade Federal Fluminense.

Carvalho, Luiz Fernando Medeiros de. 1980. *Ismael Silva: samba e resistência*. Rio de Janeiro: José Olympio.

Carvalho, Maria Alice Rezende de. 1994. *Quatro vezes cidade*. Rio de Janeiro: Sette Letras.

Castro, Ruy. 2004. *Carnaval no fogo: crônicas de uma cidade excitante demais*. São Paulo: Companhia das Letras.

Caulfield, Sueann. 2000a. 'O nascimento do Mangue: raça, nação e o controle da prostituição no Rio de Janeiro, 1850–1942'. *Tempo* 9: 43–63.

Caulfield, Sueann. 2000b. *In Defense of Honor: Sexual Morality, Modernity, and Nation in Early Twentieth Century Brazil*. Durham, NC: Duke University Press.

Cavalcanti, Nireu Oliveira. 2004. *Crônicas: históricas do Rio colonial*. Rio de Janeiro: FAPERJ, Civilização brasileira.

Cendrars, Blaise. 1924. *Feuilles de route*. Paris: Au sans pareil.

Certeau, Michel de. 1980. *L'Invention du quotidien*. Paris: Union générale d'éditions.

—— 1984. *The Practice of Everyday Life*. Berkeley, Calif.: University of California Press.

Chagas, João Pinheiro. 1897. *De bond: alguns aspectos da civilisação brazileira*. Lisbon:

Livraria Moderna.

Chalhoub, Sidney. 1986. *Trabalho, lar e botequim: o cotidiano dos trabalhadores no Rio de Janeiro da belle époque*. São Paulo: Editora brasiliense.

—— 1990. *Visões da liberdade: uma história das últimas décadas da escravidão na corte*. São Paulo: Companhia das Letras.

—— 1996. *Cidade febril: cortiços e epidemias na Corte imperial*. São Paulo: Companhia das Letras.

—— 2003. *Machado de Assis, historiador*. São Paulo: Companhia das Letras.

Chambers, Iain. 2008. *Mediterranean Crossings*. Durham, NC: Duke University Press.

Chasteen, John Charles. 2004. *National Rhythms, African Roots: The Deep History of Latin American Popular Dance*. Albuquerque: University of New Mexico Press.

Chazkel, Amy. 2011. *Laws of Chance: Brazil's Clandestine Lottery and the Making of Public Life*. Durham, NC: Duke University Press.

Coaracy, Vivaldo. 1965. *Memórias da cidade do Rio de Janeiro*. Rio de Janeiro: Livraria José Olympio.

Coelho, Jacinto do Prado. 1965. *O Rio de Janeiro na Literatura Portuguesa*. Lisbon: Comissão Nacional das Comemorações do IV Centenário do Rio de Janeiro.

Comissão de Melhoramentos da Cidade do Rio de Janeiro. 1875. *Primeiro relatório da Comissão de Melhoramentos da Cidade do Rio de Janeiro*. Rio de Janeiro: Imprensa Nacional.

Conde, Maite. 2012. *Consuming Visions: Cinema, Writing, and Modernity in Rio de Janeiro*. Charlottesville: University of Virginia Press.

Conley, Tom. 2000. 'Introduction'. *The Certeau Reader*. Graham Ward, ed. Oxford: Blackwell Publishers.

—— 2007. *Cartographic Cinema*. Minneapolis, Minn.: University of Minnesota Press.

Corboz, André. 2001. *Le Territoire comme palimpseste et autres essais*. Besançon: Imprimeur.

Costa, Haroldo. 2007. *Política e religiões no Carnaval*. São Paulo: Irmãos Vitale.

Costa, Virgilio. 1999. *O Mangue: imagem de libertinagem e pobreza no Rio de Janeiro modernista (1920–1930), ou, Os horizontes do modernismo*. Rio de Janeiro: Fundação Casa de Rui Barbosa, Ministério da Cultura.

Costallat, Benjamim. 1990. *Mistérios do Rio*. Rio de Janeiro: Departamento Geral de Documentação Cultural.

Coustet, Robert. 1979. 'Grandjean de Montigny, urbanista'. *Uma cidade em questão I: Grandjean de Montigny e o Rio de Janeiro*. Rio de Janeiro: Pontifícia Universidade Catolica.

Cruls, Gastão. 1949. *Aparência do Rio de Janeiro; notícia histórica e descritiva da cidade*. Rio de Janeiro: José Olympio.

Cunha, Euclides da. 1985 [1902]. *Os sertões*. Walnice Nogueira Galvão, ed. São Paulo: brasiliense.

Cunha, Leonardo Moreira da. 2006. 'Selvagens, atroadores e belos: a ambigüidade nas representações dos grupos carnavalescos populares pela imprensa carioca do início do século XX'. Dissertation, Pontifícia Universidade Católica do Rio de Janeiro.

Cunha, Maria Clementina Pereira. 2001. *Ecos da folia: uma história social do carnaval carioca entre 1880 e 1920*. São Paulo: Companhia das Letras.

Dabadie, F. 1859. *A travers l'Amérique du Sud*. Paris: F. Sartorius.

Damazio, Sylvia F. 1996. *Retrato social do Rio de Janeiro na virada do século*. Rio de Janeiro: EdUERJ.

Dávila, Jerry. 2003. *Diploma of Whiteness: Race and Social Policy in Brazil, 1917–1945*. Durham, NC: Duke University Press.

Davis, Darién J. 2009. *White Face, Black Mask: Africaneity and the Early Social History of Popular Music in Brazil*. East Lansing: Michigan State University Press.

De Boeck, Filip, and Marie-Francoise Plissart. eds. 2004. *Kinshasa: Tales of the Invisible City*. Tervuren: Royal Museum for Central Africa.

Debord, Guy. 1992. *La Société du spectacle*. Paris: Gallimard.

—— 2000. *Society of the Spectacle*. Trans Ken Knabb. London: Rebel Press.

Debret, Jean Baptiste. 1954. *Viagem pitoresca e histórico ao Brasil*. Trans Sérgio Milliet. São Paulo: Martins.

Deckker, Zilah Quezado. 2001. *Brazil Built: The Architecture of the Modern Movement in Brazil*. New York: Spon.

Deleuze, Gilles. 1988. *Foucault*. Trans. and ed. Seán Hand. Minneapolis: University of Minnesota Press.

Dent, Hastings Charles. 1886. *A Year in Brazil, With Notes on the Abolition of Slavery, the Finances of the Empire, Religion, Meteorology, Natural History, etc*. London: Kegan Paul, Trench and Co.

Derrida, Jacques. 1978. *Writing and Difference*. Trans Alan Bass. University of Chicago Press.

—— 1981. *Dissemination*. Trans Barbara Johnson. University of Chicago Press.

Di Cavalcanti, Emiliano. 1964. *Reminiscências líricas de um perfeito carioca*. Rio de Janeiro: Editora Civilização brasileira.

Diefendorf, J. M. 1989. 'Urban Reconstruction in Europe after World War II'. *Urban Studies* 26.1: 128–43.

Dines, Alberto. 2004. *Morte no paraíso: a tragédia de Stefan Zweig*. Rio de Janeiro: Rocco.

Diniz, André. 2007. *O Rio musical de Anacleto de Medeiros: a vida, a obra e o tempo de um mestre do choro*. Rio de Janeiro: Jorge Zahar Editor.

Diniz, Edinha. 1984. *Chiquinha Gonzaga: uma história de vida*. Rio de Janeiro: Editora Codecri.

Dodsworth, Henrique. 1955. *A Avenida Presidente Vargas: aspectos urbanísticos, jurídicos, financeiros e administrativos de sua realização*. Rio de Janeiro: Jornal do Comércio.

Draper, Jack Alden. 2010. *Forró and Redemptive Regionalism from the Brazilian Northeast: Popular Music in a Culture of Migration*. New York: Peter Lang.

Dunlop, Charles. 1973. *Os meios de transporte do Rio antigo*. Rio de Janeiro: Grupo de Planejamento Gráfico Editores.

Ebel, Ernst. 1828. *Rio de Janeiro und seine Umgebungen im Jahr 1824*. St Petersburg: Kayserliche Akademie der Wissenschaften.

Edgerton, Samuel Y. 1987. 'From Mental Matrix to *Mappamundi* to Christian Empire: The Heritage of Ptolemaic Cartography in the Renaissance'. *Art and Cartography: Six Historical Essays*. University of Chicago Press.

Edmundo, Luiz. 1950. *Recordações do Rio antigo*. Rio de Janeiro: Biblioteca do Exército Editora.

Eisenman, Peter. 2007. *Written into the Void: Selected Writings, 1990–2004*. New Haven, Conn.: Yale University Press.

Eneida. 1987. *História do carnaval carioca*. Rio de Janeiro: Editora Record.

Ermakoff, George. 2006. *Rio de Janeiro. 1840–1900: uma crônica fotográfica*. Rio de Janeiro: G. Ermakoff Casa Editorial.

Ewbank, Thomas. 1856. *Life in Brazil; or, A Journal of a Visit to the Land of the Cocoa and the Palm*. New York: Harper & Brothers.

Faria, Gentil Luiz de. 1988. *A presença de Oscar Wilde na 'belle époque' literária brasileira*. São Paulo: Editora Pannartz.

Farias, Edson. 2006. *O desfile e a cidade: o carnaval-espetáculo carioca*. Rio de Janeiro: E-papers.

Fauchereau, Serge. 2010. *Avant-gardes du XXe siècle: arts & littérature, 1905–1930*. Paris: Flammarion.

Fausto, Boris. 2006. *Getúlio Vargas*. São Paulo: Companhia das Letras.

Fenerick, José Adriano. 2005. *Nem do morro, nem da cidade : as transformações do samba e a indústria cultural (1920–1945)*. São Paulo: Annablume; FAPESP, 2005.

Ferraz de Macedo, Francisco. 1873. *Da prostituição em geral, e em particular em relação á cidade do Rio de Janeiro: prophylaxia da syphilis: estudo contendo a historia da prostituição desde os priscos tempos até Luiz XVI*. Rio de Janeiro: Typographia Academica.

Ferreira, Felipe. 2004. *O livro de ouro do carnaval brasileiro*. Rio de Janeiro: Ediouro.

Fischer, Brodwyn M. 2008 *A Poverty of Rights: Citizenship and Inequality in Twentieth-Century Rio de Janeiro*. Palo Alto, Calif.: Stanford University Press.

Fletcher, James C. 1868. *Brazil and the Brazilians: Portrayed in Historical and Descriptive Sketches*. London: Sampson, Low, Son & Co.

Fleuiss, Max. 1928. *História da cidade do Rio de Janeiro*. São Paulo: Melhoramentos.

Ford, Henry. 1933. *O judeu internacional*. Trans L. G. Porto Alegre: Livraria do Globo.

Forjaz, Maria Cecília Spina. 1977. *Tenentismo e política: tenentismo e camadas médias urbanas na crise da Primeira República*. Rio de Janeiro: Paz e Terra.

Foucault, Michel. 2000. *Aesthetics, Method and Epistemology*. London: Penguin.

França Júnior, Joaquim José de. 1926. *Folhetins*. Rio de Janeiro: J. R. Santos.

Franco, Jean. 2002. *The Decline and Fall of the Lettered City: Latin America in the Cold War*. Cambridge, Mass.: Harvard University Press.

Frank, Waldo. 1943. *South American Journey*. New York: Duell, Sloan and Pearce.

Fraser, Valerie. 2000. *Building the New World: Studies in the Modern Architecture of Latin America, 1930–1960*. New York: Verso.

Freire, Felisberto. 1914. *História da cidade do Rio de Janeiro*. Rio de Janeiro: s. ed.

Freitag, Barbara. 2009. *Capitais migrantes e poderes peregrinos: o caso do Rio de Janeiro*. Campinas: Papirus.

Freud, Sigmund. 1961 [1923–5]. 'A Note Upon the "Mystic Writing-Pad"'. *The Standard Edition of the Complete Psychological Works of Sigmund Freud*. Trans James Strachey, vol. 19. London: Hogarth Press.

—— 1962. *Civilization and its Discontents*. Trans James Strachey. New York: W. W. Norton.

—— 1978 [1900]. *The Interpretation of Dreams*. Trans A. A. Brill. New York: Modern Library.

Freyre, Gilberto. 1975. *Tempo morto e outros tempos: trechos de um diário de adolescência e primeira mocidade*. Rio de Janeiro: Olympio.

—— 2003 [1933]. *Casa-grande & senzala*. São Paulo: Global Editora.

Fridman, Fania. 2007. *Paisagem estrangeira: memórias de um bairro judeu no Rio de Janeiro*. Rio de Janeiro: Casa da Palavra.

Fry, Peter. 2005. *A persistência da raça: ensaios antropológicos sobre o Brasil e a África austral*. Rio de Janeiro: Civilização brasileira.

Fryer, Peter. 2000. *Rhythms of Resistance: African Musical Heritage in Brazil*. Hanover, NH: University Press of New England.

Gallo, Antonella. ed. 2004. *Lina Bo Bardi Architetto*. Venice: Marsilio.

Galvão, Walnice Nogueira. 2000. *Le Carnaval de Rio: trois regards sur une fête brésilienne*. Paris: Éditions Chandeigne.

Gardel, André. 1996. *O encontro entre Bandeira e Sinhô*. Rio de Janeiro: Departamento Geral de Documentação e Informação Cultural, Divisão de Editoração.

Genette, Gérard. 1983. *Nouveau discours du récit*. Paris: Editions du Seuil.

Gerson, Brasil. 1965. *História das ruas do Rio*. Rio de Janeiro: Livraria brasiliana.

Ginzburg, Carlo. 1980. *The Cheese and the Worms: The Cosmos of a Sixteenth-Century Miller*. Trans John Tedeschi and Anne Tedeschi. Baltimore, Md.: Johns Hopkins University Press.

Gledson, John. 1986. *Machado de Assis: Ficção e História*. Rio de Janeiro: Paz e Terra.

—— 2006. *Por um novo Machado de Assis*. São Paulo: Companhia das Letras.

Goeldi, Oswaldo. 1995. *Oswaldo Goeldi: um auto retrato*. Rio de Janeiro: Centro Cultural Banco do Brasil.

Goldberg, Isaac. 1930. *A Chronicle of the American Popular Music Racket*. New York: John Day.

Gomes, Renato Cordeiro. 1996. *João do Rio: vielas do vício, ruas da graça*. Rio de Janeiro: Relume Dumará.

Gonçalves Pinto, Antônio. 1936. *O Choro: reminiscências dos chorões antigos*. Rio de Janeiro. s.n.

Gonçalves, Renata de Sá. 2003. *Os Ranchos pedem passagem*. Rio de Janeiro: IFCS/UFRJ.

Goodhew, David. 2004. *Respectability and Resistance: A History of Sophiatown*. Westport, Conn.: Praeger.

Gottlieb, Jack. 2004. *Funny, it Doesn't Sound Jewish: How Yiddish Songs and Synagogue Melodies Influenced Tin Pan Alley, Broadway, and Hollywood*. Albany, NY: State University of New York.

Graham, Sandra Lauderdale. 1988. *House and Street: The Domestic World of Servants and Masters in Nineteenth-Century Rio de Janeiro*. New York: Cambridge University Press.

Green, James Naylor. 1999. *Beyond Carnival: Male Homosexuality in Twentieth-Century Brazil*. University of Chicago Press.

Guimarães, Antônio Sérgio Alfredo. 2002. *Classes, raças e democracia*. São Paulo: Editora 34.

Guimarães, Francisco [Vagalume]. 1933. *Na roda do samba*. Rio de Janeiro: Typographia São Benedito.

Guimarães Júnior, Luís. 1987. *A família Agulha: romance humorístico*. Rio de Janeiro: Presença.

Haberly, David T. 1983. *Three Sad Races: Racial Identity and National Consciousness in Brazilian Literature*. New York: Cambridge University Press.

Hanchard, Michael George. 1994. *Orpheus and Power: The Movimento Negro of Rio de Janeiro and São Paulo, Brazil, 1945–1988*. Princeton, NJ: Princeton University Press.

Harvey, David. 2003. *Paris, Capital of Modernity*. New York: Routledge.

Hedrick, Charles W. 2000. *History and Silence: Purge and Rehabilitation of Memory in Late Antiquity*. Austin: University of Texas Press.

Heidegger, Martin. 2001. *Poetry, language, thought.* Trans Albert Hofstadter. New York: Perennical Classics, 2001.

Helmer, Stephen. 1985. *Hitler's Berlin: The Speer Plans for Reshaping the Central City.* Ann Arbor, Mich.: UMI Research Press.

Henderson, James. 1821. *A History of the Brazil; Comprising its Geography, Commerce, Colonization, Aboriginal Inhabitants.* London: Longman, Hurst, Rees, Orme, and Brown.

Hertzman, Marc A. 2008. 'Surveillance and Difference: The Making of Samba, Race, and Nation in Brazil'. Dissertation, University of Wisconsin-Madison.

—— 2013. *Making Samba: A New History of Race and Music in Brazil.* Durham, NC: Duke University Press.

Heywood, Linda M., and John K. Thornton. 2007. *Central Africans, Atlantic Creoles, and the Foundation of the Americas, 1585–1660.* New York: Cambridge University Press.

Holanda, Sérgio Buarque de. 2006 [1936]. *Raízes do Brasil.* São Paulo: Companhia das Letras.

—— 2012. *Roots of Brazil.* Trans Harvey Summ. Notre Dame, Ind.: University of Notre Dame Press.

Holloway, Thomas H. 1993. *Policing Rio de Janeiro: Repression and Resistance in a 19th-Century City.* Palo Alto, Calif.: Stanford University Press.

Huyssen, Andreas. 2003. *Present Pasts: Urban Palimpsests and the Politics of Memory.* Palo Alto, Calif.: Stanford University Press.

Jacob, Christian. 2006. *The Sovereign Map: Theoretical Approaches in Cartography Throughout History.* Trans Tom Conley; Edward H. Dahl, ed. University of Chicago Press.

Jacobs, Jane. 1961. *The Death and Life of Great American Cities.* New York: Random House.

Jaguaribe, Beatriz. 1998. *Fins de século: cidade e cultura no Rio de Janeiro.* Rio de Janeiro: Rocco.

—— 2001. 'Modernist Ruins: National Narratives and Architectural Forms'. In Dilip Parameshwar Gaonkar, ed. *Alternative Modernities.* Durham, NC: Duke University Press.

—— 2007. *O choque do real: estética, mídia e cultura.* Rio de Janeiro: Rocco.

Jameson, Fredric. 1991. *Postmodernism, or, the Cultural Logic of Late Capitalism.* Durham, NC: Duke University Press.

Jasen, David A. 2003. *Tin Pan Alley: An Encyclopedia of the Golden Age of American Song.* New York: Routledge.

Jota Efegê. 1974. *Maxixe, a dança excomungada.* Rio de Janeiro: Conquista.

—— 1982. *Figuras e coisas do carnaval carioca.* Rio de Janeiro: FUNARTE.

Junqueira, Ivan. 2008. '"Uns braços": nenhum abraço'. *Revista brasileira* 12.55.

Kanter, Kenneth Aaron. 1982. *The Jews on Tin Pan Alley: The Jewish Contribution to American Popular Music, 1830–1940.* New York: Ktav Publishing House.

Karasch, Mary C. 1987. *Slave Life in Rio de Janeiro, 1808–1850.* Princeton, NJ: Princeton University Press.

Katz, Helena. , 2005 *Gang Wars: Blood and Guts on the Streets of Early New York.* Canmore, Alberta: Altitude Publishing Canada Limit.

Kessel, Carlos. 2001. *A vitrine e o espelho: o Rio de Janeiro de Carlos Sampaio.* Rio de Janeiro: Arquivo Geral da Cidade do Rio de Janeiro, Divisão de Pesquisa.

Klein, Norman. 1997. *The History of Forgetting: Los Angeles and the Erasure of Memory.* New York: Verso.

Kushnir, Beatriz. 1996. *Baile de máscaras: mulheres judias e prostituição: as polacas e suas associações de ajuda mútua*. Rio de Janeiro: Imago Editora.

Lacombe, Américo Jacobina. 1988. *Rui Barbosa e a queima dos arquivos*. Rio de Janeiro: Fundação Casa de Rui Barbosa.

Laemmert, Eduardo. 1853 and 1872. *Almanak administrativo, mercantil e industrial do Rio de Janeiro*. Rio de Janeiro: Companhia typographica do Brazil.

Lamarão, Sérgio Tadeu de Niemeyer. 1991. *Dos trapiches ao porto: um estudo sobre a área portuária do Rio de Janeiro*. Rio de Janeiro: Departamento Geral de Documentação e Informação Cultural, Divisão de Editoração.

Le Corbusier. 1967. *The Radiant City; Elements of a Doctrine of Urbanism to be Used as the Basis of Our Machine-age Civlization*. New York: Orion Press.

Lefebvre, Henri. 1970. *La révolution urbaine*. Paris: Gallimard.

—— 1991. *The Production of Space*. Trans Donald Nicholson-Smith. Cambridge, Mass.: Blackwell.

Leithold, Johann Gottfried Theodor von. 1966. *O Rio de Janeiro visto por dois prussianos em 1819*. Trans Joaquim de Sousa Leão Filho. São Paulo: Companhia Editora Nacional.

Lesser, Jeff. *Welcoming the Undesirables: Brazil and the Jewish Question*. Berkeley, Calif.: University of California Press, 1995.

Lévi-Strauss, Claude. 1992. *Tristes Tropiques*. Trans John Weightman and Doreen Weightman. New York: Penguin Books.

Levine, Robert M. 1998. *Father of the Poor?: Vargas and His Era*. New York: Cambridge University Press.

Lima, Evelyn F. Werneck. 1990. *Avenida Presidente Vargas: uma drástica cirurgia*. Rio de Janeiro: Biblioteca Carioca.

Lino, Raul. 1937. *Auriverde Jornada: recordações de uma viagem ao Brasil*. Lisbon: Edição de Valentim de Carvalho.

Lírio, Alba, Heitor dos Prazeres Filho. 2003. Heitor dos Prazeres: sua arte e seu tempo. Rio de Janeiro: SESC.

Livingston-Isenhour, Tamara Elena, and Thomas George Caracas Garcia. 2005. *Choro: A Social History of a Brazilian Popular Music*. Bloomington: Indiana University Press.

Lobo, Eulália Maria Lahmeyer. 1978. *História do Rio de Janeiro: do capital comercial ao capital industrial e financeiro*. Rio de Janeiro: IBMEC.

—— 1989. *Questão habitacional e o movimento operário*. Rio de Janeiro: Editora UFRJ.

Lobo, Manoel da Gama. 1881. *The Swamps and the Yellow Fever: with Medium, Minimum and Maximum Thermometric, Barometric and Hygrometric and Direction of Winds of the City of Rio de Janeiro during 26 Years*. New York: s.n.

Lopes, Antônio Herculano, org. *Entre Europa e África. a invenção do carioca*. Rio de Janeiro: Topbooks; Ed. Casa de Rui Barbosa, 2000.

Lopes, Nei. 2006. *Dicionário escolar afro-brasileiro*. São Paulo: Selo Negro.

—— 2009. *Mandingas da mulata velha na cidade nova*. Rio de Janeiro: Língua Geral.

Luccock, John. 1820. *Notes on Rio de Janeiro, and the Southern Parts of Brazil; Taken during a Residence Often Years in that Country, from 1808 to 1818*. London: S. Leigh.

Lynch, Kevin. 1960. *The Image of the City*. Cambridge, Mass.: MIT Press.

Lyotard, Jean François. 1977. *Rudiments païens: genre dissertatif*. Paris: Union générale d'éditions.

Macedo, Joaquim Manuel de. 1942. *Um passeio pela cidade do Rio de Janeiro*. Rio de Janeiro: Z. Valverde.

Machado, Cacá. 2007. *O enigma do homem célebre: ambição e vocação de Ernesto Nazareth*. São Paulo: Instituto Moreira Salles.

Maciel, Anor Butler. 1937. *Nacionalismo: o problema judaico no mundo e no Brasil: o nacional socialismo*. Porto Alegre: Livraria do Globo.

Magalhães Júnior, Raimundo. 1978. *A vida vertiginosa de João do Rio*. Rio de Janeiro: Civilização brasileira.

Malamud, Samuel. 1988. *Recordando a Praça Onze*. Rio de Janeiro: Livraria Kosmos Editora.

Manet, Édouard. 1928. *Lettres de jeunesse: 1848-1849 voyage à Rio*. Paris: Louis Rouart.

Maram, Sheldon. 1979. *Anarquistas, Imigrantes e Movimento Operário no Brasil, 1890-1920*. Rio de Janeiro: Paz e Terra.

Marianno Filho, José. 1943. *Debates sobre estética e urbanismo*. Rio de Janeiro: Est. de artes graf. C. Mendes Junior.

Martins, Luís. 1964. *Noturno da Lapa*. Rio de Janeiro: Editora Civilização brasileira.

Martins, Wilson. 1976. *História da inteligência brasileira*. São Paulo: Editora Cultrix.

—— 1992. *História da inteligência brasileira*. 3rd edn. São Paulo: T. A. Queiroz.

Matos, Cláudia. 1982. *Acertei no milhar: malandragem e samba no tempo de Getúlio*. Rio de Janeiro: Paz e Terra.

Máximo, João. 1990. *Noel Rosa: uma biografia*. Brasília: Editora UnB.

McCann, Bryan. 2004. *Hello, Hello Brazil: Popular Music in the Making of Modern Brazil*. Durham, NC: Duke University Press.

McLuhan, Marshall. 1967. *The Medium is the Massage*. New York: Random House.

Meade, Teresa A. 1997. *'Civilizing' Rio: Reform and Resistance in a Brazilian City, 1889-1930*. University Park, Pa.: Pennsylvania State University Press.

Mello Júnior, Donato. 1988. *Rio de Janeiro: planos, plantas, e aparências*. Rio de Janeiro: Galeria de Arte do Centro Empresarial Rio.

Mello Moraes, Alexandre José de. 1885. *Cancioneiro dos ciganos: poesia popular dos ciganos da Cidade Nova*. Rio de Janeiro: B. L. Garnier.

Melo, Hildete Pereira de, João Lizardo de Araújo, and Teresa Cristina de Novaes Marques. 2003. 'Raça e nacionalidade no mercado de trabalho carioca na Primeira República: o caso da cervejaria Brahma'. *Revista Brasileira de Economia* 57.3.

Mendes, Murilo. 1930. *Poemas, 1925-1929*. Juiz de Fora: Companhia Dias Cardoso.

—— 1994. *Poesia completa e prosa*. Rio de Janeiro: Editora Nova Aguilar.

Menezes, Lená Medeiros de. 1992. *Os estrangeiros e o comércio do prazer nas ruas do Rio, 1890-1930*. Rio de Janeiro: Arquivo Nacional, Órgão do Ministério da Justiça.

—— 1996. *Os indesejáveis: desclassificados na modernidade: protesto, crime e expulsão na Capital Federal, 1890-1930*. Rio de Janeiro: EdUERJ.

Milhaud, Darius. 1949. *Notes sans musique*. Paris: René Julliard.

Ministério do Trabalho, Indústria e Comércio. 1933. *Ao Brasil (Informações para viajantes)*. Rio de Janeiro: J. Monteiro.

Moraes, Vinicius de. 1998. *Poesia completa e prosa*. Rio de Janeiro: Nova Aguila.

Moretti, Franco. 1998. *Atlas of the European Novel, 1800-1900*. New York: Verso.

—— 2005. *Signs Taken for Wonders: On the Sociology of Literary Forms*. London: Verso.

Moura, Roberto. 1995. *Tia Ciata e a pequena África no Rio de Janeiro*. Rio de Janeiro: Prefeitura da Cidade do Rio de Janeiro, Secretaria Municipal de Cultura.

Moura, Roberto M. 1999. *Praça Onze: no meio do caminho tinha as meninas do Mangue*. Rio de Janeiro: Relume Dumará.

—— 2004. *No princípio, era a roda: um estudo sobre samba, partido-alto e outros pagodes.* Rio de Janeiro: Rocco.

Nascimento, Álvaro Pereira do. 2008. *Cidadania, cor e disciplina na revolta dos marinheiros de 1910.* Rio de Janeiro: Mauad.

Needell, Jeffrey D. 1987. *A Tropical Belle Epoque: Elite Culture and Society in Turn-of-the-Century Rio de Janeiro.* New York: Cambridge University Press.

—— 2006. *The Party of Order: The Conservatives, the State, and Slavery in the Brazilian Monarchy, 1831–1871.* Palo Alto, Calif.: Stanford University Press.

Neiva, Artur Nehl. 1944. 'Estudos sobre a imigração semita no Brasil'. *Revista de imigração e colonização* 5.2: 215–422.

Nonato, José Antonio, and Nubia Melhem Santos. eds. 2000. *Era uma vez o Morro do Castelo.* Rio de Janeiro: Ministério da Cultura, Instituto do Patrimônio Histórico e Artístico Nacional.

Norberto, Natalício, and Jonas Vieira. 1992. *Herivelto Martins: uma escola de samba.* Rio de Janeiro: Ensaio editora.

Nuttall, Sarah, and Achille Mbembe. eds. 2008. *Johannesburg: The Elusive Metropolis.* Durham, NC: Duke University Press.

O'Donnell, Julia. 2008. *De Olho na Rua: a cidade de João do Rio.* Rio de Janeiro: Zahar Editor.

—— 2013. *A Invenção de Copacabana: Culturas urbanas e estilos de vida no Rio de Janeiro.* Rio de Janeiro: Zahar, 2013.

Oliveira, Cláudia de, Monica Pimenta Velloso, and Vera Lins. 2010. *O moderno em revistas: representações do Rio de Janeiro de 1890 a 1930.* Rio de Janeiro: Garamond.

Oliveira, Josivaldo Pires de, and Luiz Augusto Pinheiro Leal. 2009. *Capoeira, identidade e gênero: ensaios sobre a história social da capoeira no Brasil.* Salvador: EDUFBA.

Orazi, Angelo. 1939. *Rio de Janeiro and Environs: Travellers' Guide.* Rio de Janeiro: Guias do Brasil, Ltda.

Painter, Borden W. 2005. *Mussolini's Rome: Rebuilding the Eternal City.* New York: Palgrave Macmillan.

Paiva, S. C. de. 1991. *Viva o rebolado!: vida e morte do teatro de revista brasileiro.* Rio de Janeiro: Nova Fronteira.

Pereira, Leonardo Affonso de Miranda. 1994. *O carnaval das letras.* Rio de Janeiro: Departamento Geral de Documentação e Informação Cultural, Divisão de Editoração.

—— 2002. *As barricadas da saúde: vacina e protesto popular no Rio de Janeiro da Primeira República.* São Paulo: Editora Fundação Perseu Abramo, 2002.

Pieroni, Geraldo. 2000. *Vadios e ciganos, heréticos e bruxas: os degredados no Brasil-colônia.* Rio de Janeiro: Bertrand Brasil.

Pinheiro, Paulo Sérgio. 1992. *Estratégias da ilusão.* São Paulo: Companhia das Letras.

Poéticas do Mangue (Fábio Magalhães, et al.). 2012. São Paulo: Imprensa Oficial do Estado de São Paulo; Museu Lasar Segall.

Prado, Antonio Arnoni. 1983. *1922-Itinerário de uma falsa vanguarda: os dissidentes, a Semana e o integralismo.* São Paulo: Brasiliense.

Prado, Paulo. 1931. *Retrato do Brasil: ensaio sobre a tristeza brasileira.* Rio de Janeiro: F. Briguiet & Cia.

Prakash, Gyan, and Kevin M. Kruse. eds. 2008. *The Spaces of the Modern City: Imaginaries, Politics, and Everyday Life.* Princeton, NJ: Princeton University Press.

Prandi, Reginaldo. ed. 2001. *Encantaria brasileira: o livro dos mestres, caboclos e encantados*. Rio de Janeiro: Pallas.

Raban, Jonathan. 1998. *Soft City*. London: Harvill Press.

Rama, Ángel. 1984. *La ciudad letrada*. Hanover, NH: Ediciones del Norte.

—— 1996. *The Lettered City*. Trans John Charles Chasteen. Durham, NC: Duke University Press.

Ramos, Arthur. 1934. *O negro brasileiro; ethnographia, religiosa e psychanalyse*. Rio de Janeiro: Civilização brasileira.

—— 1935. *O folk-lore negro do Brasil; demopsychologia e psychoanalyse*. Rio de Janeiro: Civilização brasileira.

—— 1939. *The Negro in Brazil*. Trans Richard Pattee. Washington, DC: Associated Publishers.

Rebelo, Marques. 1943. *Vida e obra de Manuel Antônio de Almeida*. Rio de Janeiro: Z. Valverde.

Recenseamento da população do Império do Brazil a que se procedeu no dia 10 de agosto de 1872. 1873-6. Rio de Janeiro: Leuzinger.

Recenseamento do Brazil realizado em 1 de setembro de 1920. 1922-30. Rio de Janeiro: Typographia da Estatistica.

Recenseamento do Rio de Janeiro (Districto Federal) realisado em 20 de setembro de 1906. 1907. Rio de Janeiro: Officina da Estatistica.

Recenseamento geral da republica dos Estados Unidos do Brazil em 31 de dezembro de 1890. 1895. *Districto federal (cidade do Rio de Janeiro)*. Rio de Janeiro: Typographia Leuzinger.

Recenseamento geral do Brasil: censo demográfico (1 de Setembro de 1940). 1952. Rio de Janeiro: Serviço Gráfico do Instituto Brasileiro de Geografia e Estatística.

Reis, João José. 2003. *Rebelião escrava no Brasil: a história do levante dos malês em 1835*. São Paulo: Companhia das Letras.

Renault, Delso. 1984. *O Rio antigo nos anúncios de jornais, 1808-1850*. Rio de Janeiro: F. Alves.

Resende, Beatriz. 1993. *Lima Barreto e o Rio de Janeiro em fragmentos*. Rio de Janeiro: Editora UFRJ.

Ribeiro, Luiz Cesar de Queiroz, and Robert Pechman. eds. 1996. *Cidade, povo e nação: gênese do urbanismo moderno*. Rio de Janeiro: Civilização brasileira.

Ribeiro, Noemi. ed. 2005. *Oswaldo Goeldi na Coleção Hermann Kümmerly*. Rio de Janeiro: Papel & Tinta.

Ribeiro, Paula. 2000. 'Saara: uma paisagem singular na cidade do Rio de Janeiro (1960-1990)'. MA dissertation, Pontifícia Universidade Católica de São Paulo.

—— 2008. 'Cultura, memória e vida urbana: judeus na Praça Onze, no Rio de Janeiro (1920-1980)'. PhD dissertation, Pontifícia Universidade Católica de São Paulo.

Riis, Jacob A. 1957. *How the Other Half Lives: Studies among the Tenements of New York*. New York: Hill and Wang.

Rio, João do. 1976. *As religiões no Rio*. Rio de Janeiro: Editora Nova Aguilar.

—— 2007. *A alma encantadora das ruas*. Belo Horizonte: Crisálida.

—— 2010. *The Enchanting Soul of the Streets*. Trans Mark Carlyon. Rio de Janeiro: Cidade Viva Editora.

Roach, Joseph. 1996. *Cities of the Dead: Circum-Atlantic Performance*. New York: Columbia University Press.

Robiano, Eugène de. 1878. *Dix-huit mois dans l'Amérique du Sud: le Brésil, l'Uruguay, la*

République Argentine, les pampas, et le voyage au Chili par la Cordillère des Andes. Paris: E. Plon.

Rocha, João Cezar de Castro, and Jeffrey T. Schnapp. 1996. 'Brazilian Velocities: On Marinetti's 1926 Trip to South America'. *South Central Review* (summer–fall).

Rocha, Oswaldo Porto. 1995. *A era das demolições: cidade do Rio de Janeiro, 1870–1920.* Rio de Janeiro: Prefeitura da Cidade do Rio de Janeiro, Secretaria Municipal de Cultura, Departamento Geral de Documentação e Informação Cultural, Divisão de Editoração.

Rodman, Selden. 1974. *Tongues of Fallen Angels.* New York: New Directions.

Rodrigues, João Carlos. 1996. *João do Rio: uma biografia.* Rio de Janeiro: Topbooks.

—— *João do Rio: vida, paixão e obra: biografia.* 2010. Rio de Janeiro : Civilização brasileira.

Rodrigubes Muller, Maria Lúcia. 2008. *A Cor da Escola: imagens da Primeira República.* Cuiabá: EdUFMT and Entrelinhas.

Roland, Maria Inês. 2000. *A Revolta da Chibata.* São Paulo: Editora Saraiva.

Romero, José Luis. 1999. *Latinoamérica, las ciudades y las ideas.* Medellín, Colombia: Editorial Universidad de Antioquia.

Rosa Duarte, Cristiane, and Fernanda Magalhães. 2009. 'Upgrading Squatter Settlements into City Neighborhoods: The Favela-Bairro Program in Rio de Janeiro'. In Vicente del Rio and William Siembieda, eds. *Contemporary Urbanism in Brazil: Beyond Brasília.* Gainesville, Fla.: University Press of Florida.

Saint-Hilaire, Auguste de. 1830. *Voyage dans les provinces de Rio de Janeiro et de Minas Geraes.* Paris: Grimbert et Dorez.

Sandroni, Carlos. 2001. *Feitiço decente: transformações do samba no Rio de Janeiro, 1917–1933.* Rio de Janeiro: Jorge Zahar Editor.

Sant'Anna, Affonso Romano de. 2002. *Nós, os que matamos Tim Lopes.* São Paulo: Expressão e Cultura.

Santa Anna, José Joaquim de. 1815. *Memória Geral sobre o Enxugo desta Cidade do Rio de Janeiro.* Rio de Janeiro: Impressão Régia.

Santos, Luis Gonçalves dos. 1825. *Memórias para servir à história do reino do Brasil, divididas em três épocas da felicidade, honra, e glória; escritas na corte do Rio de Janeiro no ano de 1821.* Lisbon: Impressão Régia.

Santos, Mílton. 1988. *Metamorfoses do espaço habitado: fundamentos teóricos e metodológicos da geografia.* São Paulo: Editora Aucitec.

—— 1993. *A urbanização brasileira.* São Paulo: Editora Hucitec.

Santos, Noronha. 1907. *Chorographia do Districto Federal: cidade do Rio de Janeiro.* Rio de Janeiro: B. de Aguila.

—— 1934. *Meios de transporte no Rio de Janeiro: historia e legislação.* Rio de Janeiro: Typographia do Jornal do Commercio.

—— 1965. *As freguesias do Rio antigo.* Rio de Janeiro: Edições O Cruzeiro.

Santucci, Jane. 2008. *Cidade rebelde: as revoltas populares no Rio de Janeiro no início do século XX.* Rio de Janeiro: Casa da Palavra.

Sarlo, Beatriz. 1988. *Una modernidad periférica: Buenos Aires, 1920 y 1930.* Buenos Aires: Ediciones Nueva Visión.

—— 2001. 'Los debates sobre Modernidad periférica, Escenas de la vida posmoderna y la cuestión del valor estético'. In Sarah de Mojica, ed. *Mapas culturales para América Latina: Culturas híbridas, No simultaneidad, Modernidad periférica.* Bogotá: Centro Editorial Javeriano: Instituto Pensar.

Sarmento, Carlos Eduardo. 2001. *O Rio de Janeiro na era Pedro Ernesto.* Rio de Janeiro: Editora FGV.

Sayers, Raymond S. 1956. *The Negro in Brazilian Literature.* New York: Hispanic Institute in the United States.

Schorske, Carl E. 1981. *Fin-de-siècle Vienna: Politics and Culture.* New York: Vintage Books.

Schreiner, Claus. 1993. *Música Brasileira: A History of Popular Music and the People of Brazil.* Trans Mark Weinstein. New York: Marion Boyars.

Schultz, Kirsten. 2001. *Tropical Versailles: Empire, Monarchy, and the Portuguese Royal Court in Rio de Janeiro, 1808–1821.* New York: Routledge.

Schwarcz, Lilia Moritz. 1999. *The Spectacle of the Races: Scientists, Institutions, and the Race Question in Brazil, 1870–1930.* Trans Leland Guyer. New York: Hill and Wang.

—— 2004. *The Emperor's Beard: Dom Pedro II and the Tropical Monarchy of Brazil.* Trans John Gledson. New York: Hill and Wang.

—— 2008. *O Sol do Brasil: Nicolas-Antoine Taunay e as Desventuras dos Artistas Franceses na Corte de D. João (1816–1821).* São Paulo: Companhia das Letras.

Schwartz, Jorge. ed. 2003. *Caixa modernista.* São Paulo: Edusp; Imprensa Oficial, Governo do Estado de São Paulo/Belo Horizonte: Editora UFMG.

Schwarz, Roberto. 1977. *Ao vencedor as batatas: forma literária e processo social nos inícios do romance brasileiro.* São Paulo: Livraria Duas Cidades.

—— 2000. *Um mestre na periferia do capitalismo.* São Paulo: Duas Cidades.

—— 2001. *A Master on the Periphery of Capitalism: Machado de Assis.* Trans John Gledson. Durham, NC: Duke University Press.

Segall, Lasar. 1977. *Mangue (textos de Jorge de Lima, Mário de Andrade, Manuel Bandeira).* Rio de Janeiro: Philobiblion.

Sennett, Richard. 1994. *Flesh and Stone: The Body and the City in Western Civilization.* New York: W. W. Norton.

Sevcenko, Nicolau. 1983. *Literatura como missão: tensões sociais e criação cultural na Primeira República.* São Paulo: Brasiliense.

—— 1984. *A revolta da vacina: mentes insanas em corpos rebeldes.* São Paulo: Brasiliense.

—— 1992. *Orfeu extático na metrópole: São Paulo, sociedade e cultura nos frementes anos 20.* São Paulo: Companhia das Letras.

—— 1998. 'A capital irradiante: técnica, ritmos e ritos do Rio'. In Nicolau Sevcenko, ed. *História da vida privada no Brasil.* São Paulo: Companhia das Letras.

—— 2000. 'Peregrinations, Visions and the City: From Canudos to Brasília, the Backlands become the City and the City becomes the Backlands'. In Vivian Schelling, ed. *Through the Kaleidoscope: The Experience of Modernity in Latin América.* New York: Verso.

—— 2003 [1983]. *Literatura como missão: tensões sociais e criação cultural na Primeira República.* 2nd edn. São Paulo: Editora Schwarcz.

Shack, William A. 2001. *Harlem in Montmartre: A Paris Jazz Story between the Great Wars.* Berkeley, Calif.: University of California Press.

Shaw, Lisa. 1999. *The Social History of the Brazilian Samba.* Aldershot: Ashgate.

Sigaud, Joseph François Xavier. 1844. *Du climat et des maladies du Brésil.* Paris: Éditions Fortin.

Silva, Eduardo. 1993. *Prince of the People: The Life and Times of a Brazilian Free Man of Colour.* Trans Moyra Ashford. New York: Verso.

—— 1997. *Dom Obá II d'Africa, o príncipe do povo: vida, tempo e pensamento de um homem livre de cor*. São Paulo: Companhia das Letras.

Silva, Hélio. 1980. *A ameaça vermelha: o Plano Cohen*. Porto Alegre: L&PM Editores.

Silva, Lúcia. 2006. *Luzes e Sombras na Cidade: no rastro do Castelo e da Praça Onze 1920–1945*. Rio de Janeiro: Departamento Geral de Documentação e Informação Cultural, Divisão de Editoração.

Silva, Maria Beatriz Nizza da. 1977. *Cultura e sociedade no Rio de Janeiro (1808–1821)*. São Paulo: Companhia Editora Nacional.

Silva Lisboa, Balthazar da. 1834–5. *Annaes do Rio de Janeiro, contendo a descoberta e conquista deste paiz, a fundação de cidade com a história civil e ecclesiastica, até a chegada d'el-rei Dom João VI, além de noticias topographicas, zooligicas e botanicas*. Rio de Janeiro: Typographia Imperial e Constitucional de Seignot-Plancher.

Simmel, Georg. 2004. 'Bridge and Door'. In Neil Leach, ed. *Rethinking Architecture: A Reader in Cultural Theory*. Routledge: New York.

Sitte, Camillo. 1945. *The Art of Building Cities; City Building According to its Artistic Fundamentals*. Trans Charles T. Stewart. New York: Reinhold Publishing Corporation.

Soares, Mariza de Carvalho. 1999. 'Nos atalhos da memória'. In Paulo Knauss, ed. *A cidade Vaidosa: imagens urbanas do Rio de Janeiro*. Rio de Janeiro: Sette Letras.

Sodré, Muniz. 1979. *Samba: o dono do corpo*. Rio de Janeiro: Codecri.

Soihet, Rachel. 2008. *A subversão pelo riso: estudos sobre o carnaval carioca da Belle époque ao tempo de Vargas*. Uberlândia: Editora da Universidade Federal de Uberlândia.

Souza, Carlos Eduardo Dias. 2009. 'A medicina e as crônicas em nome da ordem numa cidade rumo à civilização: o Rio de Janeiro entre 1850 e 1905'. *Revista Espacialidades* 2.

Souza, Percival de. 2002. *Narcoditadura: o caso Tim Lopes, crime organizado e jornalismo investigativo no Brasil*. São Paulo: Labortexto.

Stam, Robert. 1997. *Tropical Multiculturalism: A Comparative History of Race in Brazilian Cinema and Culture*. Durham, NC: Duke University Press.

Starobinski, Jean. 1973. *1789: Les Emblèmes de la raison*. Paris: Flammarion.

Stewart, C. S. (Charles Samuel). 1858. *Brazil and La Plata: The Personal Record of a Cruise*. New York : A. O. Moore, Agricultural Book.

Stuckenbruck, Denise Cabral. 1996. *O Rio de Janeiro em questão: o plano agache e o ideário reformista dos anos 20*. Rio de Janeiro: Observatório de Políticas Urbanas e Gestão Municipal.

Süssekind, Flora. 1986. *As revistas de ano e a invenção do Rio de Janeiro*. Rio de Janeiro: Nova Fronteira.

—— 1997. *Cinematograph of Words: Literature, Technique, and Modernization in Brazil*. Palo Alto, Calif.: Stanford University Press.

Taunay, Afonso de. 1947. *No Rio de Janeiro de Dom Pedro II*. Rio de Janeiro: AGIR.

Taylor, Charles. 2007. *A Secular Age*. Cambridge, Mass.: Belknap Press.

Teixeira e Sousa, Antônio Gonçalves. 1847. *As tardes de um pintor, ou as intrigas de um jesuíta* . Rio de Janeiro: s.n.

Teixeira Barbosa, Luísa. 2003. 'O Brasil e o movimento republicano português, 1880–1910'. *Revista Cultural DOM FAFES*. Ano IX, no. 10. Câmara Municipal de Fafe.

Thompson, Daniella. 2008. 'The Boeuf Chronicles; How the Ox Got on the Roof: Darius Milhaud and the Brazilian Sources of Le Boeuf sur le Toit'. *Daniella Thompson on Brazil*. January 2008. http://daniv.blogspot.co.uk/2002/04/boeuf-chronicles-pt.html.

—— 2009. 'Praça Onze in Popular Song'. *Daniella Thompson on Brazil*. January 2009. http://daniellathompson.com/Texts/Praca_Onze/praca_onze.htm.

Tinhorão, José Ramos. 1997. *Música popular: um tema em debate*. São Paulo: Editora 34.

—— 1998. *História social da música popular brasileira*. São Paulo: Editora 34.

—— 2000-2. *A música popular no romance brasileiro*. São Paulo: Editora 34.

—— 2004. *Domingos Caldas Barbosa: o poeta da viola, da modinha e do lundu, 1740-1800*. Lisbon: Editorial Caminho.

—— 2006. *Cultura popular: temas e questões*. São Paulo: Editora 34.

Tota, Antônio Pedro. 2009. *The Seduction of Brazil: The Americanization of Brazil during World War II*. Trans Lorena B. Ellis. Austin, Tex.: University of Texas Press.

Tupy, Dulce. 1985. *Carnavais de guerra: o nacionalismo no Samba*. Rio de Janeiro: ASB Arte Gráfica e Editora.

Vainfas, Ronaldo. 1999. 'Colonização, miscigenação e questão racial: notas sobre equívocos e tabus da historiografia brasileira'. *Tempo* 8: 7-22.

Valladares, Licia do Prado. 2005. *A invenção da favela: do mito de origem a favela.com*. Rio de Janeiro: Editora FGV.

Vasconcelos, Ary. 1977. *Panorama da música popular brasileira na belle époque*. Rio de Janeiro: Sant'Anna Ltda.

Vaz, Lilian Fessler. 2002. *Modernidade e moradia: habitação coletiva no Rio de Janeiro, séculos XIX e XX*. Rio de Janeiro: 7Letras.

Velloso, Mônica Pimenta. 1988. *As tradições populares na belle époque carioca*. Rio de Janeiro: FUNARTE.

—— 1996. *Modernismo no Rio de Janeiro: turunas e quixotes*. Rio de Janeiro: Editora Fundação Getúlio Vargas.

Veltman, Henrique. 1998. *A História dos Judeus no Rio de Janeiro*. Rio de Janeiro: Editora Expressão e Cultura.

Ventura, Zuenir. 1994. *Cidade partida*. São Paulo: Companhia das Letras.

Viana, Francisco José de Oliveira. 1932. *Raça e assimilação 1. Os problemas da raça. 2. Os problemas da assimilação*. São Paulo: Companhia Editora Nacional.

Vianna, Hermano. 1995. *O mistério do samba*. Rio de Janeiro: Jorge Zahar Editor.

—— 1988. *O mundo funk carioca*. Rio de Janeiro: Jorge Zahar Editor.

—— 1999. *The Mystery of Samba: Popular Music and National Identity in Brazil*. Trans John Charles Chasteen. Chapel Hill: University of North Carolina Press.

Vianna, Luiz Fernando. 2004. *Geografia carioca do samba*. Rio de Janeiro: Casa Da Palavra.

Villaça, Flávio. 1998. *Espaço intra-urbano no Brasil*. São Paulo: Studio Nobel.

Walsh, R. (Robert). 1831. *Notices of Brazil in 1828 and 1829*. Boston, Mass.: Richardson, Lord & Holbrook.

Weigel, Sigrid. 1996. *Body- and image-space: Re-reading Walter Benjamin*. Trans Georgina Paul, Rachel McNicholl and Jeremy Gaines. New York: Routledge.

Welles, Orson. 1998. *This is Orson Welles*. Jonathan Rosenbaum, ed. New York: Da Capo Press.

Whigham, Thomas. 2002. *The Paraguayan War*. Lincoln, Neb.: University of Nebraska Press.

White, Richard Dunning. 1897. *Sketches of Rio de Janeiro and Environs*. Exeter: William Pollard & Co.

Williams, Daryle. 2001. *Culture Wars in Brazil: The First Vargas Regime, 1930-1945*. Durham, NC: Duke University Press.

Wisnik, José Miguel. 1977. *O coro dos contrários: a música em torno da Semana de 22*. São Paulo: Livraria Duas Cidades.

—— 2004. *Sem receita: ensaios e canções*. São Paulo: Publifolha.

—— 2006. 'The Riddle of Brazilian Soccer: Reflections on the Emancipatory Dimensions of Culture'. *Review. Literature and Arts of the Americas* 39:2.

—— 2008. *Veneno remédio: o futebol e o Brasil*. São Paulo: Companhia das Letras.

Wolfe, Joel. 2010. *Autos and Progress: The Brazilian Search for Modernity*. New York: Oxford University Press.

Zaluar, Alba. 2004. *Integração perversa: pobreza e tráfico de drogas*. Rio de Janeiro: Editora FGV.

Zweig, Stefan. 1993. *Amok e Xadrez e fragmentos do diário*. Trans. Odilon Gallotti and Marcos Branda Lacerda; Ingrid Schwamborn, ed. Rio de Janeiro: Editora Nova Fronteira.

—— 2000 [1941]. *Brazil: A Land of the Future*. Trans Lowell Bangerter. Riverside, Calif.: Ariadne Press.

Index

Printed in the USA/Agawam, MA
May 1, 2015

613943.003